Strategies for the Technical Professional with Student Guide to Online Learning

Custom Edition

Taken from:

Power Up: A Practical Student's Guide to Online Learning
by Stacey Barrett, Catrina Poe, and Carrie Spagnola-Doyle

Cornerstone: Building on Your Best for Career Success
by Robert M. Sherfield, Rhonda J. Montgomery, and Patricia G. Moody

Cornerstone: Building on Your Best, Fourth Edition
by Robert M. Sherfield, Rhonda J. Montgomery, and Patricia G. Moody

Keys to Success: Building Successful Intelligence for College, Career, and Life, Brief Fourth Edition
by Carol Carter, Joyce Bishop, Sarah Lyman Kravits

Strategies for Active Citizenship
by Kateri M. Drexler and Gwen Garcelon

Learning Solutions

New York   Boston   San Francisco
London   Toronto   Sydney   Tokyo   Singapore   Madrid
Mexico City   Munich   Paris   Cape Town   Hong Kong   Montreal

Cover Art: Courtesy of Digital Vision/Getty Images, Stockbyte/Getty Images and PhotoDisc/Getty Images

Taken from:

Power Up: A Practical Student's Guide to Online Learning
by Stacey Barrett, Catrina Poe, and Carrie Spagnola-Doyle
Copyright © 2009 by Pearson Education, Inc.
Published by Prentice Hall
Upper Saddle River, New Jersey 07458

Cornerstone: Building on Your Best for Career Success
by Robert M. Sherfield, Rhonda J. Montgomery, and Patricia G. Moody
Copyright © 2006 by Pearson Education, Inc.
Published by Prentice Hall

Cornerstone: Building on Your Best, Fourth Edition
by Robert M. Sherfield, Rhonda J. Montgomery, and Patricia G. Moody
Copyright © 2005, 2002, 2000, 1997 by Pearson Education, Inc.
Published by Prentice Hall

Keys to Success: Building Successful Intelligence for College, Career, and Life, Brief Fourth Edition
by Carol Carter, Joyce Bishop, Sarah Lyman Kravits
Copyright © 2006, 2003, 2001, 1999 by Pearson Education, Inc.
Published by Prentice Hall

Strategies for Active Citizenship
by Kateri M. Drexler and Gwen Garcelon
Copyright © 2005 by Pearson Education, Inc.
Published by Prentice Hall

This special edition published in cooperation with Pearson Learning Solutions.

All trademarks, service marks, registered trademarks, and registered service marks are the property of their respective owners and are used herein for identification purposes only.

Pearson Learning Solutions, 501 Boylston Street, Suite 900, Boston, MA 02116
A Pearson Education Company
www.pearsoned.com

Printed in the United States of America

2 3 4 5 6 7 8 9 10   V011 14 13 12 11 10

2009220239

KW

ISBN 10: 0-558-55187-4
ISBN 13: 978-0-558-55187-2

Brief Contents

Part I

Strategies: Building on Your Best for Career Success

Excerpts taken from:

Cornerstone: Building on Your Best for Career Success
by Robert M. Sherfield, Rhonda J. Montgomery, and Patricia G. Moody

Cornerstone: Building on Your Best, Fourth Edition
by Robert M. Sherfield, Rhonda J. Montgomery, and Patricia G. Moody

Keys to Success: Building Successful Intelligence for College, Career, and Life,
Brief Fourth Edition
by Carol Carter, Joyce Bishop, Sarah Lyman Kravits

Strategies for Active Citizenship
by Kateri M. Drexler and Gwen Garcelon

Contents

PART I | Strategies: Building on Your Best for Career Success

CHAPTER THREE | Styles of Learning, Note and Test Taking Techniques 43

CHAPTER FOUR | Critical Thinking and Citing Sources 89

CHAPTER FIVE | Time Management and Teamwork 101

CHAPTER SIX | Managing Team Projects 125

CHAPTER SEVEN | Changes in the Workplace: Present and Future 133

INDEX 139

You can do it!

Portal to success

A portal is a grand and magnificent entrance into a new world. By becoming part of the ITT Technical Institute family, you have chosen to enter a portal that will lead you into a new career and different way of life. In your lifetime you will undoubtedly experience many events that can alter your views, personality, goals, and livelihood. Few decisions, however, will have as great an influence on the rest of your life as your decision to attend ITT Tech. This course, placed at the beginning of your educational journey, is the portal not only to your career but also to the rest of your life. Today you will begin preparing for the many opportunities that lie ahead. Regardless of what you might have experienced in the past—good or bad—you are entering a new era that will bring many exciting opportunities and challenges. Soon you will begin to understand yourself better and how you can realize your true potential.

Your golden potential

Have you ever thought of yourself as "golden"? More importantly, have you ever treated yourself as if you were "golden"? Consider the following true story as you begin your journey into your new career and life:

In 1957, a massive statue of Buddha was being moved from a temple in Thailand that had been abandoned in the early 1930's. The Buddha stands over 15 feet tall and measures over 12 feet in diameter. A crane had to be used to move the massive statue; but when the crane began to lift the Buddha, the weight was so great that the statue began to crack. To make matters worse, it began to rain. Concerned with the condition of the Buddha, the head monk decided to have the statue lowered so that it could be covered with a canvas until the rain stopped.

As nightfall came, the head monk took his flashlight outside to peer under the canvas to see whether the statue had begun to dry. As he moved the light from area to area, he noticed something shining in one of the cracks. He began to wonder whether something was under the clay. As he hammered and chiseled away at the crack, he found that the clay Buddha was NOT made of clay after all. The monk found that the 15-foot statue was really made of pure, 18-carat GOLD.

Many scholars and historians believe that the Buddha was cast sometime in the mid-1200's. According to one theory, in the 1700's the Siamese monks knew that the Burmese army planned to attack them and, hoping to protect their statue, they covered it in eight inches of clay, which dried and hardened like concrete. When the army attacked, all of the monks in the village were killed, leaving no one who knew the truth about the Buddha. The clay remained intact until the statue was moved on a rainy day in 1957.

Today, the Golden Buddha, which was once covered with clay and abandoned, is said to be valued at almost two hundred million dollars.

Excerpts taken from: *Cornerstone: Discovering Your Potential Learning Activity and Living Well,* Fifth Edition by Robert M. Sherfield, Rhonda J. Montgomery, and Patricia G. Moody.

YES You Can!

Your golden opportunity

We all have incredible talents, skills, and experiences that are all too often covered or underdeveloped. We move through life hiding our brightness—our golden self. As you begin to read and work through this text, think about the strengths and talents that you already have and how you can polish them and bring out their brilliance. Begin to chip away at the clay that may have been covering your true potential for years. Explore who you really are, what you have to offer to the world, and how best to live up to your golden potential. Think about the attitudes, beliefs, or behaviors that you may have to adjust to create your future success.

In discovering your potential, we also invite you to: Discover your open-mindedness

A truly educated person learns to consider a person's character rather than any one or set of factors like skin color and religion. As you become more open-minded, you will begin to understand the need to learn before judging, reason before reacting, and delve deeper before condemning. As you work to discover your potential, strive hard to develop a habit of practicing open-mindedness.

Discover your competence and ability to question

You have already established a certain level of competence or you wouldn't be here. Now is the time to push yourself to learn more than you ever have before. Your future depends on the knowledge you are gaining today. As you move through the coming months and years, don't be afraid to ask questions of others, especially your instructors. Questioning is the first step in becoming more competent and a more critical and logical thinker. Asking the right questions and listening will help you become a more active learner. You also have the opportunity to learn from your peers and their experiences.

Discover your need to be challenged

The "easy road" will never lead to greatness or help you discover your true potential. Winston Churchill said, "It is from adversity that we gain greatness." When you are struggling, remember that you are getting stronger. You are preparing for becoming the person you were meant to be. As you begin classes, talk to your instructors, and balance all the elements in your life, the experiences you have will make you stretch and ultimately lead you to another level in the search for your true potential.

Discover your ability to balance

No SINGLE thing will ever bring you joy, peace, or prosperity. Include family, friends, cultural events, social activities, work, and service to others in your daily life. Seek balance between work and play. You will endlessly search for happiness unless you have a sense of balance in your life. Harmony and balance help you reduce stress, have more time for what you love, and live well.

Discover your success and true potential

You need to define exactly what success means to you so you know where you are going. Whatever success is for you, pursue it with all of the passion and energy you have. Set your goals high and work hard to create a life that you can ultimately look back on with pride, satisfaction, and joy.

We recognize that, in order to take on your program of study, you are committing yourself to a greater amount of work than you have already been juggling. You would not commit to all of that work unless there was a major benefit when you finish. By putting in the effort now to complete your program and receive your degree, you will be in a position to realize your dreams. In your new career, you will find that your life has taken on a new meaning. Your degree will open up a new future for you that will undoubtedly lighten the load you are now carrying. Though you will find new challenges in your program and career, they will likely be interesting and exciting.

As you read about the concepts and challenges presented in this course, you will have many opportunities to personalize and mold the information to your needs. The more effort you put into doing the activities in this course and throughout your education, the more value you will gain. Our hope is that you will discover early in your education and career that the responsibility for your learning and development is primarily yours. We commend you for taking on the challenge ahead, and we are rooting for you! We'll be there along the way to help when we can, but we know the work ahead is mainly yours. The credit will be yours, as well, and we'll be there at the finish line to cheer you! You can do it, and ITT Tech can help!

and ITT Tech Can Help!

Preface

The purpose of this book and course is to help you enhance the quality of your career and life. Though the specialized skills that your future career requires will be presented throughout your education program at ITT Tech, this course is concerned with helping you build the essential skills needed for surviving and thriving in a continually changing world and workplace. Use this book to become a better student and learner, and those skills will carry into your future. By training yourself to become a more adept thinker, writer, speaker, and problem solver, you gather the tools you need to excel in many areas of your life.

Near the beginning of this text, you are asked to look within to determine your important values, because behaviors grow out of beliefs, and how we act shapes the quality of our lives. By becoming more self-aware, you can also learn more effectively and efficiently, understand your motivations and desires, and participate fully with others. Though individuals can accomplish great things, groups can usually accomplish more. This text also introduces the dynamics of working with others and how to build better working relationships.

It is our hope that this book will help you to see the possibilities of your future, anticipate and cope with new situations, guide you through difficult days, discover more about yourself and your unique gifts, develop study and learning habits that help you succeed, hone your creative and critical thinking skills, and be an effective problem solver.

⬤ Contents

What's in It for Me?

Your ITT Tech Experience

Regardless of your background or reasons for continuing your education, the experience of change is something you'll share with everyone. Will you be able to open yourself up to new people and new situations?

Welcome to the first day of the rest of your life! In your quest to realize your golden potential, you will undoubtedly find challenges ahead. Not only is the world changing rapidly, but now you will probably find that you will also begin to change. Your priorities and beliefs may be tested. In fact, you may find they are already different than they were even a few months ago. With everything in a state of flux, it becomes very important to *assess* who and where you are, *plan* for where you are going, and *apply* the plan to your life. The process of understanding and managing life change begins in this chapter. By looking at some of the elements of change, our values and how those impact motivation and self-esteem, we build a good foundation for everything that follows—in this course, in the rest of your program, and in your career.

Many students face challenges around balancing time commitments and pressures. Graduates find that their degrees have opened up a new future, the loads they were carrying before have been lightened, and in their new careers, their lives have taken on new meaning. By putting in the effort now to complete your program and receive your degree, you will be in a position to realize your dreams. Of course, the short-term process is not easy. If it were, everyone would do it. By taking on this challenge, you have put yourself into a unique category of people: career college student. It is our hope and strong belief that by investing yourself in this course, you will find the tools to make it a bit easier to be in a more unique category still: college graduate.

Before reading further, jot down some thoughts about what you want to achieve in college, what you value about being in college, what you expect from ITT Technical Institute, and what we expect from you.

So, What's This All About?

Why are you here? What is the driving force that brought you to the door of ITT Tech? Was it a desire to learn more about your field? Was it to fulfill a dream? Was it a need for a career shift? Did other major changes occur in your life? Do you need retraining for the world of work? Whatever the reason, you're here, and that is a positive and wonderful thing for you and your family.

Over 70% of entering students say that their primary reason for furthering their education is to be able to get a better job and make more money. Good news! According to the U.S. Census, people who further their education and training DO earn more than those with only a high school diploma or GED.

Beyond money, furthering your education can help you:

- Work in a career of your choosing (not just a job)
- Develop a healthier self-esteem
- Strengthen your confidence in many areas of your life
- Expand your independence (thus reducing your dependence)
- Become more knowledgeable about more things
- Increase your options for future employment
- Grow to be a role model and mentor for your family and friends

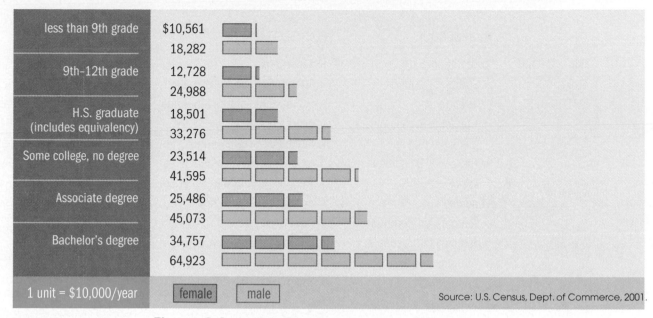

less than 9th grade	$10,561						
	18,282						
9th–12th grade	12,728						
	24,988						
H.S. graduate (includes equivalency)	18,501						
	33,276						
Some college, no degree	23,514						
	41,595						
Associate degree	25,486						
	45,073						
Bachelor's degree	34,757						
	64,923						

1 unit = $10,000/year   [female]   [male]

Source: U.S. Census, Dept. of Commerce, 2001.

Figure 1.1   Annual Earnings by Education Level and Gender

Changes in the Days to Come

(You gain strength, experience, and confidence by every experience where you really stop to look fear in the face . . . You must do the thing you think you cannot.

—Eleanor Roosevelt)

One of the first changes you may notice about college is that you have to learn to juggle several things at once, including your course work, your finances, and perhaps job responsibilities. Learning how to set priorities for your time and resources is a critical step to successfully handling this challenge. Figure 1.2 offers a guide to understanding expectations.

Attitudes That Hinder Change

You can develop attitudes that hinder change and stop growth. Such attitudes are dangerous because they rob you of opportunity, happiness, growth, and goals. These attitudes include:

- The "I can't" syndrome
- Apathy, or the "I don't care" syndrome
- Closed-mindedness
- Unfounded anxiety
- Fear of taking chances
- Loss of motivation
- The "let someone else deal with it" syndrome

If you can learn to watch out for and control these negative attitudes, you will begin to view change as a wonderful and positive lifelong event.

Change can introduce you to new people, ideas, cultures, and experiences.

	HIGH SCHOOL	POST SECONDARY	WORK
PUNCTUALITY AND ATTENDANCE	Expectations: • State law requires attendance • The hours in the day are managed for you • There may be some leeway in project dates Penalties: • You may get detention • You may not graduate • You may be considered truant • Your grades may suffer	Expectations: • Attendance and participation in class are enforced by some instructors • Some instructors will not give you an extension on due dates • You decide your own schedule and plan your own day Penalties: • You may not be admitted to class if you are late • You may fail the assignment if it is late • Repeated tardiness is sometimes counted as an absence • Most instructors do not take late assignments, especially if prior arrangements have not been made	Expectations: • You are expected to be at work and on time on a daily basis Penalties: • Your salary and promotions may depend on your daily attendance and punctuality • You will most likely be fired for abusing either
TEAMWORK AND PARTICIPATION	Expectations: • Most teamwork is assigned and carried out in class • You may be able to choose teams with your friends • Your grade reflects your participation Penalties: • If you don't participate, you may get a poor grade • You may jeopardize the grade of the entire team	Expectations: • Many instructors require group work • Your grade will depend on your participation • Your grade may depend on your entire team's performance • You may have to work on the project outside of class Penalties: • Lack of participation will probably lower your grade • Your team members will likely report you to the instructor if you do not participate and their grades suffer as a result	Expectations: • You will be expected to participate fully in any assigned task • You will be expected to rely on co-workers to help solve problems and increase profits • You will be required to attend and participate in meetings and sharing sessions • You will be required to participate in formal teams and possess the ability to work with a diverse workforce Penalties: • You will be "tagged" as non-team player • Your lack of participation and teamwork will cost you raises and promotions • You will most likely be terminated

Figure 1.2 A Guide to Understanding Expectations

	HIGH SCHOOL	POST SECONDARY	WORK
PERSONAL RESPONSIBILITY AND ATTITUDE	Expectations: • Teachers may coach you and try to motivate you • You are required to be in high school by law regardless of your attitude or responsibility level Penalties: • You may be reprimanded for certain attitudes • If your attitude prevents you from participating, you may fail the class	Expectations: • You are responsible for your own learning • Instructors will assist you, but there may be little "hand holding" or personal coaching for motivation • Continuing education did not choose you, you chose it, and you will be expected to hold this attitude toward your work Penalties: • You may fail the class if your attitude and motivation prevent you from participating	Expectations: • You are hired to do certain tasks and the company or institution fully expects this of you • You are expected to be positive and self-motivated • You are expected to model good behavior and uphold the company's work standards Penalties: • You will be passed over for promotions and raises • You may be reprimanded • You may be terminated
ETHICS AND CREDIBILITY	Expectations: • You are expected to turn in your own work • You are expected to avoid plagiarism • You are expected to write your own papers • Poor ethical decisions in high school may result in detention or suspension Penalties: • You may get detention or suspension • You will probably fail the project	Expectations: • You are expected to turn in your own work • You are expected to avoid plagiarism • You are expected to write your own papers • You are expected to conduct research and complete projects based on higher education and societal standards Penalties: • Poor ethical decisions may land you in front of a student ethics committee or a faculty ethics committee, or result in expulsion from the institution • You will fail the project • You may fail the class • You may face deportation if your visa is dependent on your student status	Expectations: • You will be required to carry out your job in accordance with company policies, laws, and moral standards • You will be expected to use adult vision and standards Penalties: • Poor ethical decisions may cause you to be severely reprimanded, terminated, or in some cases could even result in a prison sentence if your unethical behavior was also illegal.

Figure 1.2 A Guide to Understanding Expectations (*continued*)

So, I Want to Change
How Do I Do It?

After reading and reflecting thus far, you may have identified several changes that you need to make. Further, changes may have been thrust upon you by choices you or those around you have made. Although these and other events may happen to you, it's the choices that you make that will ultimately affect the outcomes in your life. The following model provides a method for dealing with and implementing change in your life and might be helpful in bringing about positive results.

The Need for Change

THE CHANGE IMPLEMENTATION MODEL

1 Determine what you need or want to change and why.

2 Research your options for making the desired changes and seek advice and assistance from a variety of sources.

3 Identify the obstacles to change and determine how to overcome them.

4 Establish a plan by outlining several positive steps to bring about the changes you identified.

5 Implement your plan for bringing about the desired change:

- Focus on the desired outcome.
- View problems as positive challenges.
- Turn your fears into energy by reducing anxiety through physical exercise, proper nutrition, and stress-management strategies.
- Associate with positive and motivated people.

1	Determine what you need or want to change and why.	You realize that you must change your study habits or fail the class. Your old study methods are not working.
2	Research your options for making the desired changes and seek advice and assistance from a variety of sources.	You look around campus to determine what services are available to you such as tutoring, learning centers, and learning communities. You also make an appointment to speak with the instructor. You talk to one of the members of a study group in class to see what benefits she is getting from the group.
3	Identify the obstacles to change and determine how to overcome them.	In the past, you have been afraid to get involved. You realize that you have never adjusted your time-management practices to post-secondary life; you are still studying on a "high school time frame." You realize that you have never reached out to classmates before. By listing the problems on paper, you see that you have to change your habits and take a risk by asking to join a study group.
4	Establish a plan by outlining several positive steps to bring about the changes you identified.	You spend a quiet evening thinking about steps that you can take to become a better student. You decide that you need to (1) approach members of the study group to ask permission to join, (2) make an appointment at the tutoring center, and (3) make a commitment to reading the assigned material every night.
5	Implement your plan for bringing about the desired change: • Focus on the desired outcome.	You know that you want and need to pass the class. This is the ultimate desired outcome, but you also know that you must change your study habits for other classes and this group may help you do so. You realize that if you can change your time and study practices, you will be successful in other areas.
	• View problems as positive challenges.	Instead of concentrating on the amount of time and energy required for the study group, you decide to look at it as a way to learn more, study better, and make new friends who have the same goals.
	• Turn your fears into energy by reducing anxiety through physical exercise, proper nutrition, and stress-management strategies.	You learn that two people from the study group also run every other morning. You decide to ask them if you can join them. You also decide that instead of going off campus to the Burger Hut, you will bring your own lunch and use this time to study for other classes.
	• Associate with positive and motivated people.	You notice that your attitude toward the class and life in general is improving because of the positive attitudes in the group. You can't believe how much you have changed in a few short weeks just by concentrating on the positive and associating with people who are motivated to succeed.

The Impact of Values

On Motivation, Goal Setting, and Self-Esteem

If you have been highly motivated to accomplish a goal in the past, this achievement was probably tied to something you valued a great deal. Most of what you do in life centers around what is truly important to you. You cannot get excited about achieving a goal or be disciplined enough to stick to it unless you definitely want to make it happen. If you really want to run a marathon, for example, you have to pay the price of long hours of practice, getting up early in the morning, and running when others are sleeping or playing. If you hate running, but you set a goal to complete a marathon in record time because your father was a champion runner and expects the same of you, you are not likely to achieve this goal. Your goals must relate to your personal value system.

Values, self-esteem, motivation, and goal setting are all mixed up together, making it difficult to separate one from the other. What you try to accomplish is directly connected to those things, ideas, and concepts that you value most. Values are central beliefs and attitudes that make you a unique person, while greatly impacting your choices and your personal lifestyle. If you cherish an attitude or belief, many of your actions will be centered around this ideal.

You were not born with your basic values. Your values were shaped to a great extent by your parents, the school you attended, the community where you grew up, and the culture that nourished you. Because of your personal background, you have developed a unique set of values. To make good decisions, set appropriate goals, and manage your priorities, you must identify those values that are central to who you are today. Until you clarify what you really value, you may try to accomplish what is important to someone else, and you will tend to wander around and become frustrated. Values, goals, and motivation bring direction to your life and help you get where you want to go.

(He who has a why to live can bear with almost any how. —Nietzsche)

As you become aware of and choose your values, they become an internal guidance system. To make good decisions, set appropriate goals, and manage priorities, it is important to identify the values that are central to who you are today and to who you want to become.

Identify Your Values

Identifying and defining **values** is usually a work-in-progress that occurs throughout your life. Because our identities are constantly open to change and re-definition, the values that we hold are also as open to change. By practicing self-reflection, you can

Figure 1.3 Wheel of Life

learn how to be more intentional in your decisions and actions. You can learn to assess how your actions are expressing the things that are important to you.

The first step in assessing values is to examine how important the various aspects of work and life are to you. Look at the preceding Wheel of Life, and consider what areas of life might have a particular significance. We may find that some areas are more important than others at varying times in our lives; however, the wheel symbolizes our lives as a whole. Keeping the wheel segments balanced, as demonstrated in our lives, will help us proceed smoothly. Start to identify values in each of the areas. For each category, identify the importance by rating it from 1 to 10, with 10 being the most important.

Category	Importance
Personal Growth	5
Money	2
Relationships	8
Education	6
Community	3
Play	4
Family	10
Spirituality	1
Health	7
Work	9

Accountable

Being Accountable may include being:

Reliable	Trustworthy
Dependable	Responsible
Loyal	Secure

Committed

Committed may mean being:

Participative	Focused
Enthusiastic	Persistent
Energetic	Productive
Faithful	

Open

Openness may include being:

Fair	Unbiased
Patient	Open-minded
Tolerant	Joyful

Honest

Honesty may include being:

Authentic	Genuine
Outspoken	Sincere
Truthful	Frank
Balanced	

Responsible

Responsibility entails taking control of our own lives without blame or victimization

Giving

Giving may include being:

Dedicated	Compassionate
Accepting	Nurturing
Contributing	Helpful
Cooperative	Generous
Appreciative	Considerate
Forgiving	Respectful
Friendly	

The previous are some sample character traits and values that can be used as a starting point in developing a list of personal values. Consider how much you value the following traits. Use these traits to help you distinguish values. For instance, you may value being reliable to your family, or being committed to your education. What are traits and values that you would add to your list?

Plan to Act with Integrity

Webster's Dictionary defines integrity as *"the state of being whole or complete; acting with moral soundness."* When your actions are an honest expression of yourself, you have personal integrity. As you become more intentional about using your values to guide your actions, you develop greater personal integrity.

Among the widely accepted qualities of morality are fairness, honesty, service, excellence, patience, and treatment of others with dignity. Consider your own definition of moral soundness in order to assess the integrity of your actions.

Congruence

Becoming more self-aware allows you to become more intentional about your choices and how they affect the quality of your life and the lives of others. Congruence means *"to be in agreement or alignment"* and is another aspect of acting with integrity. In order to achieve true congruence in your life, what you think, say and do must be in alignment.

When actions are not in alignment with values, there is internal conflict, as well as conflict within relationships. The consequences of this conflict may include stress, depression, fatigue, anger, or anxiety. Conversely, when we act in accordance with what is true for us, we experience positive feelings. These may include happiness, satisfaction, passion, certainty, and abundance. Our feelings give us immediate feedback and are important guides for acting with integrity.

The Impact of Attitude
On Motivation, Goal Setting, and Self-Esteem

Have you ever met someone who turned you off immediately with a negative attitude? Some people whine about the weather or their parents; they verbally attack people who differ from them or degrade themselves with negative remarks. Listen for the negative comments people make, and the messages they send out about themselves. When people continually feed their brains negative messages, their bodies respond accordingly.

The impact of a bad attitude on your motivation and self-esteem is overpowering. On the other hand, focusing on the positive can bring dramatic changes in your life.

We all know that life sometimes deals bad blows, but your goal should be to be positive much more often than you are negative. Positive attitudes go hand-in-hand with energy, motivation, and friendliness. People with positive attitudes are more appealing; negative people drive others away.

Listen to yourself for a few days. Are you whining, complaining, griping, and finding fault with everything and everybody around you, including yourself? Is your bad grade the instructor's fault? Is your family responsible for everything bad that ever happened to you? If these kinds of thoughts are coming out of your mouth or are in your head, your first step toward improved motivation and self-esteem is to clean up your act.

How are the friends you are making in school influencing your decisions?

To be successful at anything, you have to develop a winning attitude. You have to eliminate negative thinking. Begin today: tell yourself only positive things about yourself; build on those positives; focus on the good things; work constantly to improve.

Winners get up early with an attitude of "I can't wait for this day to start so I can have another good day." OK, OK—so you may not get up early, but you can get up with a positive attitude. Tell yourself things that will put you in the right frame of mind to succeed. When you are talking to yourself—and everybody does—feed your brain positive thoughts. Think of your brain as a powerful computer; you program it with your words, and your body carries out the program.

Pay attention to the messages you send out to others as well. What kinds of remarks do you make about yourself and about others when you are with your friends? Do you sound positive or negative? Do you hear yourself saying positive things?

Stephen Covey, in his book *Seven Habits of Highly Effective People*, refers to the concept of the "inside-out" approach. Covey relates that if you want to create change in some area of your life, focus on what you think, say and how you act in that area. For instance, if you want to have better friendships, think about and practice being a more concerned and giving friend. If you want to be a better student, think about and practice taking sole responsibility for your learning.

Overcoming Doubts and Fears

Fear is a great motivator; it probably motivates more people than anything else. Unfortunately, it motivates most people to hold back, to doubt themselves, to accomplish much less than they could, and to hide the person they really are.

One of the biggest obstacles to reaching your potential may be your own personal fears. If you are afraid, you are not alone; everyone has fears. It is interesting to note that most of our fears are learned. As a baby, you had only two fears: a fear of falling and a fear of loud noises. As you got older, you added to your list of fears. And, if you are like most people, you let your fears dominate parts of your life, saying things to yourself like: "What if I try and fail?" "What if people laugh at me for thinking I can do this?" "What if someone finds out that this is my dream?"

> They who have conquered doubt and fear have conquered failure.
> —James Allen

You have two choices where fear is concerned. You can let fear dominate your life, or you can focus on those things you really want to accomplish, put your fears behind you, and go for it. The people most successful in their fields will tell you that they are afraid, but that they overcome their fear because their desire to achieve is greater. Barbra Streisand, recording artist and stage performer, becomes physically nauseated with stage fright when she performs, yet she faces these fears and retains her position as one of the most popular entertainers of our time.

Moving Out of Your Comfort Zone

Successful people face their fears because their motivation and ambition force them out of their "comfort zones." Your comfort zone is where you know you are good, you feel confident, and you don't have to stretch your talents far to be successful. If you stay in your comfort zone, you will never reach your potential and you will deny yourself the opportunity of knowing how it feels to overcome your fears.

Deciding to go to college probably caused you some level of discomfort and raised many fears: "What if I flunk out?" "What if I can't do my job, go to school, and manage a family at the same time?" The mere fact that you are here is a step outside your comfort zone—a very important step that can change your life dramatically.

Everyone has a comfort zone. When you are doing something that you do well, and you feel comfortable and confident, you are in your comfort zone. When you are nervous and afraid, you are stepping outside your comfort zone. When you realize you are outside your comfort zone, you should feel good about yourself because you are learning and growing and improving. You cannot progress unless you step outside your comfort zone.

Dealing With Hardship and Failure

To be motivated, you have to learn to deal with failure. Have you ever given up on something too quickly, or gotten discouraged and quit? Can you think of a time when you were unfair to yourself because you didn't stay with something long enough? Did you ever stop doing something you wanted to do because somebody laughed at you or teased you? Overcoming failure makes victory much more rewarding. Motivated people know that losing is a part of winning: the difference between being a winner and being a loser is the ability to try again. If you reflect on your life, you may well discover that you gained your greatest strengths through adversity. Difficult situations make you tougher and more capable of developing your potential. Overcoming adversity is an essential part of success in college and in life. Think of a time in your life when you faced difficulties but persisted and became stronger as a result.

Motivation
What is It and How Can I Get It?

Sometimes you might hear people talk about their lack of motivation or you hear someone else referred to as a "motivated person." You might wish you were more motivated but aren't sure how to get to that point. You see people who are highly self-disciplined and you would like to be more like them, but you don't have a clue how to get started. You've probably heard that old cliché, "A journey of a thousand miles begins with a single step." It may be old and sound a little corny, but actually, it's the truth.

Abraham Lincoln

was raised in great poverty, lost the love of his life when he was 26, suffered a nervous breakdown at age 27, failed in business twice, lost eight elections, and suffered the death of two children ... all *before* he became our president and changed the face of the world.

Becoming motivated is a process—it's not one giant leap to becoming something you want to be. Motivation rarely comes overnight; rather, you become motivated by experiencing one small success after another as your confidence grows, and gradually, you try something bigger and more challenging. There are only two broad categories that will ever motivate you: a dream you have or a problem you are trying to overcome. Every goal and everything regarding motivation will fit into one of these two categories. Either dreaming of something or wanting to solve a problem is the first part of the formula for motivation. The other part is about making it happen—an action plan. Dreaming or wanting to solve a problem without action will get you nowhere. Nothing works unless you do! Motivation can be broken down into:

Desire + Courage + Goals + Discipline = Motivation

Understanding Motivation   When you act from your own values and experience self-worth from within, you are said to be internally motivated. When you act to please others, or act in alignment with the values of others, you are externally motivated.

External Motivation   Part of human nature is self-protection and the drive to sustain oneself. Many of us have learned to protect and nurture ourselves through gaining the approval of others. Children learn that they can gain love by pleasing others. The danger in **external motivation** is when we compromise our values and priorities in the pursuit of approval from others. This inevitably produces internal conflict, and the negative feelings that accompany it.

Internal Motivation   Internally motivated people consult their own guidance in decision-making. Well-being and self-worth come from within and are not dependent on the validation of others.

When your self-worth comes from within, things may change in your life, but they cannot compromise your sense of value and empowerment. A study conducted by the University of Rochester's Human Motivation Research Group found, for example, that people whose motivation was internal exhibited more interest, confidence, excitement, persistence, creativity and performance than those who were motivated by external rewards.[1]

In order to stay motivated, you have to become committed to doing something. You need to face your fears and not let them become bigger than your dreams. You need to be willing to write your dream or desire down as a goal and say it out loud to your friends and family. You need to put those goals or commitments somewhere you can see them often in order to keep you on track. You need to take the initiative to get started. You have to be willing to form good habits and replace bad habits. For example, if you are a procrastinator, you have to work hard to change the habit that gets you in trouble over and over and over again. You need to be determined to take responsibility for yourself and your habits. In other words, you need to discipline yourself. If you can keep up a good practice for 21 days, it usually becomes a habit. Tell yourself, "I can do anything for 21 days."

No one can do any of this for you. The choice to be motivated, to be successful, to reach your potential is up to you. Blaming others, making excuses, using difficult circumstances as a crutch, or quitting will never get you anywhere. If you want to be motivated and successful, *get up and get started.*

When you are sure that you are becoming more disciplined, that your work habits are getting better, your grades are improving, and you are focused on success, reward yourself. Do something that you have really wanted to do for a long time. Share your successes with a few people who really care. Be careful not to boast. If you are good, people will know it. As you grow and become more successful, you will begin to make wiser choices; you will reach bigger goals; you will be on your way to accomplishing your dreams!

Your thoughts, words and actions are energy forces, and by focusing them toward specific and intentional points, you can intensify their strength. Choose goals that are in alignment with your values and personal integrity.

Becoming Who You Want to Be
The Goal-Setting Process

Goal setting itself is relatively easy. Many people make goals but fail to make the commitment to accomplish those goals. Instead of defining their goals in concrete, measurable terms, they think of them occasionally and have vague, unclear ideas about how to attain them. The first step toward reaching a goal is the commitment to pay the price to achieve it. Opportunities abound everywhere; commitment is a scarce commodity.

> There is only one definition of success: to be able to spend your life in your own way.
>
> —Christopher Morley

Individual Goals   Individual goals are goals that are set by you, and for which you alone develop and implement a strategy. They can be goals that you have for your own development and achievement. What makes them individual goals is that you alone are responsible for achieving them.

> All things are possible until they are proved impossible—and even the impossible may only be so, as of now.
>
> —Pearl S. Buck

Collective Goals   Collective goals are set, collectively, by members of a group. Necessarily, each member of the group has a role to play in the achieving the goal. In addition, all members will gain something in common by the achievement of the goal. Collective goals can be initiated by an individual, but if they are intended to benefit a group, they should be formulated and agreed upon by the group.

Short-Term and Long-Term Goals   Having both short-term and long-term goals can be rewarding. Short-term goals are usually less complex and easier than long-term goals. We build momentum with each goal we complete, so setting short-term goals helps ensure that we'll have frequent victories.

Long-term goals (one year or longer) keep us headed in the right direction and can provide a sense of greater purpose. These goals may require a longer process in order to achieve their result, in which case it is helpful to break down the overarching, or long-term, goal into smaller goals that may be reachable in shorter periods of time. Breaking a long-term goal into smaller short-term goals can provide a sense of accomplishment if our ultimate goal requires patience and perseverance over a long period of time.

Prioritizing Goals

Most of us have several goals in different life areas that we would like to achieve. Prioritizing goals can be confusing if you think in terms of "which is more important?" Over the long term, all of your goals are probably important, or they wouldn't be goals. When prioritizing, think in terms of *timing:* "which will I focus on more right now?"

When deciding which goals to start with, consider the following:

• Will achieving certain goals first make others easier to achieve?

• Do any of your goals express values that are more important to you than others?

- Which goals will create the greatest impact on your solution with the fewest resources?
- Which goals will create long-term results?
- Which goals have the greatest chance of success?

Dealing with Conflicting Goals

Because the resources we have to spend on our goals—money, time, and energy—are limited, goals can often appear to be at odds with one another. Working on one can mean slipping on the other. Good management of your goals as a group is important for avoiding frustration.

Some suggestions for dealing with several goals at once include:

- **Stay focused.** Don't set too many goals at the same time, and make sure that your goals are in alignment with your most important values.
- **Have at least one simple goal and one difficult goal at any given time.** The simple goals motivate you as you accomplish them rapidly. The difficult goals keep you challenged and growing.
- **Have at least one short-term and one long-term goal at any given time.** As with simple goals, short-term goals help assure that you'll have frequent victories. Long-term goals keep you headed in the right direction.
- **Be flexible.** Decide which of your goals (and tasks) are most important, but be willing to change a goal or even put it on hold for a while, if necessary.
- **Look for ways to combine goals and tasks.** If you can work on two or more goals at once, you can consolidate your resources.

What Are Your Goals?

You can set many goals at this point without worrying about spreading yourself too thin because we make a distinction between setting a goal and managing a goal, or project. At this stage, think of many goals you'd like to shoot for even if you are focused on other things right now. However, also be mindful of the importance of balance. Make sure to set goals across different areas of your life: health, finance, family, relationships, personal growth, career, etc. The number of categories in which you should set goals depends on your particular situation. How well-balanced is your life right now? What are your priorities? Are you already strong in some areas, but weak in others? Answers to questions like these will give you a sense of where to focus your efforts. In general, expect to focus on a few goals in more than one category at a time. It's okay to set a lot of goals in multiple categories.

Plan for Attainable Goals

Typically, goal-setting theorists have suggested that goals have certain characteristics in order to be more easily attained. In general, goals should be:

Written

Research has shown that by simply writing down your goals, you will increase your odds of achieving them, on average, by 300 percent.[2]

A study was conducted by Yale University in 1953, and, though the study is older, it has some telling results about the importance of goals. A survey was given to the senior class, and they were asked several questions, three of which dealt with goals. The questions were:

- Have you set goals?
- Have you written them down?
- Do you have a plan to accomplish these goals?

Only three percent of the class answered "yes" to these questions. Twenty years later, the members of this class were surveyed again. The research showed that the three percent of the class who set goals were happier and more successful than those who did not have goals. In addition, the three percent who set goals had 97% of the wealth of the entire class. In other words, these three percent were wealthier than the entire rest of the class combined. This study illustrates that setting goals can lead to accomplishment and fulfillment.

Realistic

Believing that your goals are at least possible for you to achieve will motivate you. More importantly, it is you who must believe, not anyone else. However, just because you should believe that the goal is possible does not mean that you must expect it to be easy.

A goal is realistic if you stand reasonably good odds of accomplishing it, given enough time and effort on your part. You must have some control over the effort in order for goals to be realistic. The majority of the goals you set should be very realistic or you risk becoming frustrated if you do not accomplish any of them.

Challenging

Although you will want to have some easier goals, some of your goals should also be challenging. Limit the number of challenging goals or tasks to avoid becoming overwhelmed or frustrated. When goals are so challenging that you wonder whether they are realistic, it might make sense to break the goals down into smaller, incremental goals. The challenging goals force you to grow.

Measurable and Specific

Your goals should be measurable and specific enough for you to know definitively whether they have been completed. Though some goals are ongoing or will likely be works-in-progress throughout your life and may not in themselves be measurable, the individual tasks that you will later assign to these goals should be very specific and measurable.

Adaptable

The goals you set now may not be perfect, and even if they are, situations can change over time, making them imperfect. The reality is that most people's goals do change over time. In fact, goals usually should change, at least slightly, in response to things that change around you or new life events.

It's important to set goals, and to have something for which to strive, although once we set the goals, we need to detach from the outcome. You're not guaranteed specific results as you define them. But you gain the satisfaction of living your life for a higher purpose.

Time-Sensitive

When we look at goals in terms of your group of goals, you'll want many of them to have a concrete deadline. However, there may be goals that you develop that are ongoing, such as attaining excellent health or contributing to world peace. Such goals will have no end date, though they should be tracked and monitored, and the individual tasks that comprise the goals should have deadlines.

Congruous

In order to be effective, your goals should conform to your value system and be internally motivated. If you set goals that will meet someone else's expectations or that do not fit within your values, you will find it more difficult to reach them. Your goals should fit into what you want to do, be, or have in your life. If you find it difficult to develop the motivation to achieve a goal, first look at where it fits into your value system and do some self-awareness work.

For example, someone might have the goal "to buy a bigger house than my brother's." Asking the question "why a bigger house?" could shed light on the fact that your friend wants to compete with his brother. Maybe there are other issues to be addressed such as self-esteem and respect that owning a larger house will not solve. Perhaps a more congruous goal would be "to earn my brother's respect." Identifying the root goal could have a profound impact on this person's life that could not be achieved with a house of any size. Honest evaluation of why you want to achieve the goal can lead to insights and personal discovery.

Positive

Goals also have a greater ability to motivate us subconsciously if they are stated in a positive, proactive way. You may notice this in advertising messages. Nike says "Just Do It" instead of "Stop Sitting There." If your goal is to stop procrastinating, how can you state your ultimate goal, or what you really want, in a positive way? "I want to move with speed and direction in all my tasks and responsibilities" is more proactive. Negatively framed goals require not doing something, and thus focus our attention on what we don't want instead of on a positive vision. Positive goals keep us clear and focused on the images of what we want.

Determine the Values Behind Your Goals

Determining the Values Behind the Goal

For each of the goals you set, see if you can determine its underlying values.

For example:

Goal	Corresponding Value
Graduating in May	Being committed, perseverance, responsibility, patience

Goal	Corresponding Value
_____	_____
_____	_____
_____	_____
_____	_____

Loving Yourself More
Ten Ways to Increase Your Self-Esteem

If you were asked to name all the areas of your life that are impacted by self-esteem, what would you say? The correct answer is, "Everything." Self-esteem and self-understanding are two of the most important components of your personal makeup! In other words, you have got to know and love yourself! Did you know that your IQ score might not be as important as knowing your own talents and strengths and having healthy self-esteem? A student can be brilliant in terms of mental ability, but may perform at a very low capacity because of unhealthy self-esteem. Unhealthy self-esteem and a lack of self-understanding are also connected to loneliness and depression. "Self-esteem is the armor that protects kids from the dragons of life: drugs, alcohol, delinquency and unhealthy relationships" (McKay and Fanning, 2000).

- **Take control of your own life.** If you let other people rule your life, you will always have unhealthy self-esteem. You will feel helpless and out of control as long as someone else has power over your life. Part of growing up is taking control of your life and making your own decisions. Get involved in the decisions that shape your life. Seize control—don't let life happen to you!

- **Adopt the idea that "you are responsible for you."** The day you take responsibility for yourself and what happens to you is the day you start to develop your self-esteem. When you can admit your mistakes and celebrate your successes knowing you did it your way, you will learn to love yourself much better.

- **Refuse to allow friends and family to tear you down.** You may have family or friends who belittle you, criticize your decisions, and refuse to let you make your own decisions. Combat their negativity by admitting your mistakes and shortcomings to yourself and by making up your mind that you are going to overcome them. By doing this, you are taking their negative power away from them. Spend less time with people who make you feel small and insecure and more time with people who encourage you.

- **Control what you say to yourself.** "Self-talk" is important to your self-esteem and to your ability to motivate yourself positively. Your brain is like a powerful computer and it continually plays messages to you. If these self-talk messages are negative, they will have a detrimental impact on your self-esteem and on your ability to live up to your potential. Make a habit of saying positive things to yourself: "I will do well on this test because I am prepared." "I am a good and decent person, and I deserve to do well."

- **Take carefully assessed risks often.** Many people find risk taking very hard to do, but it is one of the very best ways to raise your self-esteem level. If you are going to grow to your fullest potential, you will have to learn to take some calculated risks. While you should never take foolhardy risks that might endanger your life, you must constantly be willing to push yourself out of your comfort zone. Every day, force yourself to take a little step outside your comfort zone.

- **Don't compare yourself to other people.** You may never be able to "beat" some people at certain things. But it really does not matter. You only have to beat yourself to get better. If you constantly tell yourself that you "are not as handsome as Bill" or "as smart as Mary" or "as athletic as Jack," your inner voice will begin to believe these statements, and your body will act accordingly. One of the best ways to improve self-esteem and to accomplish goals is simply to get a little better every day without thinking about what other people are doing. If you are always practicing at improving yourself, sooner or later you will become a person you can admire—and others will admire you, too!

- **Develop a victory wall or victory file.** Many times, you tend to take your accomplishments and hide them in a drawer or closet. Put your certificates, letters of praise, trophies, and awards out where you can see them on a daily basis. Keep a file of great cartoons, letters of support, or friendly cards so that you can refer to them from time to time.

- **Keep your promises and be loyal to friends, family, and yourself.** If you have ever had someone break a promise to you, you know how it feels to have your loyalty betrayed. The most outstanding feature of one's character is one's ability to be loyal, keep one's promises, and do what one has agreed to do. Few things can make you feel better about yourself than being loyal and keeping your word.

- **Win with grace—lose with class.** Everyone loves a winner, but everyone also loves a person who can lose with class and dignity. On the other hand, no one loves a bragging winner or a moaning loser. If you are engaged in sports, debate, acting, art shows, or math competitions, you will encounter winning and losing. Remember, whether you win or lose, if you're involved and active, you're already in the top 10 percent of the population.

- **Set goals and maintain a high level of motivation.** Find something that you can be passionate about; set a realistic goal to achieve this passion, and stay focused on this goal every day. By maintaining a high level of motivation, you will begin to see your goals come to fruition and feel your self-esteem soar. Setting a goal and achieving it is one of the most powerful ways to develop healthy self-esteem.

Endnotes

[1] Ryan, Richard M. and Edward L. Deci, "Self Determination Theroy and the Facilitation of Intrinsic Motivation, Social Development, and Well-Being," American Psychologist 55, 1 (January 2000) 68–78.

[2] Ziglar, Zig. Sucess and the Self-Image. New York: Simon & Schuster, 1995.

Taking A Tour of ITT Technical Institute Resources

Objectives

In this section, you will learn how to

- Introduction to the Student Portal
- E-mail options from inside and outside the Student Portal
- Get help if you run into problems
- Explore the ITT Technical Institute Virtual Library
- Use the Virtual Library to locate and analyze information from traditional, electronic, and personal resources
- Locate and utilize necessary ITT Tech resources

Introduction to the Student Portal

What's in It for Me?

The ITT Technical Institute Student Portal is your gateway into a world of resources. It is a comprehensive Web site that provides up-to-the-minute information about events at your school, as well as access to your ITT Tech e-mail account, an extensive virtual library, an online career center, and more. From here, you can access campus announcements, your school calendar, world and local news, career announcements, and more. You can also manage frequently accessed Web links and bookmarks, purchase Dell computers at a discount, check the weather, and search for jobs. As long as you remain a student you can access the Student Portal. After you graduate, you can continue to use the Student Portal indefinitely as a point of access to your frequently needed resources, and we are continuing to develop this important tool. You may see changes occurring over the coming weeks, so keep checking in to see what we've added. Though most of the basics introduced here will stay exactly the same, some may change if we find a better way of providing information to you. If it should happen that something is not exactly the same as what's shown in this manual, you can go to the Search feature or spend some time clicking around the different features in the site to find what you need.

Getting Started

ITT Technical Institute continues to strive to make your Student Portal user-friendly and dynamic. While we will explore the different features you may find that additional helpful features have been added in our technical-driven environment. We have become use to change. Change requires awareness and adaptation. As we explore the student resources be aware of the change and adapt your process. Let's get started!

Home Page

The easiest way to explore the features of a portal is to have it open on your computer. So let's go to the portal now.

The home page is the first page you see when you log on to the Student Portal. It contains links to all content available in the Student Portal.

Locate the navigation bar. This allows you to navigate through the portal, go to the ITT Tech Virtual Library and access additional information. There is often more than one navigation bar. So make sure you explore the entire site.

Surveys

We value your feedback on courses and other services. You will be surveyed shortly after the enrollment process at ITT Tech and again shortly before you graduate. Also, every academic quarter you will be surveyed with respect to each course you complete. Here are some sections to explore:

School News

The *School News* section contains time-sensitive information about events and happenings occurring at your school. For example, if bad weather causes classes to be cancelled, that information may appear here.

What's Happening

The *What's Happening* feature provides a list of articles from different campus areas such as Career Services, Registrar, Finance, Academic Affairs, and others. To read one of the articles, click on the title.

U.S. and International News Headlines

U.S. and International News Headlines is a list of current news items from various national news sources.

Career Opportunities

Career Opportunities contains job information from employers nationwide. Look for Career Bank, ITT Tech's online jobs database and career information center.

Computer Use Policy

The *Computer Use Policy*, located in the "Help Center," (located in the ITT-Tech Student Portal) outlines appropriate use of ITT Technical Institute's resources, electronic mail, software, and computing systems.

Feedback

The *feedback* feature provides an opportunity for you to submit your suggestions, comments, and general feedback.

If you have problems . . .

If you have trouble logging into the Student Portal, there is a Help Menu from the login page that will allow you to contact a help source for login or user-name/password questions. Sometimes a problem can occur if you are attempting to log in using a browser that is not supported by the Student Portal.

Compatible Browsers

The Student Portal supports the following browsers:

- Microsoft Internet Explorer 5.5 or higher

Configuring Your Browser to Accept Cookies

In order to use the Student Portal, you must configure your browser to accept cookies. The Student Portal uses cookies to manage content for you, and you must configure your browser to do one of the following:

- Accept all cookies
- Notify you each time a cookie is offered so that you can decide whether to accept it or not

Configuring Cookies in Internet Explorer 5.x

To Allow All Cookies

1. In your browser window, from the Tools menu, click Internet options.
2. Click the Security Tab.
3. Click the Custom Level button.
4. Under Allow Cookies that are stored on your computer, click Enable.
5. Under Allow per-session cookies (not stored), click Enable.
6. At the bottom of the Security Settings window, click OK.
7. At the bottom of the Internet Options window click OK.

To Be Notified Each Time a Cookie Is Offered

1. In your browser window, from the Tools menu, click Internet options.
2. Click the Security Tab.
3. Click the Custom Level button.
4. Under Allow Cookies that are stored on your computer click Disable.
5. Under Allow per-session cookies (not stored), click Enable.
6. At the bottom of the Security Settings window, click OK.
7. At the bottom of the Internet Options window click OK.

Configuring Cookies in Internet Explorer 6.x

To Allow All Cookies

1. In your browser window, from the Tools menu, click Internet options.
2. Click the Privacy tab.
3. Click the Advanced button.
4. Click the Override automatic cookie handling box to deselect this option.
5. At the bottom of the Advanced Privacy window, click OK.
6. At the bottom of the Internet Options window, click OK.

To Be Notified Each Time a Cookie Is Offered

1. In your browser window, from the Tools menu, click Internet options.
2. Click the Privacy tab.
3. Click the Advanced button.
4. Click the Override automatic cookie handling box to select this option.
5. Under First-party cookies, click Block to select this option.
6. Under Third-party cookies, click Block to select this option.
7. Click Always Allow Session Cookies to select this option.
8. At the bottom of the Advanced Privacy window, click OK.
9. At the bottom of the Internet Options window, click OK.

Necessary Software

You will need Adobe Acrobat Reader is needed in order to utilize some features of the Student Portal. You can download a copy from **www.adobe.com**.

There is also a Help menu accessible from the top navigation bar of the home page if you have trouble finding something on the site. From this menu, read the frequently asked questions (FAQs) to see if your question is answered. If it's not, contact the ITT-Tech Student Portal Customer Service line at 877-456-7134.

Explore E-mail Options
What's in It for Me?

ITT Technical Institute has partnered with Microsoft's Hotmail/Passport tool called Live@EDU to provide e-mail accounts for all ITT Tech students. The standardized e-mail address will be given to you when you sign up for classes and will be yours for as long as you're a student. Once you graduate, you get to keep the e-mail address forever. Information that is critical to your success as a student at ITT Tech will be given to you through your ITT Tech e-mail account. Your instructors and staff will use this account as a primary communication tool, so be sure to check it daily. You can use the e-mail account for personal use, as well, as long as you follow Microsoft's Privacy and Terms of use agreements, found on the Student Portal. You will notice that you are redirected to Hotmail.com when you click the e-mail link on the Student Portal.

Getting Started

Access your e-mail account from the Student Portal home page and signing in. Your username will be your entire e-mail address.

The first time you login to your ITT Tech e-mail account, you will use a temporary password. Remember, the initial password is the last two digits of your year, month, and date of birth (yymmdd) followed by your last name. (If your last name is longer than six characters, it will only be the first six.) For example: If Christopher Columbus was born on October 31, 1451, his initial password will be 511031columb. (All passwords are case sensitive and set to be lower case.)

During the initial login process, you will be required to change this password to one of your own choosing, which you will use when you login every time.

You will now need to explore the email page and follow the directions.

If you have problems . . .

During your initial login to your account, you will be asked to reset your password and also provide two methods to be able to obtain/reset your password if it is ever forgotten. You will be asked for an alternate e-mail address and also a Security Question and answer. http://www.hotmail.com

If you still have trouble contact an ITT Tech representative at 877-456-7134 to request your password be reset. Note: This option may take 24 hours to complete. When you call, you will be asked questions to verify your identity before the e-mail address will be given to you.

Introduction to the Virtual Library – Part 1
What's in It for Me?

First, early man discovered fire. Now, we have discovered an online library and nothing will ever be the same. Sure, you can survive in the world without fire or your online library, but why would you want to? The sooner you learn what is available from the ITT Technical Institute Virtual Library, the sooner you can take advantage of one of the greatest tools developed for students in this day and age. Once you start using it, you'll understand why students rave about it and can't believe they could have gotten along without it.

The Virtual Library provides library resources and services such as those you would expect to find in a traditional library. The difference is that everything is accessible through a computer over the Internet and is available 24 hours a day, seven days a week. Your Virtual Library provides access to rich databases that provide a mix of searching and information delivery to bring documents directly to your desktop. The collection includes full-text online books, periodical databases providing access to full-text magazines and journals, authoritative encyclopedias, subject dictionaries and other reference resources, and links to Web sites selected for relevance to ITT Tech programs of study. In addition, the Virtual Library provides traditional library services in the online environment. Information seekers receive support through our "Ask a Librarian" reference service and curriculum-specific research guides, tutorials, and collections of frequently asked questions and answers.

Use of the Virtual Library is limited to students, faculty, and staff of ITT Technical Institute and ITT Educational Services. ITT Tech graduates can continue to use the Virtual Library after they complete their degree program, although some resources may be unavailable to alumni accounts.

Getting Started

You can access the ITT Technical Institute Virtual Library from any computer with an Internet connection in several ways, including:

- From the navigation bar of the Student Portal
- From the ITT Technical Institute home page (**www.itt-tech.edu**)
- From **http://library.itt-tech.edu**

Access

To access the Virtual Library, please use the link available from the ITT Tech Student Portal.

Exploring the ITT Tech Virtual Library

Books

If you are looking for comprehensive information on a topic, then check the book collections for relevant titles. Books are useful for research when you need:

- in-depth coverage of a topic
- background or historical information on a topic
- to explore broader, narrower and related issues
- bibliographies of related books and reference sources

Periodicals

If you are looking for information on a very new or current topic, then check the periodical databases for articles from magazines, journals, and newspapers, Articles are the best choice when you need:

- information about current topics or events
- information with a narrow or specific focus
- scholarly (peer-reviewed) or popular publications

Reference Resources

The term "reference resources" refers to a collection of frequently used sources that enable users to quickly retrieve a variety of data for research and study. Encyclopedias, dictionaries, directories, and other reference resources provide convenient access to overviews of topics, explanatory information, quick facts, statistics, and definitions. Check reference resources when you need:

- authoritative information on a topic
- basic, overview, or introductory information
- to identify subtopics or related ideas

Resources Selected for Each School of Study

Online resources are organized to serve each School of Study. From the library homepage, select the School of Study that matches your academic program of study. School of Study pages provide access to relevant databases, professional organizations, selected textbooks, tutorial links, and other recommended links selected for curricula support.

Research Help

How To Guides listed on the Research Help page of the Virtual Library are online tools that will answer many questions about library resources and services. The **Student Research Guides** are available to provide online assistance to students are the first stage of research. The guides cover topics that represent common assignments made by ITT Technical Institute faculty.

Finding Information in the ITT Technical Institute Virtual Library

Finding information in the Virtual Library is very similar to finding information in a traditional library. The information is organized to help you locate what you are looking for quickly and easily. The resources include Books, Periodicals, Reference Resources. To find information from Books, Periodicals, and Reference Resources, start with the following information:

Books

Read the books you need immediately online! Several collections of online books are available for reference and research. The books have been selected for support of ITT Technical Institute curricula. Each title is full-text and includes the illustrations, charts, diagrams, and photographs of the print counterpart. The functionality of online books makes them ideally suited for reference and research. Users are able to quickly search for specific information using keywords, either in a single title or across a group of titles.

Periodicals

Selected magazine, journal, and newspaper articles are available from the periodical databases. The databases provide indexing that allows users to search efficiently and effectively for subjects, titles, authors, and sources. The databases offer a wide variety of publications and topic areas useful to ITT Tech students and faculty.

Reference Resources

The term Reference Resources refers to a collection of frequently used sources that enable users to quickly retrieve a variety of data for reference and research. Access to encyclopedias, dictionaries, directories, and other reference sources provides convenient online support for many of the information needs of the students, faculty, and staff of ITT Technical Institutes.

If you have problems . . .

If you don't find what you are looking for, ask for assistance from a Learning Resource Center (LRC) staff member at your school. LRC staff will help you use the resources and services of the Virtual Library. You may also receive assistance online from the **Ask a Librarian** service accessible from the navigation bar of the Virtual Library.

The **Ask a Librarian** service can provide:

- Assistance with developing an effective search strategy whether you are using the periodical databases or the Internet
- Answers to reference questions
- Information about the databases and resources found in the Virtual Library

Using the Virtual Library – Part 2
Using the 360 Search, the Library Catalog, and E-Journal Look-up:

These search tools will help you locate specific online books and articles important to your academic success.

Library Catalog

The Virtual Library catalog is a listing of records for online books licensed by the Virtual Library. The catalog can be searched by author, title, publisher, subject, or keyword. Access the Library Catalog from the library's SEARCH page.

To perform a simple search in the catalog, type any work or phrase in the search box and click the "Search" button. This performs a general keyword search to locate any books with the search term in the title, as a subject, or as an author. Advanced search gives you the advantage of combining different categories such as 'Author' AND 'Title' OR 'Subject' enabling you to search multiple terms simultaneously.

The records returned in the results list are called brief records. Click on any brief record to open up a full record for the book. The full record includes assigned subject headings, classification numbers, and a direct link to the online book.

360 Search

The library includes a federated search engine that will search all the subscription information resources. This search engine allows you to search one, several, or all premium online resources at the same time. The description of each resource will help you determine the best choices for your research topic.

- The Basic search page includes a simple search box for you to begin your search query.
- The Advanced search page includes four search boxes to create a custom search query.
- The 'Search by Subject' option allows you to select a group of resources best matching your research needs. For example, search all resources related to general education. The relevance of the results should be increased be searching specific subject categories.

E-Journal Portal

E-Journal Lookup is a tool to help you identify full-text magazines and journals in the various subscription periodical databases. Some full-text magazines and journals may be available in more than one database. Access the E-Journal Look-up from the library's SEARCH page. There are several ways to find magazines and journals:

- Find an e-journal by title
- Find an e-journal by browsing
- Find an e-journal by subject

If your searches of the E-Journal Look-up do not yield the particular magazine or journal you are seeking, it may not be available full-text in our subscription database. However, it may be available in the campus Learning Resource Center, so be sure to check with the campus LRC staff. Another option may be to visit nearby area libraries to see if they have journal you want.

Additional Search Tips:

The following basic techniques are common to many databases and online resources:

- Identify the main concepts of the question or topic of research.
- Develop a list of terms or phrases that describe the concept or topic.
- Combine search terms in different ways; that is, search synonyms in various combinations.
- Use truncation. Truncation is used to find various word endings and plurals. It works when you enter the root of a word and put the truncation symbol at the end. The search results will contain the root word with any ending. Therefore, using truncation broadens your search. The * symbol is used for truncation in many databases. For example, a search for 'comput*' will retrieve computer, computers, and computing.
- Search specific fields. Most databases have dropdown menus next to the search box where a particular field can be specified (for example, title, author, or subject). Most databases also have an advanced search feature that allows several search terms in different fields for an even more precise set of results.
- Use Boolean operators such as AND, OR, and NOT to specify the relationship between search terms.
- Use phrases searching to narrow search results; many databases use quotation marks to designate phrases, other may provide a dropdown 'exact phrase' option.
- Avoid stop words. Common stop words are: a, an, the, in, of, on, are, be, if, into, is.

Accessing Other Campus Resources
Explore the Career Bank

The Career Bank is ITT Technical Institute's online jobs database and career information tool. Though you probably don't need this immediately, know that ITT Tech students and graduates can upload resumes, search for jobs, apply online for jobs, research companies, learn about occupations and employment trends, and access other resources to help in a career search.

If you are accessing the Career Bank through Student Portal you can just click on the Career Bank link and you will not have to login again. If you are outside the Student Portal, you can go to **http://itt.erecruiting.com** and login using your ITT Tech username and password.

If you have problems . . .

On the *School Info* page, you have the option to click the link to *Campus Director or District Manager* to submit a question or comment. If you need immediate help, call your campus directly.

If you have trouble with the Career Bank, contact the network administrator or Career Services at your school, or call 877-456-7134.

Summary

You're off and running, now! In this chapter, you learned about the Student Portal and what is accessible from there. You learned about the various e-mail options inside and outside of the ITT Technical Institute Student Portal. You explored the Virtual Library and saw some of the vast amount of resources held within it that will make your life as a student much more rewarding. You also learned how to use the Student Portal to access other campus resources you may need and what you can do if you need help. You can extend your learning by reviewing and practicing the variations of the skills presented in the lessons.

Visual Summary

An illustrated introductory feature graphically presents the concepts and features you will learn, including the final results of completing the project.

Step-by-Step Tutorials

Hands-on tutorials let you learn by doing and include numbered instructions.

If you have problems . . .

These short troubleshooting notes help you anticipate or solve common problems quickly and effectively.

Skill Drill

Extensive end-of-project exercises emphasize hands-on skill development. Challenge exercises provide more difficult exercises to really put your skills to the test.

chapter 2 | Strategies for Independent Learning

 Contents

What's in It for Me?

To be successful, you have to last

Have you ever given up on something in the past and regretted it later? Do you ever think back and ask yourself, "What would my life be like if only I had done X or Y?" Have you ever made a decision or acted in a way that cost you dearly? If so, then you now know the value of persistence.

Persistence. The word itself means that you are going to stay—that you have found a way to stick it out, found a way to make it count, and found a way *not to give up.* That is what this chapter is all about—finding out how to make career college work for you. It is about giving you advice up front that can save your education and your future dreams.

> Before everything else, **getting ready** is the secret to success.
>
> —Henry Ford

Dropping out of school is not uncommon. As a matter of fact, *over 40 percent of the people who begin college never complete their programs.* Don't be mistaken in thinking that they dropped out because of their inability to learn. Many leave because they made serious and irreparable mistakes early.

Some students leave because they did not know how to manage their time. Some leave because they couldn't get along with an instructor. And still, some leave because they simply could not figure out how "the system" worked, and frustration, anger, disappointment, and fear got the better of them.

You do not have to be one of these students. This chapter and *indeed this book* are geared to help you AVOID those mistakes. They are geared to help you make the decisions that will lead to completion of your degree.

What You Need to Know Up Front

Policies and Procedures of ITT Tech

Familiarizing yourself with the policies and procedures of your college can save you a great deal of grief and frustration in the long run. Policies and procedures vary from institution to institution, but regardless, it is your responsibility to know what you can expect from your institution and what your institution expects from you. These policies can be found in the school catalog (traditional and online).

Though the ITT Tech campuses can vary in their rules, some universal policies include:

- Most colleges adhere to a strict drop/add date. Always check your schedule of classes for this information.
- Most colleges have an attendance policy for classroom instruction.
- Most colleges have a strict refund policy.
- Most colleges have an academic dishonesty policy.
- Most colleges have a standing drug and alcohol policy.
- Colleges do not put policies into place to hinder your degree completion; rather, the purpose is to ensure that all students are treated fairly and equitably.

The Golden Rule of Classroom Etiquette

You may be surprised, but the way you act in (and out of) class can mean as much to your success as what you know. No one can make you do anything or act in any way that you do not want. The following tips are provided from years of research and conversations with thousands of instructors teaching across America. Knowing this isn't enough, though. You have to be the one who chooses whether to use this advice.

- Bring your materials to class daily: texts, notebooks, pens, calculators, and syllabi.
- Come to class prepared: read your text and handouts, do the assigned work at home, bring questions to be discussed.
- Turn in papers, projects, and assignments on time. Many instructors do not accept late work.
- Participate in class. Ask questions, bring current events to the discussion, and contribute with personal experiences.
- Ask your instructor about the best time to come in for help. The time before and after class may not be the most appropriate time. Your instructor may have "back-to-back" classes and may be unable to assist you.
- If you are late for class, enter quietly. Do not walk in front of the instructor, don't let the door slam, don't talk on your way in, and take the seat nearest the door. Make every effort not to be late to class.
- Wait for the instructor to dismiss class before you begin to pack your bags to leave. You may miss important information or you may cause someone else to miss important information.
- Never carry on a conversation with another student while the instructor or another student is talking.
- Do not sleep in class.
- If for any reason you must leave during class, do so quietly and quickly. It is customary to inform the instructor that you will be leaving early before class begins.
- If you make an appointment with an instructor, keep it. If you must cancel, a courtesy call is in order.
- If you don't know how to address your instructor; that is, by Mr., Mrs., Miss., Ms., or Dr., ask them which they prefer.
- You should not wear sunglasses, oversized hats, strong cologne or perfume, skates, or earphones to class.
- Be respectful of other students. Treat diversity with dignity and respect.
- Mind your manners. Profanity and obscene language may offend some people. You can have strong, conflicting views without being offensive.
- Turn off your cell phone or beeper. If you have a home or work situation that requires that you "stay connected," put the device on vibrate.
- Remember that respect for others on your part will afford you the opportunity to establish relationships that otherwise you might never have had.
- Call you instructor or program to notify them if you are going to be late or absent. Remember that this is your job and you need to be accountable.
- Come dressed according to the dress code, if the school has one. Dress for success!

Large lecture classes often have a lab component, also, in which instruction is much more focused.

Won't You Stay for a While?

Persisting in College

The age-old "scare tactic" for first-time students, "Look to your left, look to your right—one of those people will not graduate with you," is not far from the truth. But the good news (actually, the great news) is that you do not have to become a statistic. You can make it through your classes and graduate. You have the power to get through your program. Sure, you may have some catching up to do. You may have to work harder and longer, but the beauty of college is that if you want help, you can get help.

Below, you will find some powerful, helpful tips for persisting in college. Using only a few of them can increase your chances of graduating. Using all of them virtually assures it!

- **Visit your advisor or counselor** frequently and establish a relationship. Take his or her advice. Ask questions. Use your advisor or counselor as a mentor.

- **Make use of every academic service** that you need that the college offers, from tutoring sessions to writing centers; these are essential tools to your success.

- Work hard to **learn and understand your "learning style."** This can help you in every class in which you enroll.

- Work hard to **develop a sense of community.** Get to know a few people on campus such as a special faculty member, a secretary, another student, or anyone who you can turn to for help.

- **Join a club or organization.** Research proves that students who are connected to the campus through activities drop out less often.

- **Watch your finances carefully.** Don't get "credit-carditis." If you see yourself getting into financial trouble, seek counseling immediately! Poor financial management can cost you success as quickly as failing classes.

- Concentrate on setting realistic, achievable goals. **Visualize your goals.** Write them down. Find a picture that represents your goal and post it so that you can see your goal every day.

- Work hard to develop and **maintain a sense of self-esteem and self-respect.** The better you feel about yourself, the more likely you will reach your goals.

- **Learn to budget your time** as wisely as you budget your money. You've made a commitment to college and it will take a commitment of time to bring your dream to fruition.

- If you have trouble with an instructor, don't let it fester. Make an appointment to **speak with the instructor** and work through the problem.

- If you get bored in class or feel that the class is not going to benefit you, remember that it is a required class and **you will always have a few boring classes** during your college experience. Stick to it and it will be over soon.

ITT Tech Can Help!

How to Find Available Resources

Motivating yourself to make it through the tough times at school will be a big factor in your success in college and life. You're not alone, though! We're here to help you along the way. There are many resources at your college; some of these will focus on academic life, while other may focus on social, personal or career success. It is your responsibility to explore your school to determine what resources are available to you. If you're having trouble, talk to a staff member at the college. Ask questions and be proactive in getting the help you need.

Your Catalog

Your college catalog is one of the most important publications you will read during your education. It describes the rules, regulations, policies, procedures, and requirements of the college and your program. It is imperative for you to keep the college catalog that was issued when you begin because program requirements can sometimes change. Most colleges require that you graduate under the rules and requirements stated in the catalog under which you entered.

The catalog includes information about adding and dropping classes, probation, plagiarism, attendance, course descriptions, program requirements, faculty credentials, and college accreditation. It is an important tool.

ITT Tech is committed to helping you throughout your program and your career. You will have the opportunity to explore the resources we have put into place for you in depth during the lab portion of this course. Some of ITT Tech's goals for our students in providing these resources include helping them to:

- Graduate with a profound understanding in their area of study
- Achieve continuing career success
- Understand the value of and the means to continue learning throughout their careers
- Become proactive users of technology
- Prepare for future stages in life

To help you accomplish these goals, we offer a variety of resources. Of course, the only way these can help you is if you utilize them. The single most valuable ability you have that can make the greatest contribution to your education and life success is the ability to ask for help.

Faculty and Staff

Your academic deans and instructors are primary resources to which you can turn for help when you need it. Your instructors should give you their contact information, including their e-mail address, on the first day of class. Faculty e-mail addresses follow a standard format in most cases. The format is first initial of the first name plus last name followed by @itt-tech.edu. For example, John Doe's e-mail address would be jdoe@itt-tech.edu. Exceptions to this format can occur when faculty members have similar names. This is usually resolved by adding a middle initial. We recommend that you verify e-mail addresses with your instructors prior to sending e-mail.

Virtual Library

Recognizing that your learning will continue throughout your career, ITT Tech offers all students and graduates a membership to the robust and very informative ITT Tech Virtual Library.

As a graduate of ITT Tech, you can rely on the resources found here long after you've left school. Can you picture yourself on the job finding out that you need to do a presentation the next day using Microsoft PowerPoint but you can't remember how to use it? No problem. Go to the Virtual Library and take the tutorial. Do you need to brush up on AutoCAD, a programming language, or electronics? That information is here, too. If you find yourself needing to research the latest business developments in the big computer manufacturing companies, you can do a search of the latest business articles. And, if you need in-depth knowledge and analysis of a certain subject before a meeting, you may be able to read a book on just that subject online when you need it.

The ITT Tech Virtual Library gives you access to rich databases that provide a mix of searching and information delivery to bring documents directly to your computer. The collection includes full-text online books, periodical databases providing access to full-text magazines and journals, authoritative encyclopedias,

Research all possible avenues of financial aid.

subject dictionaries and other reference resources, and links to Web sites selected for relevance to ITT Tech programs of study. In addition, the Virtual Library provides traditional library services in the online environment. Information seekers receive support through the "Ask a Librarian" reference service and curriculum-specific research guides, tutorials, and collections of frequently asked questions and answers.

Learning Resource Center (LRC)

Help is also available through the Learning Resource Center at your school. The LRC staff can help you find the answers to most of your school-related questions. They can help you with research, as well, by helping you use the resources and services of the Virtual Library.

The LRC also has a tremendous amount of information on hand. Ask the staff of the LRC at your school to show you the LRC catalog of holdings. Each book, video, magazine, and CD-ROM in the LRC's collection is listed in this catalog, and the staff can show you how to locate the items in the LRC. If the LRC does not own the particular item you are looking for, it may be possible for the LRC staff to borrow items from other local libraries on your behalf.

Student Portal

The Student Portal provides access to general information and information that is specific to your school. Here you can see events that are coming up, helpful hints, a school calendar with important dates listed, and more. You can also access your ITT Tech e-mail account here.

Yes You Can!
TIPS FOR SUCCESS

Consider the following tips for making the most of your relationships with your instructors:

- Make an effort to get to know your instructor outside the classroom if possible.
- Come to class prepared, bringing your best to the table each class session.
- Answer questions and ASK questions in class.
- Ask for help if you see things getting difficult.
- Never make excuses; talk and act like an adult.
- Volunteer for projects and co-curricular opportunities.
- Be respectful.

and ITT Tech Can Help!

Your Responsibility: Ask for Help

Many students find that they are afraid to ask for help when they don't understand something, whether it is information they learn in a class, general information about their program of study, or specific features of a new technology. When you do not understand something, there may be others who do not understand it as well. By asking questions, you may help other students. If fear keeps you from asking questions about something you don't fully comprehend, you may hinder your education and cheat yourself out of valuable information. You are investing your valuable resources in order to complete your program, and it is your right and your responsibility to find the information you need. Your instructors, deans, academic counselors and the entire administration are here to help you. They want to be helpful and are waiting for the opportunity. Even if you feel like you should already know the answer, if you don't know it-ask someone! If you don't get the answer you need, ask someone else.

What's in It for Me?
Technology is Your Friend

Technology enables adult learners to further their education using the convenience of the computer and the Internet. Motivated students can take courses, and sometimes complete programs online, interact with other students and their instructors via e-mail, and access an online library to help with research. Some courses are taught only in the classroom, some are taught only online, and others may use a combination of an online component and classroom time. The last kind of course is sometimes called "blended."

Many students like the idea of the convenience and easy access of online course offerings. Are you the type of student who likes the idea of going to class first thing while you're still in your pajamas, or late at night when everyone in your family has gone to bed? Online students appreciate that they don't have to be somewhere at any particular time and can go to class when, and where, they choose. The online class is always open. You can participate in online discussion forums; answer questions your instructor has posted; and turn in your assignments as you complete them.

In today's workplace, employees are often required to work with people from all over the country and world, virtually. Great online communication skills are assets you'll never regret developing.

From the Far Away… Nearby
Succeeding in Distance Education and Independent Study Courses

Independent study courses or courses taught by distance learning are great for students who work or who have families and small children. These courses have flexible hours and few, if any, class meetings and allow you to work at your own pace.

However (and this is a *big* however): Do not let anyone try to tell you that these courses are easier than regular classroom offerings! They are not.

Independent study and distance-learning courses are usually more difficult. You need to be a self-starter and highly motivated to complete and do well in these courses.

Consider the following tips when registering for independent study or distance education classes:

- If at all possible, review the material for the course before you register. This may help you in making the decision to enroll.

Research suggests that stress can trigger chemical releases in the body that might cause forgetfulness. Learning to relax, breathe properly, and maintain perspective can help reduce stress during tests.

- Begin before the beginning! If at all possible, obtain the independent study packet or distance-learning materials before the term begins and start working. You may think you can wait because you have the entire term, but time will quickly slip by.

- Make an appointment to meet the instructor as soon as possible. Some colleges will schedule a meeting for you. If it is not possible to meet, at least phone the instructor and introduce yourself.

- Communicate with your advisor from time to time via e-mail if possible.

- Develop a schedule for completing each assignment and stick to it! Don't let time steal away from you. This is the biggest problem with these courses.

- Keep a copy of all work mailed, e-mailed, or delivered to the instructor or the college. When possible, send your materials by certified mail to ensure their delivery.

- Always mail, e-mail, or deliver your assignment on time or even early if possible. Remember that you have deadlines and the mail system can be slow. Allow time in your schedule for revisions.

- Try to find someone who is registered for the same course so that you can work together or at least have a phone number to call if you run into a problem.

Online Learning Challenges

Learning in an online environment is challenging because it requires commitment and a learning style that is suited for learning in a new way.

Online courses can be delivered in a couple of different ways. They may be:

- **Asynchronous**–this is the anytime, any place method used in most online courses.

- **Synchronous**–this is a same-time method that some online courses use in which the class is expected to "meet"—usually via an online meeting platform— for a lecture.

Communication in online courses can also occur in the same two ways:

- **Asynchronous**–students can communicate using the anytime, any place method by leaving messages on a bulletin board–type system and responding to others' postings. This allows students with different schedules and in different time zones to hold a "conversation" and exchange ideas and opinions.

- **Synchronous**–Students can communicate in a synchronous (real-time) fashion in some online courses by agreeing to "meet" at a certain time for a conference call or online chat.

Important Skills in an Online Environment

Surprise!

Students who do particularly well in an online course do not necessarily have the most outstanding computer skills. What successful online students do have in common is the willingness to:

- **Take responsibility for their own learning**–They tend to *want* to learn and engage in learning in many aspects of their lives, not just in their courses.

- **Learn new subjects and expand their ideas**–They're interested in many subjects and want to master more things.

- **Adapt to a new environment**–Success in their learning doesn't seem to depend on the subject matter as much as on the desire to learn. Successful online students want to learn how the online courses are set up and seek to master their new learning environment.

- **Manage their time and study habits**–Online learning requires that students be self-directed. To learn in this type of environment, students have to manage their time and energy.

- **Be patient in communication**–Because the online class and communication are usually asynchronous, students might have to wait for responses from other students or the instructor.

Most online courses incorporate a lot of reading. Sometimes, it can be a heavier reading load than on-site courses demand. For a single course, you might need to devote 10 to 15 hours a week doing the reading, writing, and online discussion assignments. In addition, when taking an online course, you must:

- Create a comfortable environment for learning
- Arrange a consistent schedule
- Use available resources for learning
- Communicate your study times and goals to your family and employer
- Reflect on your learning
- Maintain a record of your learning
- Communicate with your instructor
- Keep yourself informed
- Print out the syllabus and keep track of upcoming expectations

Note-taking for Online Courses

When taking notes in an online course, you may be able to use a notes feature within the online course management system. Most likely, however, if you do this, you will be able to access your notes only when you are logged in. To review your notes at any time, use a word processing program, such as Microsoft Word. Change the size of the screen using the minimize/maximize button, and then click and drag the corner of the screen to reshape it. Do the same with your Web browser and position the screens next to each other. Toggle, or go back and forth, between screens using your mouse. Take notes in Word and save them in a Notes folder you create.

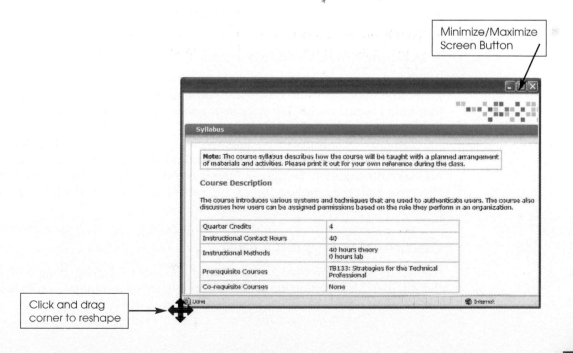

Minimize/Maximize Screen Button

Click and drag corner to reshape

Position screens next to each other on your computer desktop.

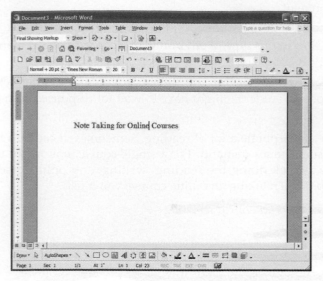

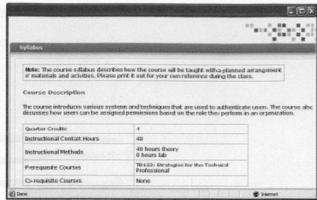

Online Collaboration

Unless you're enrolled in correspondence study or pure independent study (which is never the case at ITT Tech), communication with your instructor and other students is critical. Both online and classroom students benefit immensely from interaction, for social *and* intellectual reasons. Because the online environment is less conducive to social engagement, it is all the more important that you exert effort to communicate with your peers and instructors. You must seek out help on your own when you run into problems, and call ITT Tech when you need questions answered. This is especially important in the early days of the term.

Strive to communicate actively with your instructor in an online course and establish a rapport early. E-mail and ask questions.

Through good online learning communication, you will:

- Contribute to a culture of learning
- Learn and be able to follow online "classroom" procedures
- Empathize with and relate to other students
- Offer opinions and feedback
- Demonstrate your knowledge of content

Remember, instructors are people, too! Just like students, some instructors are good communicators and others are not. Online instructors are as varied as those that hold classes on site. Tell your instructors what you need, and follow up if you don't receive an adequate or timely response.

Using technology does not automatically improve communication, though it may be faster and easier. Faulty assumptions and misunderstandings are very common in online communication. Because electronic communication lacks important nonverbal cues, the sender of a message needs to go above and beyond nonelectronic communication efforts to help others understand a message.

Communicating Via E-mail

Netiquette is the term used for the code of conduct for getting along with others on the Internet. Most Netiquette standards simply involve common sense: being polite and considerate to others.

COURSE NUMBER:
TB139

COURSE NAME:
Strategies for Learning in a Technical Environment

SCHOOL NAME:
ITT Technical Institute

ISBN 0-536-39699-X

90000

9 780536 396990

Do:

- Keep messages brief and to the point unless otherwise asked.
- Use simple, clear, and concise language.
- Avoid profanity, sarcasm, and negativity in your responses.
- Remember that the recipient of your e-mail may forward it to someone else. Write carefully in case your message ends up in the wrong hands.
- Keep it neutral. Attempts at humor sometimes translate poorly in e-mail messages.
- Be objective and polite.
- Know your audience. Should your tone be formal or less formal?
- Write substantive messages. Do not fill up other people's inboxes with e-mails to say "I agree" or "I couldn't have said it better!"
- Post only appropriate and relevant responses.
- Read others' messages before posting a message.

Try NOT to:

- Type in all caps, which is the same thing as shouting in the online world.
- Forward messages or copy someone else's writing without his or her permission.
- Send a message or post a response if you are angry or frustrated. Write your message, but leave it in the Drafts folder until some time has passed. Read it again and modify it as you think best.

Though no other Netiquette rules apply to the online classroom, there are some more guidelines to consider when interacting with others online. These include:

- Be specific about what you want from people.
- Send messages only to people who need to be included. Send sensitive feedback only to the person who requested it.
- Use urgent and important tags sparingly.
- Ask for confirmation of receipt of messages.
- If sending a document for comments, note how you would like each participant to annotate a document (underline, bold, color, caps).
- Include the entire message "chain" so all recipients have the context for the message.
- Write expressively to help build relationships.

Communicating Via Chat

Chat rooms allow smaller groups to "talk" to each other by typing messages that appear immediately on each participant's computer. Chat rooms might be used by an entire class or a class group in a synchronous environment. Chats can take place using instant messaging systems or a number of Web-based software programs.

Using List Serves or a Discussion List   A common discussion method is e-mail, usually through a Listserv. Listservs use the Internet to distribute e-mail to groups of people. Students or the instructor create messages on new topics or respond to messages that others have sent. The Listserv forwards any new postings to all the members of the class. These are usually arranged by date.

Using Bulletin Board Systems   One of the central features of online courses is the discussion board, which enables two or more students to have a conversation by posting responses to each other. This is often called a threaded discussion. One person posts a statement onto the bulletin board, and others then join in at a later time by posting responses. All members of the group can read these postings. As an online student, you can choose when to contribute to any "thread" of comments on the discussion board. Your participation in these discussions is how you gain "visibility" in the class. Adding a posting is like participating in a class discussion on-site. Much of the instructor's assessment of your knowledge will be based on your contribution to these class discussions. Online students often are graded, in part, on the quality of their responses to instructor-posted questions.

Remember, there is a difference between contribution and participation. Although instructors may require a certain number of posts, they will judge you by the *quality* of those posts.

Receiving Lecture Materials and Assignments and Transmitting Homework

You may be asked to send your assignments as attachments to e-mail, in the text of an e-mail, using FTP (file transfer protocol), posting to the Web, or via fax. Your instructor will tell you which method you should use in the course and give you instructions for how to do it. For attachments to be opened, both the sender and receiver must have compatible software. The software you were given at the beginning of the term will be compatible with that of your instructor. Once you complete your work in the program you're using (Word, Excel, Access), save the file, close it, and go to the program you will use to send it. If you're using e-mail, go to your e-mail program. Compose an e-mail to your instructor. Explain what the e-mail attachment is in the body of the e-mail. Then attach the file you saved using the method your e-mail requires. If you're using FTP, go to that program. You'll need the specific address your instructor provided at the beginning of the course.

Suggestions for voice mail include:

- State your name and telephone number at the beginning and ending of the message.

- Keep the message short and to the point.

- Be clear about what you need, and when you need it.

- State whether the person should respond.

- Think about who will receive your message if you are sending a broadcast message.

Suggestions for telephone conferences include:

- Limit participation to no more than eight speaking participants.

- Have a clear agenda and purpose.

- Before you speak, state who you are.

- The facilitator should summarize the conversation at the end of the meeting.

Contents

What's in It for Me?
Making the Most of Your Strengths

Many students, especially those who are returning to classes for the first time in years, often wonder if they know how to learn. You may be asking yourself, "Is there one 'best' way of learning?" The answer is no. It depends on so many variables. There are a number of theories about how learning styles, personal intelligences, personality typing, past experiences, and attitude affect how people process new information. Though not everyone agrees on every theory, there are some common elements among most of them.

The idea behind the study of learning styles, personal intelligences, and personality is something that educators have known for a very long time: students learn in different ways in different situations. While some students may not like the lecture format in class, for instance, others relish it. Some students learn best by touching and doing, while others learn best by listening and reflecting. Some students learn best with a group of people sitting outside under the trees, while others must be alone in the library. Other factors that determine how well students learn seem to include their motivation for learning, the physical setting they are in, their decision-making skills, and their commitment to their long-term goals.

What almost everyone agrees upon is that, in order to most effectively learn, students need a good reason for learning new material as well as a variety of methods, or styles, they can draw upon when needed. Many people have a predominant learning style that they favor and can use certain study techniques that accommodate this style. However, classes are taught in many different ways depending on the instructor. Some instructors lecture, others demonstrate or lead students to self-discovery; some focus on principles; some use applications; some emphasize memory and others understanding. When mismatches exist between a student's primary learning style and the teaching style of the instructor, the student may become bored and inattentive in class, do poorly on tests, get discouraged about the courses, the curriculum, and themselves, and in some cases drop out of school. In order to protect your future career and be in charge of your own learning, it will be helpful if you can use several styles of learning.

By understanding your primary learning style and developing additional ways to learn, evidence indicates that you will likely:

- Experience an increased comfort level and willingness to learn
- Practice different ways of thinking and solving problems, which will be quite useful as you move to become a fully effective professional
- Experience increased motivation and achievement in a whole range of activities
- Gain an understanding of how people differ, which will aid you in becoming a more effective team member
- Take control of your own learning and future

Discovering and Polishing Your Talents

In this section, we present three self-assessments to help you better understand your dominant intelligences, personality type, and learning style. This is not a hard science, and there are no right or wrong answers. It is possible that the conclusions you come to from doing these activities may not even be accurate. These assessments are just meant to be a guide—to give you something to think about regarding how you best learn and how others may best learn. These assessments are in no way intended to label you. They are not a measure of your intelligence. These are based on theories that have been both praised and criticized. They are also not meant to be used as a static indicator of who you are. Learning styles and personalities change over the years. They do not measure your worth or your capacities as a student. They are included so that you might gain a better understanding of your multiple intelligences and identify your learning styles and your personality type. Use them as tools to help you explore who you are and how you learn. We hope that by the end of this section, you will have experienced a "wow" or an "ah-ha!" moment as you explore and discover new and exciting possibilities for your education path.

Following each of the self-review activities, there are suggestions for how to use your strengths in different situations that we hope you will find informative and helpful. Many students have met with great success by identifying and molding their study environments and habits to reflect their primary learning styles and personality types. By recognizing and expanding their repertoire of learning techniques, many students have also been able to adapt more easily to different instructors.

Looking at Yourself in a New Way
Understanding Multiple Intelligences

There are many ways to learn how to ski. The learning technique that works best for you depends on many different factors, which may vary from situation to situation.

In 1983, Howard Gardner, a Harvard University professor, developed a theory called multiple intelligences. In his book *Frames of Mind*, he outlines seven intelligences that he feels are possessed by everyone:

- Visual/spatial
- Verbal/linguistic
- Musical/rhythm
- Logic/math
- Body/kinesthetic
- Interpersonal
- Intrapersonal

In 1996, he added an eighth intelligence: naturalistic. His conclusion, in short, is that when you have done things that have come easily for you, you are probably drawing on one of your intelligences that is well developed. On the other hand, if you have tried to do things that are very difficult to master or understand, you may be dealing with material that calls on one of your less-developed intelligences. If playing the piano by ear comes easily to you, your musical/rhythm intelligence may be very strong. If you have trouble writing or understanding poetry, your verbal/linguistic intelligence may not be as well developed. This does not mean that you will never be able to write poetry; it simply means that you have not fully developed your skills in tis area.

ASSESS: YOUR MULTIPLE INTELLIGENCES

1. Your Multiple Intelligences Survey (2005) by Robert M. Sherfield, Ph.D. Based, in part, on *Frames of Mind* by Howard Gardner, 1983. Read each statement carefully and thoroughly. After reading the statement, rate your response using the scale to the right. There are no right or wrong answers. This is not a timed survey.

	Never or Almost never	Sometimes	Often
	1	2	3

1. _____ When someone gives me directions, I have to visualize them in my mind in order to understand them.

2. _____ I know where everything is in my home such as supplies, gloves, flashlights, camera, and CDs.

3. _____ I like to draw pictures, graphs, or charts to better understand information.

4. _____ I enjoy working puzzles or mazes.

5. _____ I enjoy and learn more when seeing movies, slides, or videos in class.

_____ TOTAL for **VISUAL/SPATIAL**

1. _____ I enjoy crossword puzzles and games like Scrabble.

2. _____ I am a good speller.

3. _____ I have a good memory for names and dates.

4. _____ I am a good storyteller.

5. _____ I am a very good listener, and I enjoy listening to others' stories.

_____ TOTAL for **VERBAL/ LINGUISTIC**

1. _____ I enjoy dancing and can keep up with the beat of the music.

2. _____ I often sing or hum to myself in the shower or car, or while walking or just sitting.

3. _____ When I hear music, I "get into it" by moving, humming, tapping, or even singing.

4. _____ I can easily remember the words and melodies of songs.

5. _____ I need to study with music.

_____ TOTAL for **MUSICAL/RHYTHM**

1. _____ I like to repair things that are broken such as toasters, small engines, bicycles, and cars.

2. _____ I use a lot of gestures when I talk to people.

3. _____ I enjoy playing competitive sports.

4. _____ I usually touch people or pat them on the back when I talk to them.

5. _____ I enjoy physical activities such as bicycling, jogging, dancing, snowboarding, skateboarding, or swimming.

_____ TOTAL for **BODY/KINESTHETIC**

1. _____ I enjoy leadership activities.

2. _____ I can recognize and empathize with people's attitudes and emotions.

3. _____ I communicate very well with other people.

4. _____ I understand my family and friends better than most other people do.

5. _____ I am good at solving people's problems/conflicts.

_____ TOTAL for **INTERPERSONAL**

1. _____ I have the ability to get others to listen to me.

2. _____ I prefer to study alone.

3. _____ I know what I want, and I set goals to accomplish it.

4. _____ I don't always talk about my accomplishments with others.

5. _____ I have to have time alone to think about new information in order to remember it.

_____ TOTAL for **INTRAPERSONAL**

	Never or Almost never	Sometimes	Often
	1	**2**	**3**

1. _____ I have little or no trouble conceptualizing information or facts.

2. _____ I am a very logical, orderly thinker.

3. _____ I learn better by asking a lot of questions.

4. _____ I enjoy solving problems in math and chemistry and working with computer programming problems.

5. _____ I enjoy games like Clue, Battleship, Chess, and Rubik's Cube.

_____ TOTAL for **LOGIC/MATH**

1. _____ I enjoy working with nature, animals, and plants.

2. _____ I can name many different things in the environment such as clouds, rocks, and plant types.

3. _____ I have some interest in herbal remedies and natural medicines.

4. _____ I would rather work outside around nature than inside around people and equipment.

5. _____ I enjoy sorting and organizing information, objects, and collectibles.

_____ TOTAL for **NATURALISTIC**

Plan to Make the Most of the Eight Intelligences

The "Smart" descriptors were adapted from Thomas Armstrong (1994).

Visual/Spatial (*Picture Smart*).   Thinks in pictures; knows where things are in the house; loves to create images and work with graphs, charts, pictures, and maps.

Verbal/linguistic (*Word Smart*).   Communicates well through language, likes to write, is good at spelling, great at telling stories, loves to read books.

Musical/Rhythm (*Music Smart*).   Loves to sing, hum, and whistle; comprehends music; responds to music immediately; performs music.

Logic/Math (*Number Smart*).   Can easily conceptualize and reason, uses logic, has good problem-solving skills, enjoys math and science.

Body/Kinesthetic (*Body Smart*).   Learns through body sensation, moves around a lot, enjoys work involving the hands, is graced with some athletic ability.

Interpersonal (*People Smart*).   Loves to communicate with other people, possesses great leadership skills, has lots of friends, is involved in extracurricular activities.

Intrapersonal (Self-Smart). Has a deep awareness of own feelings, is very reflective, requires time to be alone, does not get involved with group activities.

Naturalistic (Environment Smart). Has interest in the environment and in nature; can easily recognize plants, animals, rocks, and cloud formations; may like hiking, camping, and fishing.

Making It Work for You
Using Multiple Intelligences to Enhance Studying and Learning

ABILITIES AND SKILLS ASSOCIATED WITH EACH INTELLIGENCE	STUDY TECHNIQUES TO MAXIMIZE EACH INTELLIGENCE
Verbal–Linguistic • Analyzing own use of language • Remembering terms easily • Explaining, teaching, learning, using humor • Understanding syntax and word meaning • Convincing someone to do something	**Verbal–Linguistic** • Read text; highlight no more than 10% • Rewrite notes • Outline chapters • Teach someone else • Recite information or write scripts/debates
Musical–Rhythmic • Sensing tonal qualities • Creating/enjoying melodies, rhythms • Being sensitive to sounds and rhythms • Using "schemas" to hear music • Understanding the structure of music	**Musical–Rhythmic** • Create rhythms out of words • Beat out rhythms with hand or stick • Play instrumental music/write raps • Put new material to songs you already know • Take music breaks
Logical–Mathematical • Recognizing abstract patterns • Reasoning inductively and deductively • Discerning relationships and connections • Performing complex calculations • Reasoning scientifically	**Logical–Mathematical** • Organize material logically • Explain material sequentially to someone • Develop systems and find patterns • Write outlines and develop charts and graphs • Analyze information
Visual–Spatial • Perceiving and forming objects accurately • Recognizing relationships between objects • Representing something graphically • Manipulating images • Finding one's way in space	**Visual–Spatial** • Develop graphic organizers for new material • Draw mind maps • Develop charts and graphs • Use color in notes to organize • Visualize material (method of loci)
Bodily–Kinesthetic • Connecting mind and body • Controlling movement • Improving body functions • Expanding body awareness to all senses • Coordinating body movement	**Bodily–Kinesthetic** • Move or rap while you learn; pace and recite • Use "method of loci" or manipulatives • Move fingers under words while reading • Create "living sculptures" • Act out scripts of material, design games
Intrapersonal • Evaluating own thinking • Being aware of and expressing feelings • Understanding self in relation to others • Thinking and reasoning on higher levels	**Intrapersonal** • Reflect on personal meaning of information • Visualize information/keep a journal • Study in quiet settings • Imagine experiments
Interpersonal • Seeing things from others' perspectives • Cooperating within a group • Communicating verbally and nonverbally • Creating and maintaining relationships	**Interpersonal** • Study in a group • Discuss information • Use flash cards with others • Teach someone else
Naturalistic • Deep understanding of nature • Appreciation of the delicate balance in nature	**Naturalistic** • Connect with nature whenever possible • Form study groups of people with like interests

Adapted from Lazear, Seven Pathways of Learning, 1994

Figure 3.1 How to Put Your Multiple Intelligences to Work for You

Assess your personality with the Personality Spectrum

Personality assessments help you understand how you respond to the world around you—including information, thoughts, feelings, people, and events. The assessment used in this chapter is based on one of the most widely used personality inventories in the world—the Myers-Briggs Type Inventory, developed by Katharine Briggs and her daughter, Isabel Briggs Myers. It also relies upon the work of David Keirsey and Marilyn Bates, who combined the 16 Myers-Briggs types into four temperaments and developed an assessment called the Keirsey Sorter based on those temperaments.

The Personality Spectrum assessment adapts and simplifies their material into four personality types—Thinker, Organizer, Giver, and Adventurer—and was developed by Dr. Joyce Bishop. The Personality Spectrum helps you identify the kinds of interactions that are most, and least, comfortable for you. Figure 3.2, on page 52, shows techniques that improve performance, learning strategies, and ways of relating to others for each personality type.

PERSONALITY SPECTRUM

STEP 1. Rank order all 4 responses to each question from most like you (4) to least like you (1) so that for each question you use the numbers 1, 2, 3, and 4 one time each. Place numbers in the boxes next to the responses.

4 most like me   **3** more like me   **2** less like me   **1** least like me

1. I like instructors who
   a. ☐ tell me exactly what is expected of me.
   b. ☐ make learning active and exciting.
   c. ☐ maintain a safe and supportive classroom.
   d. ☐ challenge me to think at higher levels.

2. I learn best when the material is
   a. ☐ well organized.
   b. ☐ something I can do hands-on.
   c. ☐ about understanding and improving the human condition.
   d. ☐ intellectually challenging.

3. A high priority in my life is to
   a. ☐ keep my commitments.
   b. ☐ experience as much of life as possible.
   c. ☐ make a difference in the lives of others.
   d. ☐ understand how things work.

4. Other people think of me as
   a. ☐ dependable and loyal.
   b. ☐ dynamic and creative.
   c. ☐ caring and honest.
   d. ☐ intelligent and inventive.

5. When I experience stress I would most likely
   a. ☐ do something to help me feel more in control of my life.
   b. ☐ do something physical and daring.
   c. ☐ talk with a friend.
   d. ☐ go off by myself and think about my situation.

6. I would probably not be close friends with someone who is
   a. ☐ irresponsible.
   b. ☐ unwilling to try new things.
   c. ☐ selfish and unkind to others.
   d. ☐ an illogical thinker.

7. My vacations could be described as
   a. ☐ traditional.
   b. ☐ adventuresome.
   c. ☐ pleasing to others.
   d. ☐ a new learning experience.

8. One word that best describes me is
   a. ☐ sensible.
   b. ☐ spontaneous.
   c. ☐ giving.
   d. ☐ analytical.

STEP 2. Add up the total points for each letter.

TOTAL FOR   **a.** ☐ Organizer   **b.** ☐ Adventurer   **c.** ☐ Giver   **d.** ☐ Thinker

STEP 3. Plot these numbers on the brain diagram on page 51.

SCORING DIAGRAM FOR PERSONALITY SPECTRUM

Write your scores from p. 75 in the four squares just outside the brain diagram—Thinker score at top left, Giver score at top right, Organizer score at bottom left, and Adventurer score at bottom right.

Each square has a line of numbers that go from the square to the center of the diagram. For each of your four scores, place a dot on the appropriate number in the line near that square. For example, if you scored 15 in the Giver spectrum, you would place a dot between the 14 and 16 in the upper right-hand line of numbers. If you scored a 26 in the Organizer spectrum, you would place a dot on the 26 in the lower left-hand line of numbers.

Connect the four dots to make a four-sided shape. If you like, shade the four sections inside the shape using four different colors.

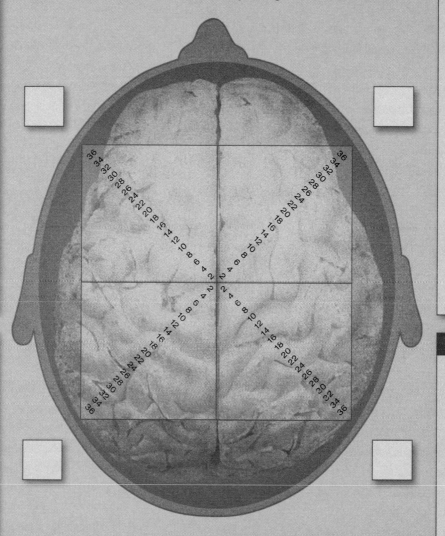

THINKER

Technical
Scientific
Mathematical
Dispassionate
Rational
Analytical
Logical
Problem Solving
Theoretical
Intellectual
Objective
Quantitative
Explicit
Realistic
Literal
Precise
Formal

GIVER

Interpersonal
Emotional
Caring
Sociable
Giving
Spiritual
Musical
Romantic
Feeling
Peacemaker
Trusting
Adaptable
Passionate
Harmonious
Idealistic
Talkative
Honest

ORGANIZER

Tactical
Planning
Detailed
Practical
Confident
Predictable
Controlled
Dependable
Systematic
Sequential
Structured
Administrative
Procedural
Organized
Conservative
Safekeeping
Disciplined

ADVENTURER

Active
Visual
Risking
Original
Artistic
Spatial
Skillful
Impulsive
Metaphoric
Experimental
Divergent
Fast-paced
Simultaneous
Competitive
Imaginative
Open-minded
Adventuresome

For the Personality Spectrum,
26–36 indicates a strong tendency in that dimension,
14–25 a moderate tendency,
and below 14 a minimal tendency.

Source for brain diagram: Understanding Psychology, 3/e, by Morris, © 1996.
Adapted by permission of Prentice-Hall, Inc., Upper Saddle River, NJ.

CHARACTERISTICS OF EACH PERSONALITY TYPE

Thinker

- Solving problems
- Developing models and systems
- Analytical and abstract thinking
- Exploring ideas and potentials
- Ingenuity
- Going beyond established boundaries
- Global thinking—seeking universal truth

Organizer

- Responsibility, reliability
- Operating successfully within social structures
- Sense of history, culture, and dignity
- Neatness and organization
- Loyalty
- Orientation to detail
- Comprehensive follow-through on tasks
- Efficiency
- Helping others

Giver

- Honesty, authenticity
- Successful, close relationships
- Making a difference in the world
- Cultivating potential of self and others
- Negotiation; promoting peace
- Openness
- Helping others

Adventurer

- High ability in a variety of fields
- Courage and daring
- Hands-on problem solving
- Living in the present
- Spontaneity and action
- Ability to negotiate
- Nontraditional style
- Flexibility
- Zest for life

STUDY TECHNIQUES TO MAXIMIZE PERSONALITY TYPES

Thinker

- Find time to reflect independently on new information
- Learn through problem solving
- Design new ways of approaching issues
- Convert material into logical charts
- Try to minimize repetitive tasks
- Look for opportunities to work independently

Organizer

- Try to have tasks defined in clear, concrete terms so that you know what is required
- Look for a well-structured, stable environment
- Request feedback
- Use a planner to schedule tasks and dates
- Organize material by rewriting and organizing class or text notes, making flash cards, or carefully highlighting

Giver

- Study with others
- Teach material to others
- Seek out tasks, groups, and subjects that involve helping people
- Find ways to express thoughts and feelings clearly and honestly
- Put energy into your most important relationships

Adventurer

- Look for environments that encourage nontraditional approaches
- Find hands-on ways to learn
- Seek people whom you find stimulating
- Use or develop games and puzzles to help memorize terms
- Fight boredom by asking to do something extra or perform a task in a more active way

Joyce Bishop, *Keys to Success,* © 2001

Figure 3.2 How to Put Your Personality Spectrum to Work for You

What Are the Benefits of Knowing How you Learn?

Generally, self-knowledge helps you make choices that boost your strong areas and help you to manage weaker ones. For example, understanding what you value can help you choose friends who cheer on your successes as well as friends who broaden your horizons with their different perspectives. Likewise for learning style: When you know your Multiple Intelligences and personality traits, you can choose strategies that will help you learn more, remember better, and use your knowledge more successfully—in any academic or workplace situation.

Study benefits

Knowing how you learn helps you choose study techniques that capitalize on your strengths. For example, if you learn successfully from a linear, logical presentation, you can look for order (for example, a chronology or a problem–solution structure) as you review notes. If you are a strong interpersonal learner, you can try to work in study groups whenever possible.

Learning style also points you toward strategies that help with tasks and topics that don't come so easily. An Adventurer who does *not* respond well to linear information, for example, has two choices when faced with logical presentations. She can apply her strengths to the material—for example, she might find a hands-on approach. Or she can work on her ability to handle the material by developing study skills that work well for linear learners.

When you study with others, understanding of diverse learning styles will help you assign tasks effectively and learn more comprehensively. An interpersonal learner might take the lead in teaching material to others; an Organizer might be the schedule coordinator for the group; a musical learner might present information in a new way that helps to solidify concepts.

Classroom benefits

Your college instructors will most likely have a range of teaching styles (an instructor's teaching style often reflects his or her dominant learning style). Your particular learning style may work well with some instructors and be a mismatch with others. After several class meetings, you should be able to assess an instructor's teaching styles (see Figure 3.3). Then you can use what you know to maximize styles that suit you and compensate for those that don't.

Although presentation styles vary, the standard lecture is still the norm in most classrooms. For this reason, the traditional college classroom is generally a happy home for the verbal or logical learner and the Thinker and Organizer. However, many students learn best when interacting more than a lecture allows. What can you do if your styles don't match up with those of your instructor?

Play to your strengths

For example, an Organizer with an instructor who delivers material in a random way might rewrite notes in an outline format to bring structure to concepts and insert facts where they fit best. Likewise, a Giver taking a straight lecture course with no student-to-student contact might meet with a study group to go over the details and fill in factual gaps.

Work to build weaker areas

> Learning is not attained by chance, it must be sought for with ardor and attended to with diligence.
> —Abigail Adams

As a visual learner reviews notes from a structured lecture course, he could outline them, allot extra time to master the material, and work with a study group. A Thinker, studying for a test from notes delivered by an Adventurer instructor, could find hands-on ways to review the material (for example, for a science course, working in the lab).

TEACHING STYLE	WHAT TO EXPECT IN CLASS
LECTURE, VERBAL FOCUS	Instructor speaks to the class for the entire period, with little class interaction. Lesson is taught primarily through words, either spoken or written on the board, overhead projector, handouts, or text.
GROUP DISCUSSION	Instructor presents material but encourages class discussion.
SMALL GROUPS	Instructor presents material and then breaks class into small groups for discussion or project work.
VISUAL FOCUS	Instructor uses visual elements such as diagrams, photographs, drawings, transparencies.
LOGICAL PRESENTATION	Instructor organizes material in a logical sequence, such as by time or importance.
RANDOM PRESENTATION	Instructor tackles topics in no particular order, and may jump around a lot or digress.

Figure 3.3 Instructors Often Rely On One or More Teaching Styles

Ask your instructor for additional help

If you are having trouble with coursework, communicate with your instructor through e-mail or face-to-face during office hours. This is especially important in large lectures where you are anonymous unless you speak up. The visual learner, for example, might ask the instructor to recommend graphs or figures that illustrate the lecture.

Instructors are unique. No instructor can give each of a diverse group of learners exactly what each one needs. The flexibility that you need to mesh your learning style with instructors' teaching styles is a tool for career and life success. Just as you can't hand-pick your instructors, you will rarely, if ever, be able to choose your supervisors or their work styles.

Workplace benefits

Knowing how you learn brings you these benefits in your career:

- **Better performance through self-awareness.** Since your learning styles are essentially the same as your working styles, knowing how you learn will help you identify career and work environments that suit you. Knowing your strengths will help you use and highlight them on the job. When a task involves one of your weaker skills, you can either take special care to accomplish it or suggest someone else who is a better fit.

- **Better teamwork.** The more attuned you are to abilities and personality traits, the better you will be at identifying the tasks you and others can best perform in team situations. For example, a Giver might enjoy helping new hires get used to the people and environment. Or a supervisor directing an intrapersonal learner might offer the chance to take material home to think about before a meeting.

ASSESS: WHAT CAN YOU LEARN ABOUT PERSONALITY

To begin, take the following PAP assessment.

#2. The Personality Assessment Profile (PAP) (2005) by Robert Sherfield, Ph.D. Based in part on the Myers Briggs Type Indicator (MBTI) by Katherine Briggs and Isabel Briggs-Myers. Read each statement carefully and thoroughly. After reading the statement, rate your response using the scale to the right. There are no right or wrong answers. This is not a timed survey.

Never or Almost never	Sometimes	Often
1	2	3

1. _____ I am a very talkative person.
2. _____ I am a very friendly and social person.
3. _____ I like to express my feelings and thoughts.
4. _____ I like to work with a group of people.
5. _____ I can be myself when I'm around others.

_____ TOTAL for **EXTROVERT**

1. _____ I am a more reflective person than a verbal person.
2. _____ I enjoy listening to others more than talking.
3. _____ I enjoy a great deal of tranquility and quiet time to myself.
4. _____ I would rather work independently.
5. _____ I can be myself when I am alone.

_____ TOTAL for **INTROVER**

1. _____ I value truth and justice over tact and emotion.
2. _____ One of my motivating forces is to do a job well.
3. _____ I make decisions with my brain.
4. _____ I am quick to criticize others.
5. _____ I think that if someone breaks the rules, the person should be punished.

_____ TOTAL for **THINKING**

1. _____ I find it easy to empathize with other people.
2. _____ I like to be recognized for, and I am motivated by, my accomplishments and awards.
3. _____ I make decisions with my heart.
4. _____ I compliment others very easily and quickly.
5. _____ I think that if someone breaks the rules, we should look at the person who broke the rules, examine the rules, and look at the situation at hand before a decision is made.

_____ TOTAL for **FEELING**

1. _____ I look to the future, and I can see possibilities.
2. _____ I enjoy being around and working with people who are dreamers and have a great deal of imagination.
3. _____ I like to create new ideas, methods, or ways of doing things.
4. _____ I learn best by relying on my gut feelings or intuition.
5. _____ I live in the future, planning and dreaming.

_____ TOTAL for **INTUITION**

1. _____ I am a very factual and literal person.
2. _____ I enjoy being around and working with people who have a great deal of common sense.
3. _____ I am a very pragmatic and realistic person.
4. _____ I learn best if I can see it, touch it, smell it, taste it, or hear it.
5. _____ I live in the here and now, in the present

_____ TOTAL for **SENSING**

continued on next page

Never or Almost never | Sometimes | Often
1 | 2 | 3

1. _____ I enjoy having freedom from control.

2. _____ I like to plan out my day before I go to bed.

3. _____ I am a very disciplined and orderly person.

4. _____ My life is systematic and organized.

5. _____ I do my work, then I play.

_____ TOTAL for **JUDGING**

1. _____ I enjoy having freedom from control.

2. _____ When I get up on a non-school or non-work day, I just like to let the day "plan itself."

3. _____ I don't make a lot of plans.

4. _____ I don't really pay attention to deadlines.

5. _____ I play, then do my work.

_____ TOTAL for **PERCEIVING**

Pap Scores

Personality Indicator

Look at the scores on your PAP. Is your score higher in the E or I line? Is your score higher in the S or N line? Is your score higher in the T or F line? Is your score higher in the J or P line? Write the code to the side of each section below.

Is your higher score   E or I   Code _____
Is your higher score   S or N   Code _____
Is your higher score   T or F   Code _____
Is your higher score   J or P   Code _____

Understanding Personality Typing (Typology)

The questions on the PAP helped you discover whether you are extroverted or introverted (E or I), sensing or intuitive (S or N), thinking or feeling (T or F), and judging or perceiving (J or P). These questions were based, in part, on work done by Carl Jung, Katharine Briggs, and Isabel Briggs-Myers. What personality typing can do is to "help us discover what best motivates and energizes each of us as individuals" (Tieger and Tieger, 2001).

Plan to Understand Personality Categories

Let's take a look at the four major categories of typing. Notice that the stronger your score in one area, the stronger your personality type is for that area. For instance, if you scored 15 on the E (extroversion) questions, this means that you are a strong extrovert. If you scored 15 on the I (introversion) questions, this means that you are a strong introvert. However, if you scored 7 on the E questions and 8 on the I questions, your score indicates that you possess almost the same amount of extroverted and introverted qualities. The same is true for every category on the PAP.

J. K. Rowling

was dismissed from a secretarial job because her boss caught her writing stories on her computer at work. She supported herself and her family on unemployment pay while she wrote the first *Harry Potter.* Today, she continues to write and is a billionaire.

E Versus I (Extroversion/Introversion)

This category deals with the way we *interact with others and the world around us.*

Extroverts prefer to live in the outside world, drawing their strength from other people. They are outgoing and love interaction. They usually make decisions with others in mind. They enjoy being the center of attention. There are usually few secrets about extroverts.

Introverts draw their strength from the inner world. They need to spend time alone to think and ponder. They are usually quiet and make decisions alone.

S Versus N (Sensing/Intuition)

This category deals with the way we *learn and deal with information.*

Sensing types gather information through their five senses. They have a hard time believing something if it cannot be seen, touched, smelled, tasted, or heard. They like concrete facts and details. They do not rely on intuition or gut feelings. They usually have a great deal of common sense.

Intuitive types are not very detail-oriented. They can see possibilities, and they rely on their gut feelings. Usually, they are very innovative people. They tend to live in the future and often get bored once they have mastered a task.

T Versus F (Thinking/Feeling)

This category deals with the way we *make decisions.*

Thinkers are very logical people. They do not make decisions based on feelings or emotion. They are analytical and sometimes do not take others' values into consideration when making decisions. They can easily identify the flaws of others. They can be seen as insensitive and lacking compassion.

Feelers make decisions based on what they feel is right and just. They like to have harmony, and they value others' opinions and feelings. They are usually very tactful people who like to please others. They are very warm people.

J Versus P (Judging/Perceiving)

This category deals with the way we *live.*

Judgers are very orderly people. They must have a great deal of structure in their lives. They are good at setting goals and sticking to their goals. They are the type of people who would seldom, if ever, play before their work was completed.

Perceivers are just the opposite. They are less structured and more spontaneous. They do not like timelines. Unlike the judger, they will play before their work is done. They will take every chance to delay a decision or judgment.

With this information, you can make some decisions about your study habits and even your career choices. For instance, if you scored very strong in the extroversion section, it may not serve you well to pursue a career where you would be forced to work alone. It would probably be unwise to try to spend all of your time studying alone. If you are a strong extrovert, you would want to work and study around people.

Making It Work for You

Having identified your personality type, use the suggestions on the following pages to enhance studying using your present personality type, while improving your study skills using your less dominate type.

Type	Current Suggestions	Improvement
Extrovert	Study with groups of people in cooperative learning teams.	Work on listening skills.
	Seek help from others.	Be sure to let others contribute to the group.
	Discuss topics with friends.	Force yourself to develop solutions and answers before you go to the group.
	Establish debate or discussion groups.	Spend some time reflecting.
	Vary your study habits; meet in different places with different people.	Let others speak before you share your ideas and suggestions.
	Discuss new ideas and plans with your friends.	Work to be more patient.
		Think before acting or speaking.
Introvert	Study in a quiet place, undisturbed by others.	Get involved in a study group from time to time.
	When reading and studying, take time for reflection.	Allow others inside your world to offer advice and opinions.
	Use your time alone to read and study support and auxiliary materials.	Share your opinions and advice with others more often.
	Set aside large blocks of time for study and reflection.	Seek advice from others.
		Use mnemonics to increase your memory power.
		Instead of writing responses or questions, speak aloud to friends and peers.
Sensor	Observe the world around you.	Try to think about the information in an abstract form.
	Experience the information to the fullest degree; feel it and touch it.	Think "What would happen if . . ." Let your imagination run wild.
	Explain to your study group or partner the information in complete detail.	Think about the information in the future tense. Let your gut feelings take over from time to time.
	Apply the information to something in your life that is currently happening.	Take more chances with the unknown.
	Create a study schedule and stick to it.	Trust your feelings and inspirations.
	If your old study habits are not working, stop and invent new ways of studying. Explore what others are doing.	Think beyond reality. Don't oversimplify.
Intuitive	After studying the information or data, let your imagination apply this to something abstract.	Work on becoming more detail-oriented.
	Describe how the information could be used today, right now, in your life at the moment.	Look at information through the senses.
	Describe how this information could help others.	Verify your facts.
	View new information as a challenge.	Think in simple terms.
	Vary your study habits; don't do the same thing all the time.	Think about the information in a logical and analytical way.
	Rely on your gut feelings.	Try to explain new information in relation to the senses.

Continued

Type	Current Suggestions	Improvement
Thinker	Make logical connections between new information and what is already known.	Try to see information and data in more abstract terms.
	Remain focused.	Look for the "big picture."
	Explain the information in detailed terms to a study group.	Develop a passion for acquiring new information.
	Put things in order.	Think before you speak.
	Study with people who do their part for the group.	Strive to be more objective and open.
Feeler	Establish a supportive and open study group.	Strive to look at things more logically.
	Teach others the information.	Work to stay focused.
	Continue to be passionate about learning and exploring.	Praise yourself when others do not.
	Explain the information in a cause/effect scenario.	Try to be more organized.
	Focus on the "people" factor.	Work to stick to policies, rules, and guidelines.
		Don't give in to opposition just for the sake of harmony.
		Don't get caught up in the here and now; look ahead.
Judger	Set a schedule and stick to it.	Take your time in making decisions.
	Strive to complete projects.	Complete all tasks.
	Keep your study supplies in one place so that you can locate them easily.	Look at the entire situation before making a judgment.
	Prioritize tasks that need to be completed.	Don't act or make judgments too quickly.
	Create lists and agendas.	Don't beat yourself up if you miss a deadline.
Perceiver	Study in different places with different people.	Become more decisive.
	Since you see all sides of issues, share those with your study group for discussion.	Finish one project before you begin another.
	Obtain as much information as possible so that you can make solid decisions.	Don't put off the harder subjects until later; study them first.
	Create fun and exciting study groups with snacks and maybe music.	Learn to set deadlines.
	Be the leader of the study team.	Create lists and agendas to help you stay on target.
	Allow yourself a great deal of time for study so that you can take well-deserved breaks.	Do your work; then play.

ASSESS: HOW CAN YOU USE LEARNING STYLES?

To begin, take the following Learning Style Assessment # 3.
Learning Style Assessment (2006) by Kateri Drexler
Based in part on the Solomon and Felder's Index of Learning Styles
Read each statement carefully and thoroughly. After reading the statement, rate your response using the scale to the right. There are no right or wrong answers. This is not a timed survey.

Never or Almost never	Sometimes	Often
1	2	3

1. _____ I tend to understand details of a subject but may be fuzzy about its overall structure.

2. _____ Once I understand all the parts, I understand the whole thing.

3. _____ When I solve math problems I usually work my way to the solutions one step at a time.

4. _____ When I'm analyzing a story or a novel I think of the incidents and try to put them together to figure out the themes.

5. _____ It is more important to me that an instructor lay out the material in clear sequential steps.

_____ TOTAL for Sequential

1. _____ I tend to understand the overall structure but may be fuzzy about details.

2. _____ Once I understand the whole thing, I see how the parts fit.

3. _____ When I solve math problems I often just see the solutions but then have to struggle to figure out the steps to get to them.

4. _____ When I'm analyzing a story or a novel I just know what the themes are when I finish reading and then I have to go back and find the incidents that demonstrate them.

5. _____ It is more important to me that an instructor give me an overall picture and relate the material to other subjects.

_____ TOTAL for Global

1. _____ I understand something better after I try it out.

2. _____ When I am learning something new, it helps me to talk about it.

3. _____ In a group working on learning difficult material or a tough project, I am more likely to jump in and contribute ideas.

4. _____ In classes I have taken I have usually gotten to know many of the students.

5. _____ I would rather first try things out.

_____ TOTAL for Active

1. _____ I understand something better after I think it through.

2. _____ When I am learning something new, it helps me to think about it.

3. _____ In a group working on learning difficult material or a tough project, I am more likely to sit back and listen.

4. _____ In classes I have taken I have rarely gotten to know many of the students.

5. _____ I would rather first think about how I'm going to do it.

_____ TOTAL for Reflective

1. _____ I would rather be considered realistic.

2. _____ I find it easier to learn facts.

3. _____ If I were a teacher, I would rather teach a course that deals with facts and real life situations.

4. _____ In reading nonfiction, I prefer something that teaches me new facts or tells me how to do something.

5. _____ I prefer the idea of certainty.

_____ TOTAL for Sensing

1. _____ I would rather be considered innovative.

2. _____ I find it easier to learn concepts.

3. _____ If I were a teacher, I would rather teach a course that deals with ideas and theories.

4. _____ In reading nonfiction, I prefer something that gives me new ideas to think about.

5. _____ I prefer the idea of theory.

_____ TOTAL for Intuitive

	Never or Almost never	Sometimes	Often
	1	2	3

1. _____ When I think about what I did yesterday, I am most likely to get a picture.

2. _____ I prefer to get new information in pictures, diagrams, graphs, or maps.

3. _____ In a book with lots of pictures and charts, I am likely to look over the pictures and charts carefully.

4. _____ I like teachers who put a lot of diagrams on the board.

5. _____ When I see a diagram or sketch in class, I am most likely to remember the picture.

_____ TOTAL for Visual

1. _____ When I think about what I did yesterday, I am most likely to get words.

2. _____ I prefer to get new information in written directions or verbal information.

3. _____ In a book with lots of pictures and charts, I am likely to focus on the written text.

4. _____ I like teachers who spend a lot of time explaining.

5. _____ When I see a diagram or sketch in class, I am most likely to remember what the instructor said about it.

_____ TOTAL for Verbal

Plan to Understand the Different Learning Styles

Sequential and Global Learners

This category deals with the way we *learn information as a whole.*

Sequential learners tend to gain understanding in linear steps, with each step following logically from the previous one. They follow logical pathways to find solutions. Sequential learners may not fully understand the material but they can nevertheless do something with it (like solve the homework problems or pass the test) because the pieces they have absorbed are logically connected. Sequential learners may know a lot about specific aspects of a subject but may have trouble relating them to different aspects of the same subject or to different subjects.

Global learners tend to learn in large jumps, absorbing material almost randomly without seeing connections, and then suddenly "getting it." They may be able to solve complex problems quickly or put things together in novel ways once they have grasped the big picture, but they may have difficulty explaining how they did it. What makes you global or not is what happens before the light bulb goes on. Strongly global learners who lack good sequential thinking abilities, on the other hand, may have serious difficulties until they have the big picture. Even after they have it, they may be fuzzy about the details of the subject.

Active and Reflective Learners

Active learners tend to retain and understand information best by doing something active with it—discussing or applying it or explaining it to others. "Let's try it out and see how it works" is an active learner's phrase. Active learners tend to like group work. Sitting through lectures without getting to do anything physical but take notes is hard for both learning types, but particularly hard for active learners.

Reflective learners prefer to think about it quietly first. "Let's think it through first" is the reflective learner's response. Reflective learners would rather avoid group work. They prefer working alone.

Sensing and Intuitive Learners

Sensing learners tend to like learning facts; intuitive learners often prefer discovering possibilities and relationships. Sensors often like solving problems by well-established methods and dislike complications and surprises. They are likely to resent being tested on material that has not been explicitly covered in class. Sensors tend to be patient with details and good at memorizing facts and doing hands-on (laboratory) work; Sensors tend to be practical and careful. Sensors don't like courses that have no apparent connection to the real world.

Intuitors like innovation and dislike repetition. Intuitive learners may be better at grasping new concepts and are often comfortable with abstractions and mathematical formulations. Intuitors tend to work faster and to be more innovative. They don't tend to like courses that involve a lot of memorization and routine calculations.

Visual and Verbal Learners

Visual learners remember best what they see—pictures, diagrams, flow charts, time lines, films, and demonstrations. In most college classes very little visual information is presented: students mainly listen to lectures and read material written on chalkboards and in textbooks and handouts. Unfortunately, most people are visual learners, which means that most students do not get nearly as much as they would if more visual presentation were used in class.

Verbal learners get more out of words—written and spoken explanations. Everyone learns more when information is presented both visually and verbally.

Making It Work for You
Using the Learning Styles to Learn More Effectively

Having identified your primary learning style, use the suggestions on the following pages to enhance studying using your present style, while improving your study skills using your less dominant type.

Type	Current Suggestions	Improvement
Sequential	Most college courses are taught in a sequential manner. If you are a sequential learner and you have an instructor who jumps around from topic to topic or skips steps, you can: Ask the instructor to fill in the skipped steps, or fill them in yourself by consulting references. Take the time to outline the lecture material for yourself in logical order, when you are studying.	Strengthen your global thinking skills by relating each new topic you study to things you already know. The more you can do so, the deeper your understanding of the topic is likely to be. Skim through the entire chapter of what you will be covering in class to get an overview.
Global	Realize that you need the big picture of a subject before you can master details. If your instructor plunges directly into new topics without explaining how they relate to what you already know, you can: Skim through the entire chapter of what you will be covering in class to get an overview. Immerse yourself in individual subjects for large blocks instead of spending a short time on every subject every night. Ask the instructor to help you see connections or consult additional resources to help you see them.	Prepare outlines of lecture material for yourself in logical order. Practice patience. Recognize that understanding of the big picture will come in time.
Active	If you are an active learner in a class that allows little or no class time for discussion or problem-solving activities, you should try to compensate for these lacks when you study by: Studying in a group in which the members take turns explaining different topics to each other. Work with others to guess what you will be asked on the next test and figure out how you will answer.	The next time you are about to take some action, try taking a minute to reflect on what you're going do.
Reflective	If you are a reflective learner in a class that allows little or no class time for thinking about new information, you should try to compensate for this lack when you study by: Stopping periodically during reading to review what you have read and to think of possible questions or applications. Writing short summaries of readings or class notes in your own words. Doing so may take extra time but will enable you to retain the material more effectively.	Get involved with a study group periodically. Actively participate in class discussions, recognizing that you reserve the right to change your mind about a topic later if you choose to.

Type	Current Suggestions	Improvement
Sequential	Sensors remember and understand information best if they can see how it connects to the real world. If you are in a class where most of the material is abstract and theoretical, you can: Ask your instructor for specific examples of concepts and procedures, and find out how the concepts apply in practice. Try to find some in your course text or other references or by brainstorming with friends or classmates.	If you overemphasize sensing, you may rely too much on memorization and familiar methods and not concentrate enough on understanding and innovative thinking. Ask your instructor for interpretations or theories that link the facts, or try to find the connections yourself.
Intuitive	Many college lecture classes are aimed at intuitors. However, if you are an intuitor and you happen to be in a class that deals primarily with memorization and rote substitution in formulas, you can: Ask your instructor for interpretations or theories that link the facts, or try to find the connections yourself. Be careful on tests and not get impatient with details. Take time to read the entire question before you start answering questions and be sure to check your results.	If you overemphasize intuition, you may miss important details or make careless mistakes in calculations or hands-on work. Think of exciting ways to memorize information that will be needed. Use mnemonic devices or flash cards.
Visual	If you are a visual learner, try to: Find diagrams, sketches, schematics, photographs, flow charts, or any other visual representation of course material that is predominantly verbal. Ask your instructor, consult reference books, and see whether any videotapes or CD-ROM displays of the course material are available. Prepare a mind map by listing key points, enclosing them in boxes or circles, and drawing lines with arrows between concepts to show connections. Color-code your notes with a highlighter so that everything relating to one topic is the same color.	Write summaries or outlines of course material in your own words.
Verbal	If you are a verbal learner, you can: Write summaries or outlines of course material in your own words. Work in groups and gain an understanding of material by hearing classmates' explanations. Summarize your understanding to your classmates.	Prepare a mind map by listing key points, enclosing them in boxes or circles, and drawing lines with arrows between concepts to show connections. Actively look for diagrams, sketches, schematics, photographs, flow charts, or any other visual representation of course material and seek to understand them

What Are Some Other Learning Styles?

There are many learning styles theories. The important thing to help you during your education is to recognize that you may have a dominant style. Fit your education around that when you can, and try to develop your other learning styles as much as possible. The following two theories may provide additional insight into how you process information.

Introduction to a Cognitive Learning Style

Kolb's Learning Style Inventory is one of the dominant approaches to categorizing cognitive styles. There are four basic learning styles: converger, diverger, assimilator, and accommodator. Their characteristics are described below:

Converger

The convergent learner uses active experimentation and abstract conceptualization. This style has great advantages in decision making, problem solving, traditional intelligent tests, and practical applications of theories. People with this style are typically superior in technical tasks and problems and inferior in social and interpersonal matters. They tend to choose to specialize in physical sciences.

Diverger

The divergent learning style has the opposite learning advantages over converger. This style depends mainly on concrete experience and reflective observation; it has great advantages in imaginative abilities and awareness of meaning and values. People with this tend to be imaginative, people- or feeling-oriented; they tend to choose to specialize in liberal arts and humanities.

Assimilator

People primarily using the assimilator learning style tend to focus more on the logical soundness and preciseness of ideas, rather than their practical values; they tend to choose to work in research and planning units.

Accommodator

The accommodative learning style has the opposite learning advantages over assimilation. These learners tend to intuitively solve problems in a trial-and-error manner, depending mainly on other people for information rather than on their own thinking. Therefore, persons with this style tend to deal with people easily and can excel in action oriented jobs, such as marketing and sales.

Introduction to an Experiential Learning Style

Theorists in the experiential learning tradition identify four types of learning style: the activist learner, the reflective learner, the theorist learner and the pragmatic learner. The following table outlines those activities that will be most or least appropriate for each type of learner.

Activist style	
Learns best from activities where:	*Learns least from activities where:*
there are new experiences/problems, etc.;	learning involves a passive role, e.g. listening to lectures, reading, explanations;
they can become engrossed in short tasks, games, competitive teamwork tasks, etc.;	they are not directly involved;
there is excitement/drama/crisis and things chop and change with a range of diverse activities to tackle;	they are required to assimilate, analyze and interpret lots of data;
there is chance of limelight, e.g. leading discussions, giving presentations;	they are required to engage in solitary work, i.e. reading, writing, thinking on their own;
they are involved with other people, e.g. bouncing ideas off them, solving problems as part of a team.	they are asked to repeat the same activity over and over again.

Continued

Reflector style

Learns best from activities where:	Learns least from activities where:
they are encouraged to watch/think/chew over activities;	they are forced into the limelight;
they are able to listen/observe a group;	they are worried by time pressures or rushed from one activity to another;
they can reach a decision in their own time without pressure and tight deadlines.	they are pitched into doing something without warning.

Theorist style

Learns best from activities where:	Learns least from activities where:
they are in structured situations with a clear purpose;	they have to participate in situations that are unstructured, where ambiguity and uncertainty are high, e.g. open-ended problems;
they are required to understand and participate in complex situations;	they are faced with a hodgepodge of alternative/ contradictory techniques without exploring any in depth;
they have time to explore the associations and interrelationships between ideas, events and situations.	they find the subject matter platitudinous, shallow or gimmicky.

Pragmatist style

Learns best from activities where:	Learns least from activities where:
there is an obvious link between the subject matter and a problem set;	the learning is not related to an immediate need or relevance;
they are practicing techniques with coaching/ feedback;	there is no practice or clear guidelines on how to do it;
they are given techniques that are applicable to the real world.	they cannot see sufficient reward from the learning activity.

Note-Taking Techniques
Tips for Effective Note-Taking During Reading

Taking notes is a useful way to organize your thoughts, focus on structure and key ideas, and help commit important information to memory. There are different reasons to take notes, and note-taking techniques may differ accordingly. We may take notes in order to:

- Brainstorm
- Explore ideas and gather more information
- Synthesize ideas
- Focus on a topic's details
- Present information

There are also different situations when we take notes, the most common being:

- Reading and researching
- Listening to a lecture or presentation

The note-taking techniques discussed later in this section include:

- Mapping
- T-format, or Cornell Method
- Outlining

Which method you use will depend on what works best for you. The following chart shows how the different techniques are best applied to the particular note-taking purpose.

Primary Note-Taking Purpose	Primary Note-Taking Techniques
Brainstorm	Mapping
Explore idea and gather more information	T-format
Synthesize ideas	T-format, Mapping
Focus on a topic's details	Outlining
Present information	Outlining

While taking notes during reading allows you the luxury of going back to passages for further understanding, you may have to do more synthesizing of multiple ideas and topics.

No matter which technique you use to take notes while reading, consider the following suggestions:

- Note any terms and definitions given. You can check the definitions of unfamiliar terms, as well as names, events, dates, steps, or directions.

- Wait until you read the document at least once before marking the text. If you mark text as you are reading you may tend to over-mark. Wait until you've finished a section, then go back and highlight the key points.

- Highlight key terms and concepts, if you own your text or are able to mark up a document. Mark the examples that explain and support the important ideas. You might try using more than one highlighter color to differentiate definitions or ideas from examples.

- Highlight figures and tables, if you own the text. Whatever information you need from the tables and figures should be highlighted along with any tables that summarize the concepts discussed in the text.

- Write notes in the margin, if you're able to mark the document. Comments such as "main point" or "important definition" will help you locate key sections later on. In addition, note any questions you may have about the document's validity in the margins.

- Review the highlights and organize into notes. Be an active reader. You will not necessarily learn from what you highlight unless you review it carefully.

Listening to people from different cultures, backgrounds, and religions can open many doors.

Now Hear This!
Tips for Effective Note-Taking in Class

It is important to develop several skills you will need to take notes. *First*, you need to cultivate and build your active listening skills. *Second*, you need to overcome obstacles to effective listening, such as prejudging, talking during a discussion, and bringing emotions to the table. *Finally*, you must scan, read, and use your textbook to understand the materials presented. Following are a few more important tips for taking notes.

Attend Class

This may sound like stating the obvious, but it is surprising how many college students feel they do not need to go to class. You may be able to copy notes from others, but you may very well miss the meaning behind them. To be an effective note taker, class attendance is crucial; there is no substitute for it.

Come to Class Prepared

Do you read your assignments nightly? Instructors are amazed at the number of students who come to class and then decide they should have read their homework. Doing your homework—reading your text, handouts, or workbooks or listening to tapes—is one of the most effective ways to become a better notetaker. It is always easier to take notes when you have a preliminary understanding of what is being said. As a student, you will find fewer tasks more difficult than trying to take notes on material that you have never seen or heard before. Coming to class prepared means doing your homework and coming to class ready to listen.

Coming to class prepared also means bringing the proper materials for taking notes: your textbook or lab manual, at least two pens, enough sharpened pencils to make it through the lecture, a notebook, and a highlighter. Some students also use a tape recorder. If you choose to use a tape recorder, be sure to get permission from the instructor before recording.

Bring Your Textbook to Class

Although many students think they do not need to bring their textbook to class if they have read the homework, you will find that many instructors repeatedly refer to the text while lecturing. Always bring your textbook to class with you. The instructor may ask you to highlight, underline, or refer to the text in class, and following along in the text as the instructor lectures may also help you organize your notes.

Ask Questions and Participate in Class

Two of the most critical actions you can perform in class are to ask questions and to participate in the class discussion. If you do not understand a concept or theory, ask questions.

Don't leave class without understanding what has happened and assume you'll pick it up on your own. Many instructors use students' questions as a way of teaching and reviewing materials. Your questions and participation will definitely help you, but they could also help others who did not understand something!

Listen Up!
Building Listening Skills

Listening is one of the most important and useful skills human beings possess. For all animals, listening is a survival skill needed for hunting and obtaining food; for humans, listening is necessary for establishing relationships, growth, survival, knowledge, entertainment, and even health. It is one of our most widely used tools. How much time do you think you spend listening every day? Research suggests that we spend almost 70% of our waking time communicating, and 53% of that time is spent in listening situations (Adler, Rosenfeld, and Towne, 2001). Effective listening skills can mean the difference between success and failure, A's and F's, relationships and loneliness.

For students, good listening skills are critical. Over the course of your program, you will be given a lot of information in lectures. Cultivating and improving your active listening skills will help you to understand the lecture material, take accurate notes, participate in class discussions, and communicate with your peers.

The Difference between Listening and Hearing

We usually do not think much about listening until a misunderstanding occurs. You've no doubt been misunderstood or misunderstood someone yourself. Misunderstandings arise because we tend to view listening as an automatic response when it is instead a learned, voluntary activity, like driving a car, painting a picture, or playing the piano. Having ears does not make you a good listener.

After all, having hands does not mean you are capable of painting the *Mona Lisa*. You may be able to paint the *Mona Lisa*, but only with practice and guidance. Listening, too, takes practice and guidance. Becoming an active listener requires practice, time, mistakes, guidance, and active participation.

Hearing, however, is not learned; it is automatic and involuntary. If you are within range of a sound, you will probably hear it although you may not be listening to it. Hearing a sound does not guarantee that you know what it is or what made it. Listening actively, though, means making a conscious effort to focus on the sound and to determine what it is.

Listening Defined

According to Ronald Adler (Adler, Rosenfeld, and Towne, 2001), the drawing of the Chinese verb "to listen" provides a comprehensive and practical definition of listening (see Figure 3.4). To the Chinese, listening involves the ears, the eyes, undivided attention, and the heart. Do you make it a habit to listen with more than your ears? The Chinese view listening as a whole-body experience. People from Western cultures seem to have lost the ability to involve their whole body in the listening process. We tend to use only our ears, and sometimes we don't even use them. At its

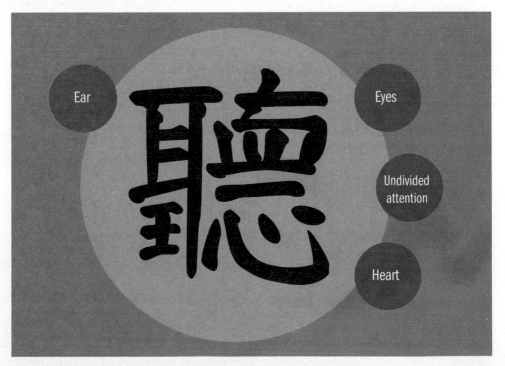

Figure 3.4   The Chinese Pictograph for "Listen"

College classes demand active critical listening skills.

core, listening is "the ability to hear, understand, analyze, respect, and appropriately respond to the meaning of another person's spoken and nonverbal messages" (Daly and Engleberg, 2002, p. 270). Although this definition involves the word "hear," listening goes far beyond just the physical ability to catch sound waves.

The first step in listening *is* hearing, but true listening involves one's full attention and the ability to filter out distractions, emotional barriers, cultural differences, and religious biases. Listening means that you are making a conscious decision to understand and show reverence for the other person's communication efforts.

Listening needs to be personalized and internalized. To understand listening as a whole-body experience, we can define it on three levels:

1. Listening with a purpose
2. Listening objectively
3. Listening constructively

Listening with a purpose suggests a need to recognize different types of listening situations—for example, class, worship, entertainment, and relationships. People do not listen the same way in every situation.

Listening objectively means listening with an open mind. You will give yourself few greater gifts than the gift of knowing how to listen without bias and prejudice. This is perhaps the most difficult aspect of listening. If you have been cut off in mid-conversation or mid-sentence by someone who disagreed with you, or if someone has left the room while you were giving your opinion of a situation, you have had the experience of talking to people who do not know how to listen objectively.

Listening constructively means listening with the attitude of "How can this be helpful to my life or my education?" This type of listening involves evaluating the information you are hearing and determining whether it has meaning to your life. Sound easy? It is more difficult than it sounds because, again, we all tend to shut out information that we do not view as immediately helpful or useful. To listen constructively, you need to know how to listen and store information for later.

What Did You Say?
Obstacles to Listening

Several major obstacles stand in the way of becoming an effective listener. To begin building active listening skills, you first have to remove some barriers.

Obstacle One: Prejudging

Prejudging means that you automatically shut out what is being said; it is one of the biggest obstacles to active listening. You may prejudge because of the content; the person communicating; or your environment, culture, social status, or attitude.

Obstacle Two: Talking

Not even the best listener in the world can listen while he or she is talking. The next time you are in a conversation with a friend, try speaking while your friend is speaking—then see if you know what your friend said. To become an effective listener, you need to learn the power of silence. Silence gives you the opportunity to think about what is being said before you respond.

TIP Tips for Overcoming Prejudging

1. Listen for information that may be valuable to you as a student. Some material may not be pleasant to hear but may be useful to you later on.

2. Listen to the message, not the messenger. If you do not like the speaker, try to go beyond personality and listen to what is being said, without regard to the person saying it. Conversely, you may like the speaker so much that you automatically accept the material or answers without listening objectively to what is being said.

3. Try to remove cultural, racial, gender, social, and environmental barriers. Just because a person is different from you or holds a different point of view does not make that person wrong; and just because a person is like you and holds a similar point of view does not make that person right. Sometimes, you have to cross cultural and environmental barriers to learn new material and see with brighter eyes.

TIP Tips for Overcoming the Urge to Talk Too Much

1. Force yourself to be silent at parties, family gatherings, and friendly get-togethers. We're not saying you should be unsociable, but force yourself to be silent for 10 minutes. You'll be surprised at what you hear. You may also be surprised how hard it is to do this. Test yourself.

2. Ask someone a question and then allow that person to answer the question. Too often we ask questions and answer them ourselves. Force yourself to wait until the person has formulated a response. If you ask questions and wait for answers, you will force yourself to listen.

Obstacle Three: Bringing Your Emotions to the Table

Emotions can form a strong barrier to active listening. Worries, problems, fears, and anger can keep you from listening to the greatest advantage. Have you ever sat in a lecture, and before you knew what was happening your mind was a million miles away because you were angry or worried about something? If you have, you know what it's like to bring your emotions to the table.

TIP Tips for Overcoming Emotions

1. Know how you feel before you begin the listening experience. Take stock of your emotions and feelings ahead of time.

2. Focus on the message; determine how to use the information.

3. Create a positive image about the message you are hearing.

Listening for Key Words, Phrases, and Hints

Learning how to listen for key words, phrases, and hints can help you become an active listener and an effective note taker. For example, if an auto mechanics instructor began a lecture saying, "There are ten basic elements to engine maintenance," you might jot down the number 10 under the heading "Maintenance" or put the numbers 1 through 10 on sequential lines of your notebook page, leaving space for notes. If by the end of class you had listed only six elements, you would know that you had missed a part of the lecture. At that point, you would need to ask the instructor some questions.

Here are some key phrases and words to listen for:

- in addition
- most important
- you'll see this again
- for example
- in contrast
- the characteristics of
- on the other hand

- another way
- such as
- therefore
- to illustrate
- in comparison
- the main issue is
- as a result of

- above all
- specifically
- finally
- as stated earlier
- nevertheless
- moreover
- because

Listening When English Is Your Second Language
Suggestions for ESL Students

For students whose first language is not English, the college classroom can present some uniquely challenging situations. One of the most pressing and important challenges is the ability to listen, translate, understand, and capture the message on paper in a quick and continuous manner. According to Lynn Forkos, Professor and Coordinator of the Conversation Center for International Students at the Community College of Southern Nevada, the following tips can be beneficial:

- Don't be afraid to **stop the instructor** to ask for clarification. Asking questions allows you to take an active part in the listening process. If the instructor doesn't answer your questions sufficiently, be certain to make an appointment to speak with him or her during his or her office hours.

- If you are in a situation in which the instructor can't stop or you're watching a movie or video in class, listen for words that you do understand and try to **figure out unfamiliar words in the context** of the sentence.

- **Enhance your vocabulary** by watching and listening to TV programs such as *Dateline, 20/20, Primetime Live, 60 Minutes,* and the evening news. You might also try listening to radio programming such as National Public Radio as you walk or drive.

- Be certain that you **write down everything** that the instructor puts on the board, overhead, or PowerPoint. You may not need every piece of this information, but this technique gives you (and hopefully your study group) the ability to sift through the information outside of class. It gives you a visual history of what the instructor said.

- Finally, if there is a conversation group or club that meets on campus, take the opportunity to join. **By practicing language,** you become more attuned to common words and phrases. If a conversation group is not available, consider starting one of your own.

Plan to Write It Right
Methods for Effective Note-Taking

There are three common note-taking systems: (1) the **out-line** technique; (2) the **Cornell**, or split-page technique (also called the **T** system); and (3) the **mapping** technique.

No matter which method you use, the L-STAR system can help you improve your note-taking skills, enhance your ability to participate in class, help other students, study more effectively, and perform well on exams and quizzes.

The L-Star System

One of the most effective ways to take notes begins with the **L-STAR** system.

L   Listening
S   Setting It Down
T   Translating
A   Analyzing
R   Remembering

Good note-taking skills help you do more than simply record what you're taught in class or read in a book so that you can recall it. These skills can also help to reinforce that information so that you actually know it.

This five-step program will enable you to compile complete, accurate, and visual notes for future reference.

L—Listening

One of the best ways to become an effective note-taker is to become an active listener. A concrete step you can take toward becoming an active listener in class is to sit near the front of the room where you can hear the instructor and see the board and over-heads. Choose a spot that allows you to see the instructor's mouth and facial expressions. If you see that the instructor's face has become animated or expressive, you can bet that you are hearing important information. Write it down. If you sit in the back of the room, you may miss out on these important clues.

S—Setting It Down

The actual writing of notes can be a difficult task. Some instructors are organized in their delivery of information; others are not. Your listening skills, once again, are going to play an important role in determining what needs to be written down. In most cases, you will not have time to take notes word for word. You will have to be selective about the information you choose to set down. One of the best ways to keep up with the information being presented is to develop a shorthand system of your own. Many of the symbols you use will be universal, but you may use some symbols, pictures, and markings that are uniquely your own.

Some of the more common symbols are:

w/	with	w/o	without
=	equals	≠	does not equal
<	less than	>	greater than
%	percentage	#	number
&	and	^	increase
+	plus or addition	−	minus or subtraction
*	important	etc	and so on
eg	for example	vs	against
esp	especially	"	quote
?	question	...	and so on

These symbols can save you valuable time when taking notes. Because you will use them frequently, it might be a good idea to memorize them. As you become more adept at note-taking, you will quickly learn how to abbreviate words, phrases, and names.

T—Translating

One of the most valuable activities you can undertake as a student is to translate your notes immediately after each class. Doing so can save you hours of work when you begin to prepare for exams. Many students feel that this step is not important, or too time-consuming, and leave it out. Don't. Often, students take notes so quickly that they make mistakes or use abbreviations that they may not be able to decipher later. After each class, go to the library or some other quiet place and review your notes. You don't have to do this immediately after class, but before the end of the day, you will need to rewrite and translate your classroom notes. This process gives you the opportunity to put the notes in your own words and to incorporate your text notes into your classroom notes. You can correct spelling, reword key phrases, write out abbreviations, and prepare questions for the next class. Sounds like a lot of work, doesn't it? It is a great deal of work, but if you try this technique for one week, you should see a vast improvement in your comprehension of material. Eventually, you should see an improvement in your grades. Translating your notes helps you to make connections among previous material and will prove a valuable gift to yourself when exam time comes.

A—Analyzing

This step takes place while you translate your notes from class. When you analyze your notes, you are asking two basic questions: (1) What does this mean? and (2) Why is it important? If you can answer these two questions about your material, you have almost mastered the information. Though some instructors will want you to spit back the exact same information you were given, others will ask you for a more detailed understanding and a synthesis of the material. When you are translating your notes, begin to answer these two questions using your notes, textbook, supple-mental materials, and information gathered from outside research. Once again, this process is not simple or quick, but testing your understanding of the material is important. Remember that many lectures are built on past lectures.

R—Remembering

Once you have listened to the lecture, set your notes on paper, and trans-lated and analyzed the material, it is time to study, or remember, the infor-mation. Some effective ways to remember information include creating a visual picture, speaking the notes out loud, using mnemonic devices, and finding a study partner.

It's as Simple as A, B, C—1, 2, 3
The Outline Technique

The outline system uses a series of major headings and multiple subhead-ings formatted in hierarchical order. The outline technique is one of the most commonly used note-taking systems, yet it is also one of the most mis-used systems. It can be difficult to outline notes in class, especially if your instructor does not follow an outline while lecturing.

DID YOU KNOW?

Ludwig van Beethoven

Born in 1770, Beethoven composed many concertos and symphonies, totaling more than 850 pages. At age 32, he began to lose his hearing and fell into deep depression that would haunt him until his death. *While completely deaf* and in poverty, he composed *The Ninth Symphony*, considered to be his most beautiful and impressive work.

When using the outline system, it is best to get all the information from the lecture and afterward to combine your lecture notes and text notes to create an outline. Most instructors would advise against using the outline system of note-taking in class, although you may be able to use a modified version. The most important thing to remember is not to get bogged down in a system during class; what is critical is getting the ideas down on paper. You can always go back after class and rearrange your notes as needed.

If you are going to use a modified or informal outline while taking notes in class, you may want to consider grouping information together under a heading as a means of outlining. It is easier to remember information that is logically grouped than to remember information that is scattered across several pages. If your study skills lecture is on listening, you might outline your notes using the headings "The Process of Listening" and "Definitions of Listening (see Figure 3.5 on next page).

It's a Split Decision
The Cornell (Modified Cornell, Split Page, or T) System

The basic principle of the Cornell system, developed by Dr. Walter Pauk of Cornell University, is to split the page into two sections, each section to be used for different information. Section A is used for questions that summarize information found in Section B; Section B is used for the actual notes from class. The blank note-taking page should be divided as shown in Figure 3.6.

Sometimes the basic Cornell layout is modified to include a third section at the bottom of the page for additional or summary comments. In such cases the layout is referred to as a "T system" for its resemblance to an upside-down T. To implement the Cornell system, you will want to choose the technique that is most comfortable and beneficial for you; you might use mapping (discussed next) or outlining on a Cornell page (see Figure 3.7).

Yes You Can!
IDEAS FOR SUCCESS

Consider the following tips for improving listening in the classroom:

- Sit near the front of the room.

- Establish eye contact with the instructor.

- Read the text or handout beforehand. Listening is aided greatly when you have advance knowledge of the subject.

- Memorize the *key words* listed previously to help you identify when important information is coming.

- Don't give up—even if the information is difficult and the instructor is hard to understand.

- Enter class with a mindset of learning. Remember, listening purposefully requires that you know the type of listening situation in which you will be involved and then prepare for that situation.

and ITT Tech Can Help!

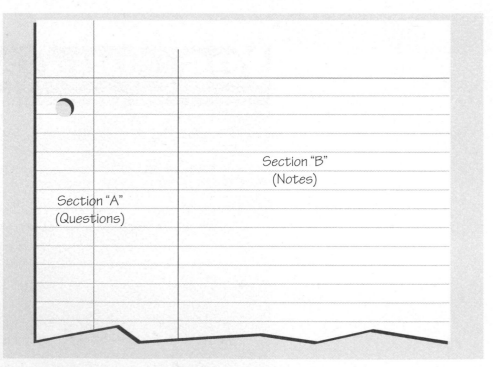

Study Skills 101   Oct. 17
                                                                  Wednesday

Topic: Listening

I. The Process of Listening (ROAR)
    A. R = Receiving
        1. W/in range of sound
        2. Hearing the information
    B. O = Organizing & focusing
        1. Choose to listen actively
        2. Observe the origin, direction & intent
    C. A = Assignment
        1. You assign a meaning
        2. May have to hear it more than once
    D. R = Reacting
        1. Our response to what we heard
        2. Reaction can be anything
II. Definitions of Listening (POC)
    A. P = Listening w/ a purpose
    B. O = Listening w/ objectivity
    C. C = Listening constructively

Figure 3.5   The Outline Technique

Section "B"
(Notes)

Section "A"
(Questions)

Figure 3.6   A Blank Cornell Frame

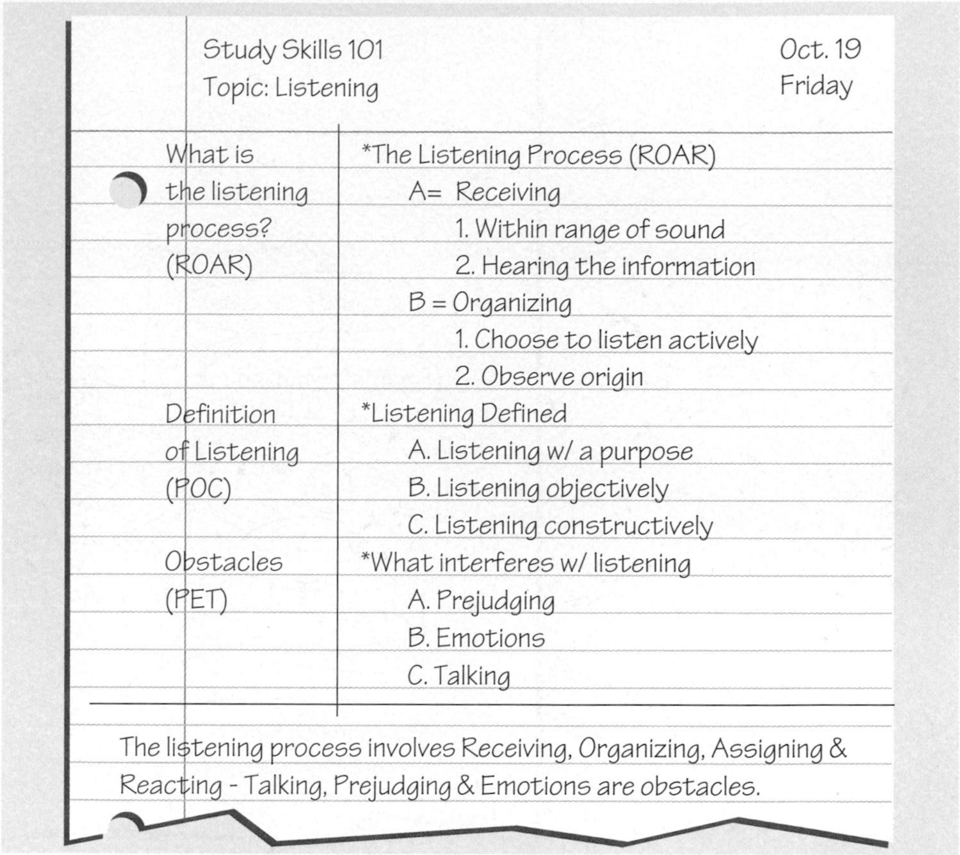

Figure 3.7 Outline Using a Cornell Frame

The figure shows handwritten notes in a Cornell frame:

Study Skills 101
Topic: Listening

Oct. 19
Friday

What is the listening process? (ROAR)	*The Listening Process (ROAR)
	A= Receiving
	   1. Within range of sound
	   2. Hearing the information
	B = Organizing
	   1. Choose to listen actively
	   2. Observe origin

Definition of Listening (POC)	*Listening Defined A. Listening w/ a purpose B. Listening objectively C. Listening constructively
Obstacles (PET)	*What interferes w/ listening A. Prejudging B. Emotions C. Talking

The listening process involves Receiving, Organizing, Assigning & Reacting - Talking, Prejudging & Emotions are obstacles.

Going Around in Circles
The Mapping System

If you are a visual learner, this system may be especially useful for you. The mapping system of note-taking generates a picture of information (see Figure 3.8). The mapping system creates a map, or web, of information that allows you to see the relationships among facts or ideas. (See Figure 3.9 for an example of mapping using a Cornell frame.) The most important thing to remember about each note-taking system is that it must work for you. Do not use a system because your friends use it or because you feel that you should use it. Experiment with each system or combination to determine which is best for you. Always remember to keep your notes organized, dated, and neat. Notes that cannot be read are no good to you or to anyone else.

What to Do When You Get Lost

Have you ever been in a classroom trying to take notes and the instructor is speaking so rapidly that you cannot possibly get all of the information? Just when you think you're caught up, you realize that he or she has made an important statement and you missed it. What do you do? How can you handle, or avoid, this difficult note-taking situation? Here are several hints:

- Raise your hand and ask the instructor to repeat the information.
- Ask your instructor to slow down.
- If he or she will do neither, leave a blank space with a question mark at the side margin. You can get this information after class. This can be a difficult task to master. The key is to focus on the information at hand. Focus on what is being said at the exact moment.

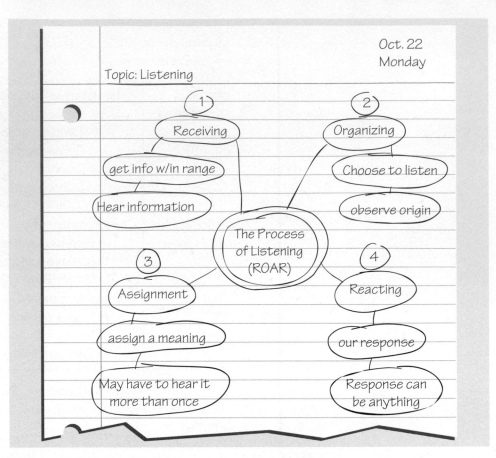

Figure 3.8 The Mapping System

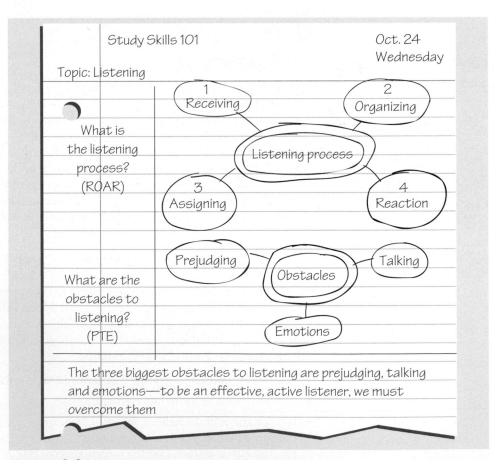

Figure 3.9 Mapping Using a Cornell Frame

- Meet with your instructor during break or immediately after class, or at the earliest time convenient for both of you.

- Form a note-taking group that meets after each class. This serves two purposes: (1) you can discuss and review the lecture, and (2) you will be able to get the notes from one of your note-taking buddies.

- Never lean over and ask questions of another student during the lecture. This will cause them to lose the information as well.

- Rehearse your note-taking skills at home by taking notes from TV news magazines or channels like the History Channel.

- Ask the instructor's permission to use a tape recorder during the lecture. Do not record a lecture without permission.

We suggest that you try to use other avenues, such as the ones listed above, instead of taping your notes. It is a time-consuming task to listen to the lecture for a second time. However, if this system works for you, use it.

Adapting Note-Taking to Different Instructor Styles

You can adjust your note-taking techniques according to the varying styles and personalities of lecturers. If your lecturer can be characterized as using primarily one of the following, use the associated tips for taking notes.

Lecturer Style	Tips for Note-Taking
Organized Lecturer	Copy all material from the board or slide.
	Understand the definition of all key words and phrases.
	Be prepared by doing background reading.
Entertaining Lecturers	Predict what an outline of the topic would look like and write this down before the lecture.
	As you listen to the lecture, remind yourself to ask "What is the point?" or "What am I learning?" "What is this story an illustration of?" "What is this example demonstrating?"
	Ask questions to clarify.
Questioning Lecturer	Record your own responses to the instructor's questions, even if you don't voice your response.
	Note when the lecturer affirms an idea ("Yes, that's right" or "Exactly, that's an important point").
	Note when the lecturer summarizes or paraphrases an idea.

What's in It for Me? Test Taking

How do you really feel about tests? Successful students realize that testing is necessary and even useful, that it has several positive purposes. Testing provides motivation for learning, offers feedback to the student and to the instructor, and determines mastery of material.

Successful people accept testing as a fact of life. You have to be tested to drive a car; to continue in school; to join the armed services; to become a teacher, a lawyer, a doctor, or a nurse; and often to be promoted at work. To pretend that testing is not always going to be a part of your life is to deny yourself many opportunities. Testing now prepares you for the world of work.

You may dread tests for a variety of reasons and may be afraid of the test itself and the questions it may pose. Test anxiety can be overcome, however, and this chapter presents several ways you can become a more confident test taker and get started on the path to success. Remember, too, some test anxiety is normal and can help you do your best!

Controlling Test Anxiety

Some students have physical reactions to testing, including nausea, headaches, and blackouts. Such physical reactions may be a result of being underprepared or not knowing how to take an exam. You reduce anxiety when you are in control of the situation, and you gain control by convincing yourself that you will be successful. If you honestly tell yourself that you have done everything possible to prepare for a test, then the results are going to be positive. Tests are a "mind game" and you can win!

It is important to realize that a test is not an indication of who you are as a person or a mark of your worth as a human being. Not everyone can be good at all things. You will have areas of strength and of weakness. You will spare yourself a great deal of anxiety and frustration if you understand from the start that you may not score 100 on every test. If you expect absolute perfection on everything, you are setting yourself up to fail. Think positively, prepare well, and do your best, but also be prepared to receive less than a perfect score on occasion.

Predicting Exam Questions

You can also reduce test anxiety by trying to predict what types of test questions the instructor will give. Instructors frequently give clues ahead of time about what they will be asking and what types of questions will be given. Several classes before the test is scheduled, find out from your instructor what type of test you can expect. Some questions you might ask are:

1. What type of questions will be on the test?
2. How long is the test?
3. Is there a time limit on the test?
4. Will there be any special instructions, such as use pen only or use a number 2 pencil?
5. Is there a study sheet?
6. Will there be a review session?
7. What is the grade value of the test?

Asking these simple questions will help you know what type of test will be administered, how you should prepare for it, and what supplies you will need. You will want to begin predicting questions early. Listen to the instructor intently. Instructors use cue phrases, such as, "You will see this again," and "If I were to ask you this question on the test." Pay close attention to what is written on the board, what questions are asked in class, and what areas the instructor seems to be concentrating on more than others. You will begin to get a feel for what types of questions the instructor might ask on the test.

It may also be beneficial for you to keep a running page of test questions that you have predicted. As you read through a chapter, ask yourself many questions at the end of each section. When it is time to study for the test, you may have already predicted many of the questions your instructor will ask.

Save all quizzes and exams that you are allowed to keep. These are a wonderful resource for studying for the next exam or for predicting questions for the course final.

Most test anxiety can be reduced by studying, predicting questions, reviewing, and relaxing.

Helpful Reminders for Reducing Test Anxiety

- Approach the test with an "I can" attitude.
- Prepare yourself emotionally for the test, control your self-talk, and be positive.
- Remind yourself that you studied and that you know the material.
- Overlearn the material—you can't study too much.
- Chew gum or eat hard candy during the test if allowed; it may help you relax.
- Go to bed early. Do not pull an all-nighter before the test.
- Eat a healthy meal before the test.
- Arrive early for the test (at least 15 minutes early).
- Sit back, relax, breathe, and clear your mind if you become nervous.
- Come to the test with everything you need: pencils, calculator, and other supplies.
- Read over the entire test first; read all the directions; highlight the directions.
- Listen to the instructor before the test begins.
- Keep an eye on the clock.
- what you know first, the questions that are easiest for you.
- Check your answers, but remember, your first response is usually correct.
- Find out about the test before it is given; ask the instructor what types of questions will be on the test.
- Find out exactly what the test will cover ahead of time.
- Ask the instructor for a study sheet; you may not get one, but it does not hurt to ask!
- Know the rules of the test and of the instructor.
- Attend the review session if one is offered.
- Know what grade value the test holds.
- Ask about extra credit or bonus questions on the test.
- When you get the test, jot down any mnemonic you might have developed on the back or at the top of a page.
- Never look at another student's test or let anyone see your test.

Three Types of Responses to Test Questions

Almost every test question will elicit one of three types of responses from you as the test taker:

- Quick-time response
- Lag-time response
- No response

Your response is a *quick-time response* when you read a question and know the answer immediately. You may need to read only one key word in the test question to know the correct response. Even if you have a quick-time response, however, always read the entire question before answering. The question may be worded in such a way that the correct response is not what you originally expected. By reading the entire question before answering, you can avoid losing points to careless error.

You have a *lag-time response* when you read a question and the answer does not come to you immediately. You may have to read the question several times or even move on to another question before you think of the correct response. Information in another question will sometimes trigger the response you need. Don't get nervous if you have a lag-time response. Once you've begun to answer other questions, you usually begin to remember more, and the response may come to you. You do not have to answer questions in order on most tests.

No response is the least desirable situation when you are taking a test. You may read a question two or three times and still have no response. At this point, you should move on to another question to try to find some related information. When this happens, you have some options:

1. Leave this question until the very end of the test.
2. Make an intelligent guess.
3. Try to eliminate all unreasonable answers.
4. Watch for modifiers within the question.
5. See if one question answers another.
6. Look for hints throughout the test.
7. Don't panic . . . simply move on.

Test-Taking Strategies and Hints for Success

The most common types of questions are:

- Matching
- True–false
- Multiple-choice
- Short answer
- Essay

Before you read about the strategies for answering these different types of questions, think about this: There is no substitute for studying! You can know all the tips, but if you have not studied, they will be of little help to you.

Strategies for Matching Questions

Matching questions frequently involve knowledge of people, dates, places, or vocabulary. When answering matching questions, you should:

- Read the directions carefully.
- Read each column before you answer.
- Determine whether there is an equal number of items in each column.
- Match what you know first.
- Cross off information that is already used.
- Use the process of elimination for answers you might not know.
- Look for logical clues.
- Use the longer statement as a question; use the shorter statement as an answer.
- Answer all the questions.

What's Sleep Got to Do with It?

You've heard the old saying, "You are what you eat." This may be true, but many sleep experts would say, "You are how you sleep." Sleep deprivation is one of the leading causes of poor productivity and academic performance, workplace and auto accidents, lack of concentration, diminished immune systems, decreased metabolism, cardiovascular problems, and even poor communication efforts.

The National Traffic Safety Administration estimates that 100,000 crashes each year are the result of sleepy drivers. These crashes cause nearly 1,600 deaths, 71,000 injuries, and $12.5 billion in property loss and diminished activity (Hidden Menace, 2003).

Mark Rosekind, Ph. D., an expert on fatigue and performance issues and a member of the board of directors for the National Sleep Foundation, states, "Without sufficient sleep it is more difficult to concentrate, make careful decisions, and follow instructions; we are more likely to make mistakes or errors, and are more prone to being impatient and lethargic. Our attention, memory, and reaction time are all affected" (Cardinal, 2003).

According to the National Sleep Foundation, the following symptoms can signal inadequate sleep:

- Dozing off while engaged in an activity such as reading, watching TV, sitting in meetings, or sitting in traffic.
- Slowed thinking and reacting.
- Difficulty listening to what is said or understanding directions.
- Difficulty remembering or retaining information.
- Frequent errors or mistakes.
- Narrowing of attention, missing important changes in a situation.
- Depression or negative mood.
- Impatience or being quick to anger.
- Frequent blinking, difficulty focusing eyes, or heavy eyelids.

Indeed, lack of sleep can decrease your ability to study, recall information, and perform well on tests and assignments. This can be especially true during midterm and final exam periods. Those late or all-night cram sessions can actually be more detrimental to your academic success than helpful. By including your study sessions in your time-management plan, you can avoid having to spend your sleep time studying.

Different people need different amounts of sleep within a 24-hour period. Some people absolutely need 8–10 hours of sleep, while others can function well on 4–6 hours. If you are not sleeping enough to rest and revive your body, you will experience sleep deprivation.

Researchers suggest that missing as little as 2 hours of sleep for one night can take as long as 6 days to recover—if it is recovered at all (Moss, 1990). It is generally estimated that 8–9 hours of good, solid, restful sleep per night can decrease your chances of sleep deprivation.

Below, you will find some helpful hints for getting a good night's rest:

- Avoid alcohol and caffeine (yes, alcohol is a depressant, but it interrupts both REM and slow-wave sleep, and caffeine can stay in your system for as long as 12 hours).
- Exercise during the day (but not within four hours of your sleep time).
- Regulate the temperature in your bedroom to a comfortable setting for you.
- Wind down before trying to sleep. Complete all tasks at least one hour prior to your bedtime. This gives you time to relax and prepare for rest.
- Avoid taking naps during the day.
- Have a set bedtime and try to stick to it.
- Take a warm bath before bedtime.
- Go to bed only when you are tired. If you are not asleep within 15–30 minutes, get up and do something restful like reading or listening to soft music.
- Use relaxation techniques such as visualization and mind travel.
- Avoid taking sleeping aids. This can cause more long-term problems than sleep deprivation.

Sample Test #1: Matching

Directions: Match the information in column A with the correct information in column B. Use uppercase letters.

LISTENING SKILLS

A

___ They can be long or short, social, academic, religious, or financial

___ A step in the change process

___ Studying cooperatively

___ Your "true self"

___ Listening with an open mind

B

A. Child within

B. Objectivity

C. Letting go

D. Group or teamwork

E. Goals

> You are fast becoming that you are going to be.
>
> —Anonymous

Strategies for True-False Questions

True–false tests ask if a statement is true or not. True–false questions can be some of the most challenging questions you will encounter on tests. Some students like them; some hate them. There is a 50/50 chance of answering correctly, but you can use the following strategies to increase your odds on true–false tests:

- Read each statement carefully.
- Watch for key words in each statement, for example, negatives.
- Read each statement for double negatives, such as "not untruthful."

Sample Test #2: True–False

Directions: Place "T" for true or "F" for false beside each statement.

NOTE-TAKING SKILLS

1. _____ Note taking creates a history of your course content.

2. _____ "Most importantly" is not a key phrase.

3. _____ You should always write down everything the instructor says.

4. _____ You should never ask questions in class.

5. _____ The L-STAR system is a way of studying.

6. _____ W/O is not a piece of shorthand.

7. _____ You should use 4-by-6-inch paper to take classroom notes.

8. _____ The outline technique is best used with lecture notes.

9. _____ The Cornell method should never be used with textbook notes.

10. _____ The mapping system is done with a series of circles.

- Pay attention to words that may indicate that a statement is true, such as "some," "few," "many," and "often."

- Pay attention to words that may indicate that a statement is false, such as "never," "all," "every," and "only."

- Remember that if any part of a statement is false, the entire statement is false.

- Answer every question unless there is a penalty for guessing.

Strategies for Multiple-Choice Questions

Many instructors give multiple-choice tests because they are easy to grade and provide quick, precise responses. A multiple-choice question asks you to choose from among usually two to five answers to complete a sentence. Some strategies for increasing your success in answering multiple-choice questions are the following:

- Read the question and try to answer it before you read the answers provided.

- Look for similar answers; one of them is usually the correct response.

- Recognize that answers containing extreme modifiers, such as *always, every,* and *never,* are usually wrong.

- Cross off answers that you know are incorrect.

- Read all the options before selecting your answer. Even if you believe that A is the correct response, read them all.

Sample Test #3: Multiple Choice

Directions: Read each statement and select the best response from the answers given below.

STUDY SKILLS

1. When reading your text, you should have

    A. an open mind.

    B. a dictionary.

    C. a highlighter.

    D. all of the above.

2. There are three types of memory; they are:

    A. short-term, sensory, computer.

    B. computer, long-term, perfect.

    C. perfect, short-term, long-term.

    D. sensory, short-term, long-term.

3. To be an effective priority manager, you have to:

    A. be very structured and organized.

    B. be very unstructured and disorganized.

    C. be mildly structured and organized.

    D. be sometimes a little of both.

    E. know what type of person you are and work from that point.

- Recognize that when the answers are all numbers, the highest and lowest numbers are usually incorrect.

- Recognize that a joke is usually wrong.

- Understand that the most inclusive answer is often correct.

- Understand that the longest answer is often correct.

- If you cannot answer a question, move on to the next one and continue through the test; another question may trigger the answer you missed.

- Make an educated guess if you must.

- Answer every question unless there is a penalty for guessing.

Strategies for Short-Answer Questions

Short-answer questions, also called fill-in-the-blanks, ask you to supply the answer yourself, not to select it from a list. Although "short answer" sounds easy, these questions are often very difficult. Short-answer questions require you to draw from your long-term memory. The following hints can help you answer this type of question successfully:

- Read each question and be sure that you know what is being asked.

- Be brief in your response.

- Give the same number of answers as there are blanks; for example, _____ and _____ would require two answers.

- Never assume that the length of the blank has anything to do with the length of the answer.

- Remember that your initial response is usually correct.

- Pay close attention to the word immediately preceding the blank; if the word is "an," give a response that begins with a vowel (a, e, i, o, u).

- Look for key words in the sentence that may trigger a response.

- Answer all the questions.

Sample Test #4: Short Answer

Directions: Fill in the blanks with the correct response. Write clearly.

LISTENING SKILLS

1. Listening is a _____ act. We choose to do it.

2. The listening process involves receiving, organizing, _____, and reacting.

3. _____ is the same as listening with an open mind.

4. Prejudging is an _____ to listening.

5. Leaning forward, giving eye contact, being patient, and leaving your emotions at home are characteristics of _____ listeners.

Strategies for Essay Questions

Most students look at essay questions with dismay because they take more time. Yet essay tests can be among the easiest tests to take because they give you a chance to show what you really know. An essay question requires you to supply the information. If you have studied, you will find that once you begin to answer an essay question, your answer will flow easily. Some tips for answering essay questions are the following:

- More is not always better; sometimes more is just more. Try to be as concise and informative as possible. An instructor would rather see one page of excellent material than five pages of fluff.

Sample Test #5: Essay

Directions: Answer each question completely. Use a separate paper if you wish.

STUDY SKILLS

1. Identify and discuss two examples of mnemonics.

_____

_____

_____

2. Discuss why it is important to use the SQ3R method.

_____

_____

_____

3. Justify your chosen notebook and study system.

_____

_____

_____

4. Compare an effective study environment with an ineffective study environment.

_____

_____

_____

_____

- Pay close attention to the action word used in the question and respond with the appropriate type of answer. Key words used in questions include the following:

discuss	illustrate	enumerate	describe
compare	define	relate	list
contrast	summarize	analyze	explain
trace	evaluate	critique	interpret
diagram	argue	justify	prove

- Write a thesis statement for each answer.
- Outline your thoughts before you begin to write.
- Watch your spelling, grammar, and punctuation.
- Use details, such as times, dates, places, and proper names, where appropriate.
- Be sure to answer all parts of the question; some discussion questions have more than one part.
- Summarize your main ideas toward the end of your answer.
- Write neatly.
- Proofread your answer.

Learning how to take a test and learning how to reduce your anxiety are two of the most important gifts you can give yourself as a student. Although tips and hints may help you, don't forget that there is no substitute for studying and knowing the material.

chapter 4 | Critical Thinking and Citing Sources

Contents

What's in It for Me?
Thinking about Thinking

Thinking is defined, according the American Heritage Dictionary, as "to reason about or reflect on; to ponder." Although critical thinking involves thinking more analytically and reflectively about an issue or problem, knowing facts and figures is also essential for clear thinking.

Benjamin Bloom created a taxonomy, or classification, for categorizing levels of thinking. At the first level, we observe and recall information. At the next level of thinking, we move into understanding meaning. The third level involves applying the information in some way. At the fourth level of thinking, we recognize patterns and can analyze information, and the fifth and sixth levels involve combining old ideas to create new ideas and recommending action. The lower levels of thinking are the foundation of critical thinking, which takes place at the higher levels in this categorization. Reflective thought must be grounded in factual knowledge. Critical thinking entails seeking to understand different aspects of an issue, and in deciding what to believe, looking not only at truths and untruths, but also at stories that display bias or are incomplete.

Almost any profession you choose to go into will require the ability to think through problems, make decisions, and apply other critical-thinking skills.

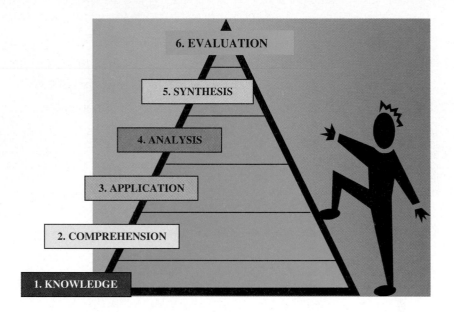

Steps in Critical Thinking

To think critically using the higher levels, we might:

- Evaluate sources of information
- Explore different points of view
- Question opinions and assumptions
- Evaluate the context
- Look for false logic and bias

Step One: Evaluate Sources of Information

Considering the source of the information is crucial to weighing the potential bias of its content. Information can be embedded in a context that manipulates the conclusion in order to serve the interests of a particular group. The higher your level of interest in an issue, the more effort you might want to expend in assessing the source.

Level of Competence	Skills Demonstrated
1. Knowledge	Observation and recall of information Knowledge of dates, events Able to: list, define, tell, describe, identify, show, label, collect, examine, quote, name
2. Comprehension	Grasp meaning Translate knowledge into new context Interpret facts Predict consequences Able to: summarize, describe, interpret, contrast, predict, associate, distinguish, estimate, differentiate
3. Application	Use information Use methods, concepts, theories Solve problems Able to: apply, demonstrate, calculate, solve, complete, relate, discover
4. Analysis	See patterns Organize parts Recognize hidden meanings Able to: analyze, separate, order, explain, connect, classify, arrange, divide, compare, infer
5. Synthesis	Use old ideas to create new ones Relate knowledge from several areas Predict Draw conclusions Able to: combine, integrate, modify, rearrange, substitute, plan, create, design, invent, compose, formulate
6. Evaluation	Compare and discriminate between ideas Assess value of theories, presentations Make choices based on reasoned argument Verify value of evidence Recognize subjectivity Able to: assess, decide, rank, grade, test, measure, recommend, convince, select, judge, discriminate, support, conclude, compare, summarize

Internet   Reference materials need to be analyzed with a critical eye. The Internet is a reference that especially warrants the use of critical thinking. Information today is readily available. By using search engines on the Internet, we can retrieve vast amounts of information on many subjects quickly and easily. However, determining the accuracy and reliability of the information is another matter. It may take less time to find information, but we must spend more time verifying the information.

Traditional newspapers rely on editors to determine the accuracy and overall quality of their articles. Many journals also rely on the peer-review process. But a great deal of online information does not go through these traditional filters.

When critically evaluating Web sites and their information, consider scrutinizing:

Accuracy

- Has the page been rated or evaluated in some manner? If so, who did the evaluation?
- Is the author's point of view clear and sound?
- Is there a bias—political, ideological, or cultural? Does the author hope to persuade you in some way?
- When was the site produced and last updated?

Authority

- Are the qualifications of the site's author or producer indicated on the page?
- Who sponsors the site? Is it a commercial or educational site, or does it appear to be created by an individual?

Completeness

- How well and thoroughly is the subject covered?
- Are the links appropriate, relevant, and comprehensive?

Content

- How many items are included on the page?
- Is a copyright notice indicated on the page?
- Does the site include a bibliography?
- Is the level of detail appropriate for the subject?

Propaganda

- Does the author present accurate descriptions of alternative views?
- Does the author attack other perspectives?
- Is the writing overly emotional?

Step Two: Maintain Objectivity

Emotions are an inescapable part of our human experience. Our feelings of happiness, excitement, surprise, anger, fear, sadness, and frustration give us the ability to relate to others' experiences. Emotions may compel us to feel compassion and reach out in times of need *or* to turn away, ignore, and stop listening to others. We may find that our own emotions, although very important in motivating us to act, can negatively affect our ability to think critically if they are so strongly felt that we lose objectivity. If we have an extreme reaction to an issue or topic, we can take that as a clue that our ability to think objectively may be compromised. In this case, it is helpful to identify our emotions and the personal issues that may be triggering them. Ultimately, knowing our *own* emotions helps us understand issues from *different* perspectives.

> Nothing in this world is bad or good but thinking makes it so.
> —William Shakespeare

Step Three: Separate Facts and Opinions

A factual statement offers proof from a source that can be verified. Assumptions, or opinions, are more often based on emotion and myth.

If a statement is based on facts, it will likely pass one or more of the following three tests:

1. Can it be observed?
2. Has it been established over the years?
3. Can it be tested?

If a statement is an opinion, it will probably meet one or more of the following criteria:

1. Others may not agree with it.
2. Superlatives like "best," "tremendous," and "outstanding" are used.
3. Opinion keywords such as "think," "believe," "assume," "imagine," "feel," "surmise," "may," or "suppose" are used.
4. It implies that the statement is true for everyone through words like "all," "none," "every," "no," "only," "nobody," "everybody," "always," and "never."

Step Four: Evaluate the Context

Candid discussions, and sometimes brutal honesty, are useful and necessary when you are addressing complex or difficult issues. However, be careful not to let emotions take over your objectivity.

When people are trying to mislead or influence others toward their point of view, they may exaggerate a story or take it out of context. Question the stories you hear. Are they representative of the problem or are they exceptions? Finding out as much information about the topic as possible will help you put the issue into a proper context.

Step Five: Recognize False Logic and Bias

By learning to recognize faulty arguments and deceptive logic, you can improve your ability to think critically about issues. The following are some common faulty persuasion techniques:

Glittering Generalities say little specifically but convey emotion. "Jim has made this country a better place."

Hasty Generalizations are conclusions based on insufficient evidence. "Windows has some serious problems—I saw an article about that."

False Dilemma poses only two choices when there are a variety of possibilities and perspectives to consider. "Get an "A" in that course and you'll be set; anything less and you won't get a good job."

Card Stacking involves presenting evidence in a partial or skewed way to promote the interests of a particular group. Saying that "the average income is rising" may be accurate when only the income level of the top ten percent of the population is considered.

Bandwagon is an approach that encourages people to do something because it is the popular thing to do. "Everybody is doing it!"(This is what your mother was referring to when she said, "If everyone jumped off a bridge would you, too?!")

Appeals to Emotion summons anger, pity or fear, including alienation, disapproval and violence, to entice support. A scare tactic is one use of an appeal to emotion. "If you don't use that minty mouthwash, you'll have bad breath and no one will like you."

Ad verecundiam is used when people invoke quotes and phrases from popular or famous people, or from those in an authoritative position, in order to support their views.

False Cause and Effect is used to insist that an event is caused by another event just because it took place afterwards.

Straw arguments are used when people attack their opponent's argument in the hopes that this will make their own arguments stronger (as opposed to focusing on the strengths of their own argument.)

Ad hominem is a persuasive technique that involves attacking the person and not the ideas. This is also called slander or name-calling.

Appeals to Tradition look at the past and suggest because things have always been done one way, they should continue to be done that way.

Step Six: Use Your Values

What you know to be true can help to guide you no matter how persuasive an argument is to the contrary. In analyzing arguments, we use more than just our intellect. Critical thinking involves tapping into our intuition and values, as well. It is important to access your core values when a good argument attempts to sway you or when you may feel intimidated without the facts and figures in front of you.

Yes You Can!
IDEAS FOR SUCCESS

Put into action the following tips for critical thinking:

- Don't let your emotions cloud the truth about a situation or problem.
- Keep an open mind about people and don't stereotype them.
- Remember that negative attitudes about people, places, and situations can get in the way of critical thinking.
- If you have difficulty thinking through a situation, use the analysis technique with an A and B column.
- Be certain to listen to all sides of the argument before making up your mind.
- Try to stay away from the "I'm right, you're wrong" mentality.
- When faced with a new situation, try to look at it differently, as you did with the penny exercise.
- Don't just accept information as real or factual. Do your homework.

and ITT Tech Can Help!

Your Role	Situation	Noncritical Thinking Response	Critical Thinker's Response
Student	Instructor is lecturing on the rising use of a particular operating system in companies.	You assume that everything your instructor tells you is true and you concentrate solely on learning the new operating system.	You consider what the instructor says; write down questions; initiate discussion with the professor, other classmates, and the IT departments where you would like to work; and you read professional journals.
Student	You read that companies are having a hard time finding technical employees.	You assume that you won't have to do any work to find a job and will be able to set your terms of employment.	You prepare yourself for what companies need; ask questions about whether this situation will always be the case; read several journals and pay particular attention to what seems standard in the industry.
Citizen	You encounter a homeless person.	You avoid the person and the issue.	You examine whether the community has a responsibility to the homeless, and if you find that it does, you explore how to fulfill that responsibility.
Consumer	You want to buy a car.	You decide on a brand-new car without thinking about how you will handle the payments.	You consider the different effects of buying a new car vs. buying a used car; you examine your money situation to see what kind of payment you can handle each month.
Employee	You hear rumors of an impending lay-off.	You become depressed and stop doing your best work.	You ask people in the industry what companies need; you determine what skills you may need; you read publications about growth sectors; you consider all options recognizing that you have the ability to adjust to change.

You may find that you silence yourself or change your opinions, sometimes, in the face of arguments over issues because you're not prepared. Trust your values to guide you in these instances, and research the needed information.

Critical thinking can be used in all areas of your life. Consider the following roles you might play and how you can more critically think about issues. The table (opposite) compares how a noncritical thinker and a critical thinker might respond to particular situations.

Creative Thinking

The best problem solvers are also creative. Creativity is the ability to create anything new, whether it is a solution, a tangible product, a work of art, an idea, a system, a program, or a format—anything at all. Everyone is creative in some way. Some people assume that the word *creative* refers primarily to visual and performing artists, writers, designers, musicians, and other who work in fields whose creative bents are obvious. However, creativity is inside everyone and exists in every field.

Creativity means thinking in fresh new ways. It requires that you loosen up your brain and be more flexible in your approaches and tactics. To begin the creative process, consider the following chart. These are some of the characteristics that creative thinkers have in common. Everyone has the capacity to be creative, though this skill takes courage.

Plan to Be Creative

Creativity is likely the most exciting trait you can develop. It can also be the most frustrating because it can be difficult to nurture. Learn to use your imagination and not be constrained by what others think. The following techniques can help you improve your creative thinking ability:

1. **Learn to brainstorm.** Some schools reinforce rigid thinking. We take multiple-choice tests, which reinforce the idea that there are only right and wrong answers. However, in life, there can be dozens of ways to solve a problem or answer a question. Brainstorming, the art of considering numerous possibilities from the silly to the practical, allows people to explore a problem or an issue from many different angles. Get in the habit of making brainstorming lists when you are trying to solve a problem. Brainstorming will give you practice at keeping your mind open to new possibilities.

2. **Think through ideas with others.** Once you've become comfortable with the process of brainstorming, learn to discuss your ideas with other people. Encourage them to open their minds, to develop their own ideas, and to help you critique and develop yours. This is an enjoyable part of teamwork and it yields the best ideas.

3. **Look for the possibilities.** See situations in terms of what they can become, not what they are at first glance. In order to go in new and different directions, you have to visualize how things could be. Don't be afraid to come up with fresh ideas.

4. **Make connections.** Creative people are good at seeing patterns in seemingly unrelated things. They perceive both similarities and differences and frequently come up with ingenious ways of capitalizing on a trend, a set of circumstances, or existing need. This is how inventions come to be.

What Problem? No Problem Here!
Steps in Problem Solving

Managing the myriad problems that arise throughout your lifetime takes skill and careful consideration. Every day you are called to make numerous decisions, for school (how to juggle your schedule to accommodate all your coursework), work (how to deal with a difficult colleague or boss), or your personal life (how to increase your income or deal with a medical problem). Being a skilled and thoughtful problem solver can help you succeed at whatever you do.

Solving problems is not always easy. Some people try to solve their problems by making a snap decision and not thinking things through. They may also do what someone else tells them without making their own judgment about what is best. They may even try to avoid the problem altogether by doing nothing and waiting for the problem to sort itself out. While these are common approaches to problem solving, they rarely lead to good results.

> The significant problems we face cannot be solved at the same level of thinking we were at when we created them.
>
> —Albert Einstein

In order to be a good problem solver, you must first be a critical thinker. We have already looked at how to become a critical thinker. Now let's apply that knowledge to the problem-solving process. To solve a problem using critical thinking, you might engage in the following activities of critical thinking:

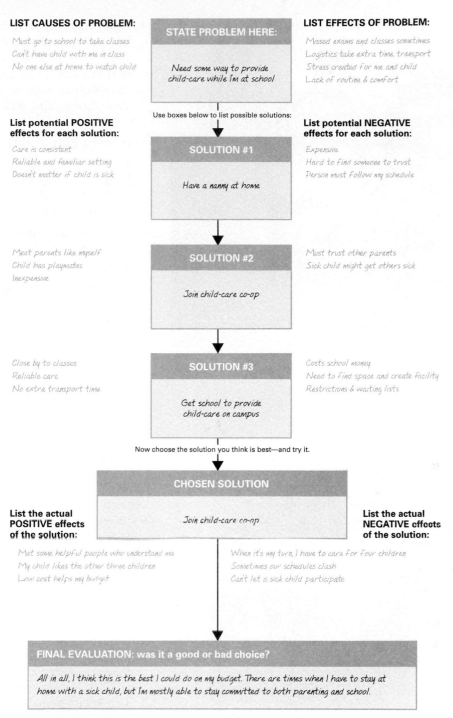

LIST CAUSES OF PROBLEM:

Must go to school to take classes
Can't have child with me in class
No one else at home to watch child

STATE PROBLEM HERE:

Need some way to provide child-care while I'm at school

LIST EFFECTS OF PROBLEM:

Missed exams and classes sometimes
Logistics take extra time, transport
Stress created for me and child
Lack of routine & comfort

Use boxes below to list possible solutions:

List potential POSITIVE effects for each solution:

Care is consistent
Reliable and familiar setting
Doesn't matter if child is sick

SOLUTION #1

Have a nanny at home

List potential NEGATIVE effects for each solution:

Expensive
Hard to find someone to trust
Person must follow my schedule

Meet parents like myself
Child has playmates
Inexpensive

SOLUTION #2

Join child-care co-op

Must trust other parents
Sick child might get others sick

Close by to classes
Reliable care
No extra transport time

SOLUTION #3

Get school to provide child-care on campus

Costs school money
Need to find space and create facility
Restrictions & waiting lists

Now choose the solution you think is best—and try it.

CHOSEN SOLUTION

Join child-care co-op

List the actual POSITIVE effects of the solution:

Met some helpful people who understand me
My child likes the other three children
Low cost helps my budget

List the actual NEGATIVE effects of the solution:

When it's my turn, I have to care for four children
Sometimes our schedules clash
Can't let a sick child participate

FINAL EVALUATION: was it a good or bad choice?

All in all, I think this is the best I could do on my budget. There are times when I have to stay at home with a sick child, but I'm mostly able to stay committed to both parenting and school.

Courtesy of Frank T. Lyman, Jr., and George Eley

Figure 4.1 Sample Problem and Solution

1. **State the problem clearly.** What are the facts of the situation? Name the problem specifically without focusing on causes or effects.

2. **Analyze the problem.** What is happening that needs to change? What are the causes and effects of the problem?

3. **Brainstorm possible solutions.** Brainstorming will help you think of similar problems and how you solved them. When brainstorming, generate possible solutions spontaneously and rapidly without immediately analyzing whether those solutions will work. During brainstorming, no idea is a bad idea! The more ideas, the better.

When solving a problem, it is helpful to look at all possible alternatives and decide on the best one. Sometimes there is one right answer, but often you'll have to settle for the best answer.

4. **Determine the criteria for your solution.** How are you going to determine which solution to choose? Are there any constraints, such as time or money, that must be overcome? Establishing criteria that the solution must meet will help you narrow down your choices and pick the best solution for the given situation.

5. **Explore each solution.** Determine how and why each possible solution would or would not work. Evaluate the negative and positive effects of each solution by applying the standards (criteria) that you previously established.

6. **Choose and execute the solution you decide is best.** Decide how you will put your solution to work.

7. **Evaluate the solution.** Look at how well your solution worked. What are the positive and negative effects of what you did? Was it a useful solution?

8. **Continue to refine the solution.** Problem solving is a process, and you may need to refine your solution to solve any remaining problems that arise.

Obstacles to Problem Solving

Problem solving isn't always easy. There are many obstacles that can hinder the process of finding good solutions. Here are some common stumbling blocks to solving problems. Watch for these pitfalls as you work to solve the problems that come your way.

1. **The perfect solution.** Believing that every problem has one perfect solution can intimidate you. If you can come up with fifty ideas, but none seems exactly right, you may want to give up. Try to refrain from looking for the perfect solution. Instead, look for the best solution, using whatever time frame you have.

2. **The smart-people complex.** If you run into a snag while trying to solve a problem, you might get yourself off the hook by deciding that only a much smarter person could solve the problem. This excuse leads to both an unsolved problem and a negative assessment of your abilities. Think positively. Believe that any person, thinking critically and carefully, can solve this problem.

3. **The first choice is the best.** If you come up with a good idea right away, it is tempting to go with it. Be sure to give each of your ideas equal time, even if the first one is good. Evaluate each so you can be sure you have covered every angle. The more solutions you generate, the better chance you have of finding the absolute best one.

4. **Focusing on the "easier" cause.** If you are not doing very well in a course, you may want to believe it is because your instructor is incompetent. It is easier to blame someone—anyone—else for the cause of a problem. However, look for the true causes. In this case, it might be because you're not studying effectively or enough. Blaming the instructor won't solve your difficulties if the true cause lies elsewhere. It also may add to the problems you are already experiencing.1

Making important decisions about what you will do to solve a problem can take time. Think through your decisions thoroughly, considering your own ideas as well as those of others you trust, but don't hesitate to act once you have your plan. You cannot benefit from your decision until you act upon it and follow through.

Citation and Plagiarism

When you get excited about writing something, it can be easy to overlook the obvious: you must give credit to the resources where you found your material. If you don't, that's called *plagiarism* and it is a very serious academic offense, sometimes resulting in expulsion from school.

It's increasingly easy to forget to cite sources with advancing technology, and with so much information and the easy cut-and-paste feature of most word processing programs.

Picture this scenario: You are reading from a Web site and you see a great quote that you'd like to use. You quickly cut and paste it into your notes. Then . . . the tea kettle starts whistling, the dog starts barking . . . you get up to get your tea . . . Once you return to your computer, you have forgotten that you needed to copy the name of the author, too. This scenario is innocent enough, but the risk of plagiarism is high. If you use the quote without including a citation, that's plagiarism.

Using some old-fashioned practices of annotating your sources or keeping note cards is a way to make sure you keep your sources straight.

The Index Card Method

Index cards can be used for detailed information that comes from specific sources. The information noted on these cards is readily accessible, easily organized, and can be used when preparing presentations and reports. Keeping a stack by your computer is handy. Simply write down quotes and the authors' names along with the source, publication dates, and any other pertinent information. Later, you can use the cards to compile your source list.

Number of Source or Author's Last Name and Date	Rating System for Value of Information	Key Word for Subtopic or Question
Most important facts:		
Paraphrased specific information:		
Summary:		
Direct quote:		
Primary source of info:		

You may not like this particular method of keeping track of sources; but however you do it, you must not forget to cite a source and commit plagiarism. You can also use a Notes program, either in Microsoft Outlook or Notepad, to keep track of citations.

If something is "common knowledge," you don't have to cite it. If the information is indisputable, such as the signing date of the Declaration of Independence, which has been recorded in many, many places, it is common knowledge.

Paraphrasing

You can also *paraphrase* a source and not cite it. Paraphrasing means you express content from a source in your own words. Alternating between direct quotes and paraphrasing is an effective writing tool to lend some variety to your writing. But, be careful to paraphrase accurately. Altering the spirit of a quote or its context is a misuse of the source.

To paraphrase, try the following steps:

- Skim the material to get the overall meaning.
- Read the material thoroughly.
- List the main ideas.
- Review the selection.
- Write your paraphrase restating the author's ideas in your own words. Stick to the basics. Don't insert your own ideas or opinions.
- Put quotations around important words taken directly from the source.
- Check your paraphrase for accuracy—could someone understand the author's meaning just from reading your paraphrase?

chapter 5 | Time Management and Teamwork

Contents

What's in It for Me?
Putting Time on Your Side

Have you ever tried to define time? This is an interesting exercise. If you stop now and try to define exactly what time is, you will probably find it difficult. Time is elusive and flexible and also restrictive and binding. Time is an unusual and puzzling resource. You can't save it in a box until you need it. You don't feel it passing by like wind in your face. It has no color. If you are in a hurry or if you are pressured to reach a deadline, time seems to fly. If you are bored or have nothing to do, it seems to creep at a very slow pace. You can't get your arms around it; yet, you know it exists. Though time is an invisible commodity, it is one of our most important resources. We all know how much trouble we can bring down on our heads when we use it poorly or waste it. The truth is, many students' worst problems start with poor use of time. Staying power actually begins with how you manage your time and get control of your life.

Some people seem to be born with the ability to get so much more done than most other people. They appear to always be calm and collected, to have it together, to reach lofty goals. Many people from this group work long hours in addition to going to school. They never appear to be stressed out, and they seem to attend all the social functions.

You are probably aware of others who are always late with assignments, never finish their projects on time, rarely seem to have time to study, and appear to have no concrete goals for their lives. Many people from this second group never make it past their first class of continuing education.

Sometimes, we get the idea that one group of people accomplishes more because they have more time or because they don't have to work or they don't have children or they are smarter or wealthier. While in some cases, this may be true, it doesn't change the fact that we all have the same amount of time each week, and we decide how to spend most of it. Even if you are rich, you can't buy more time than the allotted 10,080 minutes that each of us is given every week. So, while everyone has the same amount of time in their days and nights, the secret is that one group organizes for success, whereas the other never knows what happened to them.

Corporate managers realize the value of time because they pay consultants millions of dollars to teach their employees how to use their time more wisely. *Time is money in the business world;* employees who can produce excellent work by established deadlines are highly valued.

There is no guarantee that someone will finish an educational program just because he has enrolled. Some students lack staying power because they don't know how to manage themselves. Time must be considered one of your most valuable resources while you are in school and after you complete your program. Time management is actually about managing YOU, taking control. The sooner you get control of how you use your time, the quicker you will be on your way to becoming successful in your program and at work. Learning to manage your time is a lesson that you will use throughout your learning endeavors and beyond. It is really about self-management. Time management is paying attention to how you are spending your most valuable resource and then devising a plan to use it more effectively.

You Have All the Time There Is
Taking Control of Time and Yourself

With all the advances in technology that have given us time-saving devices, how is it that many of us feel that we have less time than ever? We may find ourselves engaged in activities that aren't totally satisfying or are in conflict with our values. As a result, we have less time to accomplish the important goals, and many of us feel overextended. Defining values and setting goals are important to managing resources, but we can lose sight of those on a daily basis when deadlines loom, urgent family needs interrupt us, and we are forced to respond to one crisis after the next. At times, there may

...ing power begins with how you manage your time, ...e to build on your best in all areas of your life— ...ol, work, family, and friends.

seem to be too much distraction at the day-to-day, hour-to-hour level to even think about the more important goals.

We can find our lives reduced to blocks of allocated time, week after week. Recognizing that time management is about managing our actions and our energy, David Allen, author of *Getting Things Done: The Art of Stress-Free Productivity*, asserts that, "it's possible for a person to have an overwhelming number of things to do and still function productively with a clear head and a positive sense of relaxed control." The key to achieving high levels of effectiveness and efficiency is to recognize that our ability to be productive is directly proportional to our ability to relax. When our actions are congruent with our values and goals, our minds become clear and we can relax with what we are doing in the moment. In this state of clarity we access the energy to get a lot done.

Have you ever done something that you love and noticed that time seemed to "stand still," or even expand? When you engage fully and consciously in the important activities of your life, you may notice this sense of relaxation, and heightened efficiency and productivity.

Plan to Get the Important Things Done

(Lost time is never found again.
—Benjamin Franklin)

Steps in Time Management Time continues on no matter what we do and is a cultural concept that has no absolute meaning on its own. Westerners, for example, think in terms of twenty-four hours in a day, seven days in a week. Those divisions, however, are arbitrary. The real issue in time management is how to make appropriate choices about what action to take at any point in time. When we are making choices that help us to move toward greater long-term fulfillment, we will naturally use our resources in the best way for us.

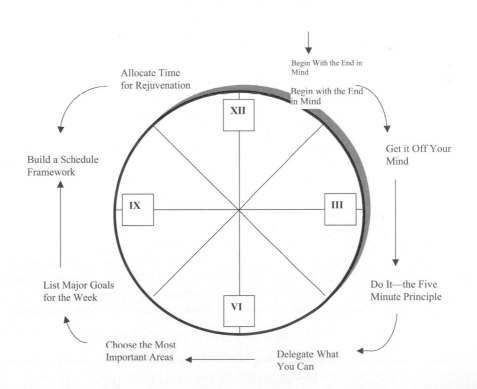

Begin with the End in Mind

Outcome thinking, or thinking to define desired results, is one of the most effective means available for turning goals into reality. After going through the goal-setting process, focusing on those goals can have a dramatically beneficial effect. Management expert Peter Drucker has written, "There is usually no right answer. Rather, there are choices, and results have to be clearly specified if productivity is to be achieved."

Getting It Off Your Mind

Write down what is most on your mind at this moment. What most bothers you, distracts you, interests you, or in some other way consumes a large part of your attention? It may be a project or problem that you are being pressed to handle, or a situation you feel you must deal with soon.

Next describe, in a single written sentence, your intended successful outcome for this problem or situation.

Finally, write down the very next physical action required to move the situation forward. If you had nothing else to do in your life, what visible action would you take?

What did you gain from going through this thinking exercise? You may be feeling a bit more in control, more relaxed, and focused. Nothing has changed in the physical realm, but your feelings about the problems may have changed by writing them down and getting them off your mind.

Get It Done; Get It Off Your Mind

There is usually an inverse proportion between how much something is on your mind and how much is getting done. If you're thinking about doing something too much, chances are that you're probably not doing it. These are open items that pull at your attention and can include everything from "get that promotion" to the more modest "complete assignment" to the smallest task such as "get gas." These open items can take up a lot of attention, adding to the anxious feeling that there is too much to do. Writing down everything you need to do will move it from your mind and make it more likely that you'll get it done.

Follow the "Five-Minute Principle"

Discipline yourself to make decisions immediately about all of the tasks you take on so you will always have a plan for actions that you can implement.

If there's anything you absolutely must do that you can do in five minutes or less, do it now.

Delegate What You Can

If there's anything that absolutely must get done soon, and you have others who are willing to help, delegate. Delegating is entrusting tasks to others. It is hard to give up control sometimes, but if you delegate properly, it can dramatically increase your overall effectiveness. Effective delegation is a three-step process:

a. Decide what you want to give to others

b. Select people with the proper skills

c. Design a plan for review of the work

Choose the Most Important Areas

Vilfredo Pareto, a nineteenth-century Italian economist and sociologist, developed a principle that has been used frequently since termed. Pareto's 80/20 Principle implies that about 20% of what we do in any given area delivers 80% of the results. Going after the "right" 20% will get you 80% of the results. This is how *to work smarter and not harder.*

	MAJOR GOALS FOR WEEK
LIFE CATEGORY 1:	1.
LIFE CATEGORY 2:	2.
LIFE CATEGORY 3:	3.
LIFE CATEGORY 4:	4.

Build a Schedule Framework

Steps six and seven in a strategic time management process include listing the major goals for the week and building out a schedule framework by day and hour. First, include the top four goals you need to accomplish this week. List those in the template. Don't worry for now about the days of the week or the time blocks. On the left hand side, incorporate the goals you have for the week by life category.

Using the following template, you can now map out what you know you need to do during the week. Include activities such as work hours, classes, study time, and all other scheduled activities.

How does your schedule match your major life goals at this moment? Are there things you can change in your schedule to better meet your main goals? It's important to know how you spend your time, but some people don't have a clue how they spend their time. That puts them at a serious disadvantage in meeting their important goals. Another pitfall in time management for students is that they sometimes are quite unprepared for the fact that their programs will probably require a lot of time outside of class. Experts advise students to count on spending at least three hours outside of class for every hour spent in class.

TIME	MONDAY	TUESDAY	WEDNESDAY	THURSDAY	FRIDAY	SATURDAY	SUNDAY
6:00AM							
7:00AM							
8:00AM							
9:00AM							
10:00AM							
11:00AM							
12:00AM							
1:00PM							
2:00PM							
3:00PM							
4:00PM							
5:00PM							
6:00PM							
7:00PM							
8:00PM							
9:00PM							
10:00PM							
11:00PM							

Some other people actually do work hard, but their work habits are so poor that they still don't produce very much. Others try to work while they are simultaneously entertaining themselves. For example, they watch TV while they read. This doesn't work! Consider first working in a quiet place where you can concentrate. Then, reward yourself with 30 minutes to watch your program or record it to watch when you know that you have a predictable dip in energy.

Allocate Time for Rejuvenation

While committing ourselves to our goals is important, if we spend too much time "on task" and not enough time just "being," we may become drained and lose motivation. We need periods of structure as well as unstructured time for rejuvenation. Build into your schedule a time where you can relax, reflect, and discover who you are.

In the *Dance of Life: the Other Dimensions of Time,* Edward T. Hall contrasts the way people of American-European heritage think about time with time concepts in other cultures. In summarizing the differences between the Hopi Indians, who "live in the eternal present," and American-European people, Hall writes: ". . . one feels that [for the Hopi] time is not a harsh taskmaster nor is it equated with money and progress as it is with [American-European people] . . . who tend to think that because nothing overt is happening, nothing is going on. With many cultures there are long periods during which people are making up their minds or waiting for a consensus to be achieved."

Julie Cameron, in her book *The Artist's Way,* describes a useful tool for tapping into the creativity available in times that we allow ourselves for rejuvenation. She suggests scheduling an *"artist date"* once a week when you spend time by yourself doing something creative, interesting, or fun.

The "P" Word: Procrastination
How to Quit Avoiding the Hard Jobs and Get Your Priorities in Order

Even with the best plan in place, we may find ourselves procrastinating. Everyone does it. Then, we worry and promise we'll never do it again if we can just get through this day. We say things to ourselves like, "If I can just live through this test, I will never wait until the last minute again." But something else comes along and we put off our school work again. Why do we do this? Why do we procrastinate when we all know how unpleasant the results can be? Why aren't we disciplined and organized and controlled so we can reap the rewards that come from being prepared?

People procrastinate for different reasons. Common reasons that students procrastinate include:

- **Superhuman expectations.** You simply overdo and put more on your calendar than Superman or Superwoman could accomplish. Many of these to-do items might not relate to your major goals. Think about the 80/20 rule.

- **Fear of failing.** You have failed a difficult subject in the past, and you are afraid it is going to happen again, so you do the natural thing and avoid unpleasant experiences. Think about how much you have already accomplished getting to this place. You have already succeeded in being here. Know that you are wiser now and that any goal can be accomplished if you approach it one step at a time.

- **Emotional blocks.** It is time to get started and you have no routine and no past regimen to get you started. You are already feeling guilty because you have wasted so much time. You feel tired, depressed, and beaten. You may feel like the job ahead is so big that you cannot get it done. The thing to do in these situations is to make yourself spend ten minutes on the task. You can do ten minutes, and at the end of that time, the job may look more approachable. You might even be able to put a game plan together for attacking the problem. If not, take a break and spend another ten minutes on it later.

- **Fear of being unworthy.** You may be telling yourself that smart people don't have to study, and everybody is smart but you. Recognize that smart people are studying or they have studied in the past and have already mastered the material you are struggling with now. Sooner or later, you must pay the price to gain knowledge. We all have different strengths. Recognize that this education is for you. If you aren't picking up a subject as well as you had hoped, study hardier. Another subject may come much easier for you than for others.

> We have only this moment, sparkling like a star in our hand . . . and melting like a snowflake. Let us use it before it is too late.
>
> —Marie Ray

Plan to Beat Procrastination

Not only is it important that you overcome procrastination for the sake of your education, but it is also equally crucial to your success at work. Procrastination is a bad habit that will haunt you until you make up your mind to overcome it. In other words, don't procrastinate in beating procrastination!

The chart on the following pages offers 25 tips that might help.

25 Ways to Beat Procrastination

- **Face up to the results of procrastination.** What will happen if you procrastinate? How will you feel if you fail the test? How miserable will you be over the weekend if you have to write a last minute paper while your family and friends get to go see a movie?

- **Concentrate on the rewards of managing yourself and your time.** Think about the rewards that you will get when you finish a difficult task. You can go to a movie or relax or spend time with your children. You can get a good grade. Think about how good you will feel when the weekend comes and your paper is finished and you don't have to spend all your time working on a project. Focus on how good you will feel when you did well on a project. While you are working, stop periodically and focus on the rewards.

- **Break up big tasks into small ones.** If you have to write a paper, can you work on one segment tonight and another one tomorrow? If you start early and finish a small segment each day, a big paper is just a series of small tasks.

- **Give yourself a time limit to accomplish a task.** Work will expand to take up as much time as we allow it to. Push yourself to work faster and more efficiently.

- **Set a regular time for study, and do not vary from it.** Determine your personal "best time" and "best place."

- **Start studying with positive, realistic thoughts.** Push negative thoughts out of your mind. Tell yourself that you are growing and becoming more competent. Remember, "You can do this."

- **Establish good study habits.**

- **Set reasonable, concrete goals that you can reach in about 20 to 25 minutes.** Then, set others for the next block of time.

- **Face fear; look it right in the face.** Make up your mind you are going to overcome fear by studying and preparing every day.

(continued)

25 Ways to Beat Procrastination, *continued*

- **Get help from your instructor.** Show the instructor what you have done and ask whether you are on the right track.

- **Avoid whining and people who whine and complain.** You have this job to do, and it is not going away.

- **Allow yourself more time than you think you need to complete an assignment or to study for a test.**

- **Practice your new study habits for 21 days.** By then, you will have gone a long way toward getting rid of your procrastination habits.

- **Actually reward yourself when you have accomplished an important body of work.** Perhaps you spent two hours looking for research articles on the Internet. Now, you deserve a reward. Watch a TV program; visit a friend for a few minutes; talk on the phone; answer your e-mail; read a book to a child. If you have not finished your work, push yourself to go back to work for a few more minutes. When you do this, you are building your discipline and staying power. Ask yourself: "Can I work just 15 more minutes?"

- **Look at this task in terms of your long-range goals.** Where does it fit in your plans of getting what you want? Does passing this test get you admitted to the job you want? Does making a B1 on this test take you one step closer to your career? Does making a good grade on this speech move you toward overcoming your fear of public speaking?

- **Avoid getting involved in too many organizations, accepting too many commitments, or overextending yourself.** Stop and think about how much you really want to do something before you accept. How much time will it take? Does it help you grow and learn? Does it fit with your goals? It's better to say "no" than to accept something that will make you miserable before you finish. "NO!" is a powerful word—use it! Weed out activities that take too much of your time and provide you very little personal reward. You only have so much personal time. Fill that time with activities that give you pleasure and energy.

- **Force yourself to jump in.** Even if your initial work is not satisfactory, you have made a start, and chances are you will get focused as you progress. Sometimes, you just have to plunge in. You can't jump off the high dive in small steps. Just do it!

- **Start on the difficult, most boring tasks first.** Sometimes, it is effective to do these difficult tasks early in the morning before breakfast. This depends on your personal "best time" to work.

- **Practice "do it now."** Do simple tasks as you get them. Practice multitasking. What things can you do at the same time? For example, you can read a chapter while the clothes are washing. You can take your children on a walk and get your own exercise at the same time.

- **Find a quiet place to study and concentrate.** Small children might not understand that Mommy or Daddy needs to study very badly. You may need to make regular visits to the library or to a computer laboratory so you can focus on your work.

- **Gain the support of your family and/or friends.** Talk to the important people in your life and let them know how important your education is to you. Ask them to help and support you.

- **Weed out your personal belongings and living space.** Clean out and organize your closets and drawer space. Give things you no longer wear to charity. Buy fewer things that require waxing, polishing, recharging, cleaning, or storing. Things become monsters that take up your valuable time. Live a simpler life.

- **Prepare to be successful by getting ready the evening before.** Be sure your car has gas; select and press your clothes; put all your materials in order; check to see if the children's necessities and clothes have been organized. Often, the first few minutes of every day determine if you are going to have a good day. Program yourself for success!

- **Take time to smell the roses.** Part of every day should belong to you to do what you want. We all need to find time for regular exercise; we need to spend quality time with people we love and enjoy; we need to pay attention to friends and relationships; we need time to focus on spiritual development. Don't overmanage yourself to the point that you lose sight of what is really important—friends and family and self!

- **Balance your load.** If you are working full-time and paying for all of your expenses, you may need to take a lighter load so you can have a life. If you are a nontraditional student who is working and has small children and a home to take care of, you might need to rethink your schedule. Very few people will ever lament that they didn't do more work. But many will be sorry they didn't spend quality time with their parents, grandparents, or small children when they could have. It is true that you can do it all, but most of us can't do it all at one time. This race is just yours. You are not racing everyone else around you—just yourself.

Tools of Time Management

Having some type of scheduling system or calendar is important when managing activities. "ABC" priority codes and daily "to-do" lists have been key techniques to help sort through choices in some meaningful way. What you may have already discovered, however, is that a calendar, though important, can really effectively help you manage only a small portion of what you need to organize and is inadequate to deal with the volume of things to do and the variable nature of priorities.

E-mail, personal digital assistants (PDAs), scheduling software, and other digital data are becoming increasingly viable means of keeping track of our actions. If you've tried to use any of these processes or tools, however, you may have found them also unable to accommodate the complexity and changing priority factors. The ability to be successful, relaxed, and in control requires that we use these tools only to help us, not limit us. They cannot prioritize for us. They cannot advise us when we need to change our plans due to unforeseen opportunities or responsibilities. They can't remember to add new activities, or develop strategies for specific goals. In other words, they can't think for us. However, they can be extremely useful in organizing much of what we need to accomplish.

Time Bandits
Watch the Number of Commitments

Much of the stress people experience comes from inappropriately managed commitments they make or accept. When we intend to do something, or commit to doing something for others and are not able to follow through, we experience conflict. We run the risk of damaging trust with ourselves and with others. Most of us are almost always juggling commitments in several different areas of our lives. A good way to estimate if you have too many commitments is to write them all down and estimate how many hours you'll be spending on them during a week's time.

Saying "no" is something many of us have a hard time doing. We want to do it all, and we don't want to disappoint others or miss out on opportunities. Check in with what is most important, and be aware of what will be compromised when you agree to something. When you are clear about who you are and what you are creating in your life, "no" becomes "yes," because you are ultimately saying "yes" to what you know will be most satisfying to you in the long term. If priorities grow out of a profound sense of values, according to management expert Stephen Covey, we will enjoy a relaxed approach to dealing with important tasks. "Only when you have the self-awareness to examine your values and create a value-centered purpose, will you have the power to say no with a genuine smile to the unimportant."

Develop Good Habits

Good habits replenish energy. These good habits are the activities that are most meaningful to you and help you accomplish your goals. One way to develop good habits is to establish rituals. Jim Lohr and Tony Schwartz write in their book *The Power of Full Engagement,* "The bigger the storm, the more inclined we are to revert to our survival habits, and the more important positive rituals become."

Avoid Crisis Management

There's a certain frenetic energy around managing a crisis that causes an illusion of importance. With this feverish pace of activity, we release stress hormones such as adrenaline, noradrenaline, and cortisol that may actually be addictive.

Stephen Covey, time-management expert, relates that if we are *overly* externally motivated, we will tend to prioritize the needs of others over our own goals and needs. If you do this, you will find yourself continually dealing with crises and interruptions and not using your time for what is most important. When you live in crisis mode, you attempt to get relief from pressing problems by becoming busy with seemingly urgent but unimportant tasks. However, if you spend your time building relationships, recognizing new opportunities, and planning and preventing crises, you will be more effective at achieving goals.

7:00	get up & shower	7:00		12:15
		7:15		12:30
	X	7:30	Walked to lunch	12:45
	Breakfast	7:45	Ate lunch 1:00	
8:00		8:00		1:15
		8:15		1:30
	Read paper	8:30	Talked w/ Joe	1:45
	Walked to class	8:45	2:00	2:00
9:00	Class	9:00	Went to book	2:15
		9:15	store	2:30
		9:30	Walked	2:45
		9:45	3:00 home	3:00
10:00		10:00	Called Ron	3:15
		10:15		3:30
		10:30		3:45
	Walked to class	10:45	4:00 Watched	4:00
11:00	Class	11:00	TV	4:15
		11:15		4:30
		11:30	Walked to	4:45
		11:45	5:00 library	5:00
12:00		12:00		5:15

Figure 5.1 Evaluating How You Really Spend Your Time

Planning and Organizing for School

Each evening, you should take a few minutes (and literally, that is all it will take) and sit in a quiet place and make a list of all that needs to be done tomorrow.

Successful time management comes from planning the NIGHT BEFORE! Let's say your list includes the following:

Research project	Exercise
Study, test on Friday	Buy birthday card for mom
Read Chapter 13	Wash the car
Meet with study group	Wash clothes
Attend class, 8:00	Buy groceries
Attend class, 10:00	Call Janice about weekend
Help child with school project	

Now, you have created a list of tasks that you will face tomorrow. Next, separate this list into three categories: **MUST** *Do, Would* **LIKE** *to Do,* and **FUN** *Breaks.*

MUST DO	WOULD LIKE TO DO	FUN BREAKS
Read Chapter 13	Research project	Wash the car
Meet with study group	Buy birthday card for Mom	Call Janice
Study, test on Friday	Wash clothes	
Exercise	Buy groceries	
Help child with school project		
Attend class, 8:00		
Attend class, 10:00		

Don't get too excited yet. Your time-management plan is not finished. You have not done the most important part yet. Now, you will need to rank the items in order of their importance. You put a 1 by the most important, a 2 by the next most important, and so forth in each category. It may look something like this:

MUST DO	WOULD LIKE TO DO	FUN BREAKS
1 Read Chapter 13	1 Research project	2 Wash the car
1 Meet with study group	2 Buy birthday card for Mom	1 Call Janice
1 Study, test on Friday	3 Wash clothes	
2 Attend class, 8:00	2 Buy groceries	
2 Attend class, 10:00		
2-Help child with school project		
3 Exercise		

Planning and Organizing for Work

Some supermen and superwomen work full-time and go to school full-time while they juggle families and other responsibilities. If kept up for a long period, you can burn out from the stress that such a pace imposes on your mind and body; and if you have children, they may be adversely affected in the short run by your overfull schedule. If you can work less or experience less stress at work, it can take away some of the pain.

Important Principles for Priority Management at Work

- Organize your materials at work as they are organized at home. If you have a desk in both places, keep your supplies in the same place in both desks. Simplify your life by following similar patterns at work and at home. Make your office or work space inviting, attractive, and stimulating. If you are a visual thinker and need to see different assignments, be considerate of others who may work close to you. Use clear plastic boxes, colored file folders, and colored file boxes to organize your projects.

- Write directions down! Keep a notebook for repetitive tasks. Keep a calendar, and be on time to meetings.
- Learn to do paperwork immediately rather than let it build up. File—don't pile!

- Never let your work responsibilities slide because you are studying on the job. Employers always notice.
- Leave the office for lunch, breaks, and short walks.
- When you are given projects that require working with others, plan carefully to do your work well and on time.
- Keep an address book (electronic or paper) handy with important phone numbers and addresses that you use frequently.
- Perform difficult, unpleasant tasks as soon as you can so you don't have them hanging over your head.
- When you plan your work schedule, allow for unexpected problems that might interfere with the schedule.
- Practice detached concern—care about your work but don't take it home with you.

Planning and Organizing at Home

Some people organize effectively at work and school but allow things to fall apart at home. Your home should be a place where you can study, relax, laugh, invite your friends, and find solitude. The following ideas about home organization will help you maximize your time.

Important Principles for Priority Management at Home

- Organize as effectively at home as you do at work.
- If applicable, divide the chores. Insist on everyone doing his or her share.

  - Plan a rotation schedule for major household chores and stick to it—do laundry on Mondays and Thursdays; clean bathrooms on Saturdays; iron on Wednesdays; and so on.
  - Organize your closet and your dresser drawers. Get rid of clothes you don't wear. Put a sign by your telephone that reads "TIME" to remind yourself not to waste it on the phone. If you can't study at home because of drop-in visitors or other housemates, go to the library.
  - Pay bills twice monthly. Pay them on time so you don't ruin your credit rating.
  - Manage your money wisely so you are not stressed by too many bills and too little money.
  - If you drive to class or work, fill up your tank ahead of time so you won't be late.
  - Keep yourself physically fit with a regular exercise plan and nutritious meals.
  - Get out of the house. Take a walk. Visit a friend.
  - If you have children, teach them to be organized so they don't waste your time searching for their shoes, books, and assignments. Help family members take responsibility!
  - You can't work, go to school, and hold everybody's hand all the time. Give each of your children a drawer in a filing cabinet. Show them how to organize their work. You will be preparing them to be successful.

DID YOU KNOW?

Jeffrey Katzenberg

Walt Disney fired Jeffrey Katzenberg in 1994. He went on to co-create Dream-Works Studio. DreamWorks now produces movies such as *Shrek, Shark Tale, Collateral, Anchorman,* and *Madagascar.*

- If you are a perfectionist and want everything in your home to be perfect, get over it!
- Get rid of the clutter in your home or apartment, basement, and closets.
- Establish a time for study hall in your home. Children do their homework, and you do yours.
- If you have a family, insist that all of you organize clothes in advance for school or work for several days.
- Put a message board in a convenient place for everyone to use.
- If your children are old enough to drive, have them run errands at the post office and grocery store.
- Carpool with other parents in your neighborhood.
- Delegate, delegate, delegate! You are not superwoman or superman. Tell your family you need help. Children can feed pets, make their own beds, fold clothes, vacuum, sweep, and cut the grass if they are old enough.
- Schedule at least one hour alone with each of your children each week. Make this a happy, special time—a fun break!
- Make meals happy, relaxed times when each person's successes are shared and celebrated. Discuss current events.
- Plan special times with your spouse or partner if you have one so that he or she does not get fed up with your going to school.
- Tell your family and friends when you have to study; ask them to respect you by not calling or dropping by at this time.
- Post a family calendar where everyone can see it. Put all special events on it—for example, Janie's recital, Mike's baseball game, Jasmine's company party.
- Put sacred days on this calendar so that your entire family has something to look forward to.

Yes You Can!
IDEAS FOR SUCCESS

Consider the following tips for managing your time and money:

- Push yourself to use your time more wisely. Can you get more done in less time by focusing on what you have learned?
- Use your time-management practices at work and for school.
- Focus on doing hard, unpleasant jobs first, then reward yourself.
- Analyze how you are actually spending your time.
- Practice the strategies you have learned for avoiding procrastination.
- Map out your activities and tasks for a week and a month at a time.

and ITT Tech Can Help!

What's in It for Me?
Becoming a Team Player

What kind of team player are you? Do you support others? Are you competitive? Do you like to work in teams?

In today's world, it is very likely that, no matter what your job, you will work on teams during your career. Teamwork is one of the business strategies of the 21st century.

Organizations are always changing the way they do business on every level. Recently, efficiency and creativity have been emphasized, particularly in how resources and outcomes are linked. Employees are directly impacted by this focus because they are expected to help achieve these shared goals.

Communication skills can prove to be very important to groups' efforts. Several researchers have found that the way team members communicate with each other is critical to the overall effectiveness of the team. The good news is that team and communication skills *can be learned and improved.*

Employers are looking for people who excel as team members.

Understanding the Types of Teams

Understanding how teams function and how you can best interact in a team is very important to your career success. A **team** is a unit of two or more people who interact and coordinate their work to accomplish a specific goal. Although they can be quite large, most teams have fewer than 15 people.

There are many types of teams:

- *Formal teams* are formed by the organization as part of the organizational structure.
- *Special purpose teams* are formed to take on a temporary project, such as solving a problem or developing a new process or system.
- *Self-directed teams* rotate jobs to produce a product or service.
- *Virtual teams* use technology to collaborate on projects.

Regardless of the type of team, effectiveness depends on the quality of team members' interactions. The teams you work on will likely be diverse, including people from different ethnic groups, education levels, and professional fields. The more you understand individual roles and the dynamics of group interaction, the more valuable and effective you can be as a team member.

What's Your Role?
Understanding Team Structure and Roles

Teams come in many shapes and sizes. They may be highly structured, which means that everyone's role on the team is predetermined and clearly defined; or they may be unstructured, which means that roles emerge as the team members begin to interact.

There are numerous roles that individuals can play as part of a team. Formal or assigned roles can include team leader, note taker, or scheduler. Informal roles develop during group interactions and generally fall into two categories: roles that focus on the accomplishment of tasks (the **task specialist role**) and roles that focus on the social and emotional needs of the group or the team's working relationships (the **socioemotional role**). The most effective teams have members who fulfill roles in both of these areas and not exclusively in one or the other.

Team members in the **task specialist** role frequently engage in the following behaviors:

Initiator: proposing solutions and opinions to team members

Information seeker: asking for task-relevant facts

Summarizer: pulling ideas together

Energizer: stimulating a team into action when interest falls

Team members in the **socioemotional role** frequently perform the following functions:

Encourager: praising others; encouraging others' ideas

Harmonizer: reconciles group conflicts; reduces tension

Compromiser: compromises opinions to go along with the group

Task Specialist Role	Socioemotional Role
Focuses on task accomplishment over members' needs	Focuses on people's needs over task accomplishment

You will likely play different roles in different groups. No matter what role you play, your participation as well as that of each other member is valuable and important to the success of the overall team. The potential of the team lies in the combination of talents, knowledge, and insights that each person brings.

Look over the different roles played by the task specialist and the socioemotional team member. Which roles do you tend to play?

Let's Work Together
Team Development Stages

FORMING

Getting to know each other

STORMING

Conflict over goals and positions

NORMING

Team cohesion is established

PERFORMING

Team goals are accomplished

After a team has been created, the team members navigate through a set of stages as they learn to become a productive unit. These stages are normal, and every team must go through them. The stages may last a short time, depending on the team members and task deadline. In the worst case, a team may never move into the performance stage. Understanding this process will help the team members move more quickly through the stages and complete their tasks.

When a team is formed, the team members must get to know each other, establish their roles and norms, divide up the work, and understand their task in order to achieve their goal(s). The following stages generally occur in sequence:

Forming In the forming stage, the members break the ice and test one another for friendship opportunities and task orientation. They determine whether each other's behaviors are acceptable. Uncertainty runs high during this stage as members wonder what the ground rules are, what their duties will be, and whether they will fit in. Social discussions should be encouraged during this stage.

Storming During this stage individual personalities emerge and people become more assertive in clarifying their roles and what is expected of them. There is conflict and disagreement, possibly over the team's tasks and goals or individual positions within the team. People may jockey for the leadership role. This stage is unavoidable, though if a team stays here for long, it may never achieve its goals. Members should propose ideas, disagree with one another, and work through the uncertainties. During this stage the members should concentrate on defining the group's goals. If people allow their egos to intrude too much, the group will be held back. On the other hand, if members do not speak their opinions about the group's mission because they are afraid of confrontation, the group could lose the benefit of stimulating ideas. Pick your battles and know why you are fighting them.

Norming During this stage, conflict is resolved. A consensus develops concerning who is the leader and members' roles. Members develop a sense of cohesion and belonging. This stage typically lasts a short time.

Performing During this stage, members focus on accomplishing the assigned tasks. Problems are solved and most discussion is based around the team goal(s). Members who have mainly played the socioemotional role will now contribute to the task. Everything is focused on getting the job done.

> No member of a crew is praised for the rugged individuality of his rowing.
>
> —Ralph Waldo Emerson

Understanding these stages of team development will help you deal with the inevitable challenges that arise in group situations. By recognizing these stages, you can see that becoming an effective team is a process of working out relationships and is not a given. Work and thought are required from the participants so they understand their roles in relation to each other and learn how to manage interaction.

Talk Among Yourselves
Team Communication

Successful interaction between team members is the key to effective teams. This successful interaction begins with communication. How effectively we communicate with those around us can make a huge difference in our success. Like learning skills, communication skills can be developed and are critical to success as a technology professional.

The word "communication" is derived from the same Latin root, *communis*, as the word "communion," which implies mutual participation. For communication to take place, whereby information is shared, the mutual participation of two or more parties is necessary. Even with active, mutual participation, however, there may at times be a gap in the communication process between what someone intends to communicate and what is actually heard.

To understand this principle, think about the telephone game in which a child whispers a message to the next child in the line, who then whispers the message to the next child, and so on down the line. The last child in line receives the message and announces it. Invariably, the message received by the last child is different from the one whispered by the first child in line. Because each of us hears and considers information through our own set of intellectual, emotional and physical filters, we may interpret messages in ways that were not intended by the people communicating the messages.

Types of Team Communication

Verbal Communication   Verbal communication is the expression of something in words or language, whether spoken, written, or thought.

Virtual Communication   Virtual communication is a form of verbal communication that is prevalent in our society today.

The two categories of virtual communication are:

Synchronous communication, which takes place at the same time—real-time interaction. This could include telephone and video conferencing, electronic display (whiteboard), and chatting.

Asynchronous communication, which takes place at different times—delayed interaction. This could include e-mail, voice-mail, group calendars and schedules, bulletin boards and Web pages, and file sharing.

Researchers have investigated how much and how quickly people reveal information about themselves and the overall impressions they make when using the computer to communicate. Many studies have found that people reveal much more information online than they would in a face-to-face interaction and even developed more socially rich relationships than people who interacted face-to-face. Developing relationships with others may take longer using virtual communication, but it does occur.

Using e-mail for messages, however, can hinder understanding. It may contribute to greater polarization of opinions; group members may take more extreme positions when putting information in writing than when communicating orally.

Nonverbal Communication   Have you ever watched comedians' faces? Sometimes their faces are reflecting something entirely different from what's actually happening. The difference between the two messages can create very funny results. Nonverbal communication works hand in hand with verbal communication to send a message. If you speak the same sentence three times—once in a loud voice while standing up, once quietly while sitting with arms and legs crossed, and once while maintaining eye contact and taking the receiver's hand—you are sending three entirely different messages.

Nonverbal communication is communication that does not rely on written or spoken words. Body posture and movement, eye contact, facial expression, seating arrangement, spatial relationships, personal appearance, response time, and tone of voice all communicate nonverbal messages. When body language contradicts verbal language, the message conveyed by the body is dominant. Consider, for example, if someone asks you how you feel, and you say "fine" even though you don't feel fine at all. In such a case, your posture, eye contact, and other body language may convey the real message loud and clear.

We also send messages with our actions. For instance, the people with whom we spend time, what we spend our money on, how we care for our health, and how we care for others are all ways in which we communicate nonverbally.

Nonverbal communication also includes internal conversations and thoughts. Our internal thought processes create emotion and energy. Even when we don't give voice to these feelings, they may influence others around us.

To improve your nonverbal communication:

- Pay attention to what other people communicate nonverbally.
- Note when someone misinterprets what you have said.
- Look for ways in which your nonverbal communication affects your message.
- Be aware of saying things with your body that contradict what you are saying; you will confuse your listeners.
- Notice the distance between you and others when you're speaking. In some cultures, casual acquaintances stand very close to one another when speaking; in others, only very intimate, personal conversations are carried out while standing close together.
- Notice your eye contact when talking and listening. American culture encourages eye contact, interpreting it as honesty and openness; other cultures frown on it, interpreting it as a sign of disrespect.

Nonverbal communication takes practice. If you have a VCR at home, put on a video and turn off the sound. Look at the nonverbal messages the actors are conveying. Another way to improve your nonverbal awareness is to play charades. Or, go to the mall and watch people as they go past. What are their mannerisms saying? Do you think you're reading them accurately? You might even want to observe yourself if you have the chance. Look at old video tapes or pictures. What are you conveying with your nonverbal signs? Remember to practice. Communication takes effort.

> As I grow older, I pay less attention to what people say: I just watch what they do.
>
> —Andrew Carnegie

Communication Styles

The first step in developing communication skills for teams is to become aware of yourself and your communication style. Self-awareness encompasses knowing your personal capabilities and your weaknesses. You have already begun this process by learning about your personality type, your intelligences, and your learning styles. The following chart will help you understand different styles of communication and suggested strategies for using them in a group.

Communication ◀

Using techniques corresponding to your stronger intelligences boosts your communication skills both as a speaker and as a listener.

INTELLIGENCE	SUGGESTED STRATEGIES	WHAT WORKS FOR YOU? WRITE NEW IDEAS HERE
Verbal–Linguistic	• Find opportunities to express your thoughts and feelings to others—either in writing or in person. • Remind yourself that you have two ears and only one mouth. Listening is more important than talking.	
Logical–Mathematical	• Allow yourself time to think through solutions before discussing them—try writing out a logical argument on paper and then rehearsing it orally. • Accept the fact that others may have communication styles that vary from yours and that may not seem logical.	
Bodily–Kinesthetic	• Have an important talk while walking or performing a task that does not involve concentration. • Work out physically to burn off excess energy before having an important discussion.	
Visual–Spatial	• Make a drawing or diagram of points you want to communicate during an important discussion. • If your communication is in a formal classroom or work setting, use visual aids to explain your main points.	
Interpersonal	• Observe how you communicate with friends. If you tend to dominate the conversation, brainstorm ideas about how to communicate more effectively. • Remember to balance speaking with listening.	
Intrapersonal	• When you have a difficult encounter, take time alone to evaluate what happened and to decide how you can communicate more effectively next time. • Remember that, in order for others to understand clearly, you may need to communicate more than you expect to.	
Musical	• Play soft music during an important discussion if it helps you, making sure it isn't distracting to the others involved.	
Naturalistic	• Communicate outdoors if that is agreeable to all parties. • If you have a difficult exchange, imagine how you might have responded differently had it taken place outdoors.	

Keeping the Peace
How to Have Difficult Conversations

Have you ever been involved in a heated conversation when you notice that you're sweating or that your stomach is tightening and you think you can feel your blood starting to boil? Kerry Patterson et al., in their book *Crucial Conversations,* call conversations that are challenging, frustrating, frightening or annoying, and, at the same time, could have an impact on the quality of your life or work **crucial conversations.** These conversations are usually about tough issues. You may experience physical responses during these conversations, such as tightening of the stomach. Look for clues that you are involved in a crucial conversation.

While it's common to want to back away from such situations, if you know how to master these types of conversations, you can engage in ways that create beneficial outcomes for all the participants. Leadership expert Stephen Covey believes that, by employing several critical communication skills, it is possible to create a level of "mutual understanding and creative synergy"[3] that moves people to agree and act on effective solutions.

Make People Feel Safe   People feel safe to share creative ideas or confrontational information when they trust that they won't be attacked or humiliated. When people feel unsafe, they generally either attack defensively or withdraw into silence. A common response is to react in kind, and the communication continues in a downward spiral.

Many times, people can receive tough feedback without becoming defensive if they believe that the giver of the feedback is trying to help or support. We can look for opportunities in such challenging conversations for greater awareness and movement toward our goals.

Ways to create or restore safety:

- Notice when others are withdrawing or attacking.
- Watch the impact you are having on others, and how you are feeling in response to others.
- Make others feel respected by recognizing your own weaknesses.
- Consider others' points of view and look for common interests.

Take Responsibility for Feelings   We all choose our response to the actions and words of others. No one can "make" us feel a certain way. How we feel is always our choice.

In responding to the actions and words of others, use "I" statements as opposed to "you" statements.

- **"I" statement:** "I feel stressed out and rushed when you give me a deadline for tasks to accomplish without checking with me about my schedule."
- **"You" statement:** "You make me feel stressed out and rushed when you give me a deadline for tasks to accomplish without checking with me about my schedule."

Accept Criticism   Understanding what criticism is and is not can help us avoid getting caught in the downward spiral of communication gone awry. Too often we take critiques personally, assuming the criticism is about us as people rather than about what we've done. You are not your project or your grade. Getting well-intentioned criticism does not mean that you have failed. It means you can do things better. Sometimes, however, people are not well meaning. They intend to put others down. Psychologist Lonnie Barbach describes these "put down" individuals as follows:

> "People who feel insecure and inadequate often get into the right/wrong battle. They try to raise their self-image by being "right." One way of proving oneself right is to make the other person wrong. Making someone feel wrong has an alienating effect."

Critically evaluate the criticism you receive. Is it from a source whom you respect? Is the criticism itself valid? Is any part of it valid? Can you use the feedback to make changes for the better? If so, then set an intention to do that. If not, then let the criticism go. In the midst of an adversarial conversation, know that you can evaluate the feedback at a later time; you do not have to respond immediately. Be aware of your physical responses, and remember to focus on the general context of the conversation.

How to Give a Useful Group Peer Review

At times in your courses and in some groups at work, you will be asked to do a peer review—to rate your team members on their contribution to the group. Usually people are quite easy on each other in these instances, and many leave the group without gaining any knowledge about how to become a better team member. The best thing you can do for each other, especially during your peer reviews in your classes, is to be honest and helpful. Use the principles of good communication to explain what you really feel about how your teammates have contributed and how they could better contribute in the future. Likewise, as you receive feedback, recognize that any criticism can ultimately help you far more than positive feedback. Practice accepting, and even welcoming, honest feedback.

Giving useful feedback requires empathy, sensitivity, and self-awareness. We can never know what is most beneficial for someone else, though we can share what works and what doesn't work for us.

Some tips for giving and receiving feedback include:

Giving Feedback to Others

- Ask whether they want feedback before offering any.
- Be mindful of the timing and environment. Avoid emotional situations and giving feedback in public settings.
- Find something positive about their performance, and comment on it.
- Give others a chance to give feedback to themselves.
- Be specific—refer to specific scenarios or situations.
- Give a suggestion for how you believe they could be more effective.

Receiving Feedback from Others

- Let others know if the timing or location doesn't work for you.
- Assume the givers have your best interests at heart.
- Be open and nondefensive.
- Ask questions if you are unclear. Strive for understanding.
- Ask how you could have done things differently.

Getting More of What You Want
The Art of Negotiation

Negotiations occur in many areas of life. We may negotiate a job offer, a relationship, or a treaty among nations. Usually in negotiation, each side takes a position, argues for it, and makes concessions to reach a compromise.

Evaluate What You Want   To negotiate, begin with understanding what you want. Negotiation leads back to our values and our understanding of those values. In the heat of a discussion about an important issue, you may feel intense emotions welling, and you may be tempted to give in or act in a way that is uncharacteristic. You may feel the need to avoid embarrassment, win, be right, or punish others. As you make an effort to discover the underlying motive, you may conclude that you're pushing harder to win an argument than it merits.

To allow for healthy dialogue to occur in these instances, step away from the interaction and look at your desires in light of the following questions. Alternatively, you can frame your desires in advance before you enter into a conversation that is likely to require negotiation. Ask yourself:

1. What do I really want for myself?

2. What do I really want for others?

Based on those answers, ask yourself how you would behave if you wanted those outcomes.

Also evaluate what you don't want to occur for yourself, others, or the relationship. Put this into the following framework:

I want _____ AND I don't want _____.

Then, you have a foundation for discovering a solution.

Foster Cooperation and Dialogue   You can think of negotiation as a compromise: the parties each have their desires and meet as close to the middle as they can get. Negotiation can also involve a synergistic process through which parties achieve the optimum solution for both.

Typical Compromise

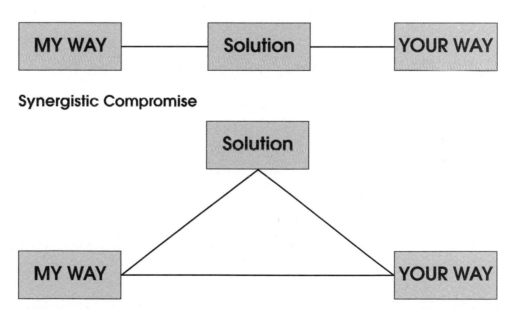

Synergistic Compromise

Synergistic compromise involves an understanding that our thoughts are interconnected, and, through an intentional dialogue, we can collaborate toward greater understanding and levels of creativity than we could access alone. A group may explore complex issues by involving people with many different points of view. But in order for dialogue to occur, the participants must agree to share their points of view while suspending their assumption that their viewpoint is correct. Participants must agree that the possibility exists for an "alternate way" that none of them had previously considered.

You are not trying to win in a dialogue. Everyone wins if you're doing it right. This type of communication is as much about a collective learning process as it is about the sharing of information.

The basic conditions necessary for effective compromise are:

- All participants suspend assumptions. Participants are aware of their programming and opinions and agree to be open to other ways of thinking.

- All participants regard each other as colleagues, peers, or equals. Every participant's input is considered equally.

- There must be a facilitator who makes sure the process is maintained and respected.

> He that complies against his will is of his own opinion still.
>
> —Samuel Butler

Conflict Is Inevitable
How Do You Deal with It?

Many people intensely dislike conflict and will go to extreme measures to avoid it. On the other hand, some people seem to thrive on conflict and enjoy creating situations that put people at odds with each other. While in college, you certainly will not be sheltered from conflicts. In fact, on a college campus where a very diverse population lives and learns together, conflict is likely to arise on a regular basis. The simple truth is, conflict is pervasive throughout our culture, and you simply cannot avoid having some confrontations with other people. Therefore, you should not try to avoid conflict; rather, you can use it to create better relationships by exploring workable solutions.

You may experience conflict in a classroom when another student takes issue with your opinions and continues to harass you about your ideas after the class is over. You could be placed on a team where conflicts arise among the members. A major conflict could erupt in the parking lot if someone thoughtlessly pulls into a parking space that you have been waiting for. You could even experience conflict with a faculty member because you intensely disagree with the grade he or she assigned you on a project. Conflict can occur in any relationship, whether it is your parents, your girlfriend or boyfriend, your best friend, a roommate, a spouse or partner, your children, or a total stranger.

Plan to Build Effective Teams
Characteristics of an Effective Team

Effective teams get results and provide satisfaction and meaning to their members. Characteristics of effective teams include:

The team has developed well-defined, elevating goals. The team goals of effective teams are usually very specific and measurable. They are also larger goals than any individual could accomplish alone and are considered by the group to be elevating and important.

Team members have clearly defined roles and responsibilities. Research has shown that people who belong to an effective team usually have a clear sense of their particular role or function on the team and the function of other members.

Team members share leadership. All members of the team are encouraged to take responsibility and give input into decision making and direction of the team. There is open exchange between members as equal colleagues or peers.

Team members prioritize collaboration and partnership. The team develops a collective vision and strategies and methods, rather than carrying out directives or acting on preformed opinions. Team members are encouraged to express their own ideas. Mutual inspiration is valued above competition.

Disorder is considered as a source of creativity. Effective teams look for opportunities in fluctuations, chaos and disturbances and use these opportunities for growth and learning.

(All for one and one for all!
—Alexander Dumas)

Team members are competent. Team members need to know not only what their assignment is but also how to perform their job. Members need adequate training in teamwork, problem-solving, and job skills in addition to being open, straightforward, supportive, action-oriented and friendly.

The team applies standards of excellence. A team is more likely to achieve its potential if it establishes high standards.

Team members give each other useful feedback. One of the ways that team members support each other in developing excellent performance is to effectively give and receive feedback. Studies show that when people are deprived of information regarding their performance, their self-confidence suffers as much as when they are given criticism. Constructive feedback, on the other hand, is an effective way to support positive growth.

Yes You Can!

Consider the following strategies when trying to resolve a conflict:

- Control yourself. Keep your words, actions, tone of voice, and body language respectful. Resist the urge to use name calling, hurtful words, and interruptions. Remember, you can't control or change anyone else.

- Establish an environment where people feel safe. This is not the time for intimidating body language, yelling, or obscenities. If you are going to resolve a conflict, you must keep your anger under control.

- Listen to what the other person has to say first. Let the other person know that you respect his or her opinions and rights.

- Avoid "gunnysacking," which is the practice of suppressing a long list of complaints and bringing them up all at one time. Sometimes, this suppressed hostility explodes and escalates.

- Try to reach some common ground. Focus your conversations on finding solutions instead of placing blame.

- Think of ways you can arrive at a "win–win" solution by first looking for common ground and things that you do agree on. Be sure you are considering the other person's needs as well as your own. Taking care of your needs and leaving the other person unhappy will only result in future conflicts that may be even worse.

● ● *and ITT Tech Can Help!*

chapter 6 | Managing Team Projects

Contents

Managing Team Projects

Understanding how teams function and how to communicate within them is just the beginning of building your team skills. Teams must also produce. They are formed to complete some type of project, utilizing the skills of the team members. Projects are the means to achieve business objectives. Project management is the process of planning, organizing and managing all the people and activities involved in a project from the project's concept to its completion. All organizations have projects. A project may be a large task or a complex activity, in fact, any work that is done to achieve an objective on time and within budget. Projects are ideas in motion. Examples of projects include efforts to: move an office to another location; put on an event; merge two organizations; institute a new training program; put together a budget; create a new product; change or produce a Web site, or put a new process into place. More and more people recognize that their ability to effectively manage projects is now key to their success within the organization. To successfully complete a project, teams must be well organized.

When you start a new project, you probably have many things going on in your mind. How long will it take? Are there enough people to do the work? How will you get it done on time?

In this section we will take a brief look at how projects can be organized and managed.

Project Phases

Well-organized projects generally involve the following steps or phases:

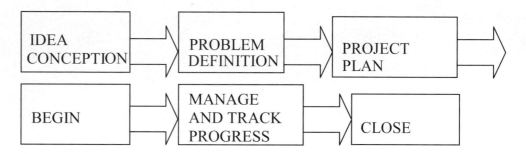

In the **conception** phase, the idea for the project comes about. What do you want to get done? Every person and every department affected by the project are also identified.

The **definition** phase includes a detailed description of the problem and the results to be produced.

The **project plan** includes a list of all the work that needs to be performed and the roles that everyone working on the project will perform. Budgets should also be established during this phase, as well as a detailed project schedule.

Once the project plan is in place, the project can **begin.**

The progress of the project is **managed and tracked** throughout the process.

The **close** of the project includes preparing any final reports as well as a post-project evaluation.

Project Planning

Perhaps the most important work in project management is done during the early phases of a project, before the actual project begins. Although many people try to shortcut these phases by moving directly into the project, experts have found that projects that are not well thought-out and planned at the beginning almost always take longer that those that are. Taking extra time at the beginning to plan saves much more time over the course of the entire project. Because of the great importance of good planning, in this section we will look in more detail at the problem definition and project plan development phases of a project.

Project management software packages that are on the market today can make the planning process easier. However, never underestimate the critical thinking that is involved with project management. As with all other forms of technology, the software can be used as a tool to help in the work, as a hammer aids in the building of a house. But, the software can no more manage the project than the hammer can design the house.

Before you can develop the project plan, you must have a clear project definition. The project definition should include the following information:

- Who is affected by the project?
- How important is this project to the company?
- What is the project trying to achieve and how will these results be measured?
- Are the objectives clear and specific? Are they '"SMART" (see the following box)?
- What are the limitations of the project in terms of time and resources?
- Will the benefits of the project be worth the costs of doing the project?

"SMART" goals have the following characteristics:

Specific: Each objective should be defined clearly, in detail.

Measurable: Each objective should have indicators that you can use to determine whether you met the objective.

Aggressive: Objectives should be worth the trouble. They should be challenging and meaningful.

Realistic: Objectives should be attainable. Excessively aggressive goals that cannot be reached, realistically, will not motivate people working on the project.

Time-Sensitive: Each objective should have a set end date.

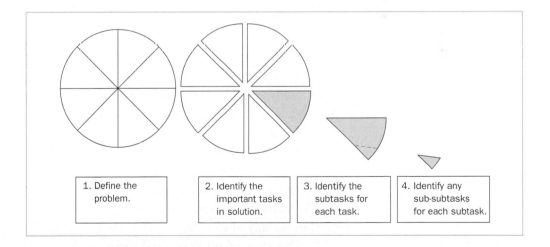

| 1. Define the problem. | 2. Identify the important tasks in solution. | 3. Identify the subtasks for each task. | 4. Identify any sub-subtasks for each subtask. |

With the project clearly defined, you can now develop your project plan. Developing the project plan means thinking about the "big picture" of the entire project as well as thinking about all the details. It involves identifying each big goal of the project and breaking it down into specific tasks. The figure on the previous page illustrates this process.

Let's look at a hypothetical team project.

Scenario   It has come to the attention of the management that there are some serious problems in communicating across departments in the company. The production department is not communicating with the marketing department, and this is hurting customer relations. The IT department is unable to process everyone's requests because there are too many requests and too few IT people. In order to stimulate more company cohesion and get everyone talking to each other, your boss has requested that you and three co-workers put on a day-long conference on best practices for working together. She would like you to have presenters from every department give an overview of what they are working on, what problems they have, and how other departments can help them. Your boss would like the conference to take place as soon as possible, ideally in the next two weeks. You quickly realize that in order to make this happen, you will have to get busy immediately.

Identify Important Tasks

After defining the problem, identify the important tasks. In our conference example, these might be:

1. Decide on a location and date for the event.
2. Find the speakers.
3. Invite attendees and advertise internally.

Identify Subtasks

Identify the steps that will make up each of your important tasks. In our example, these might include:

1. **Decide on a location and date for the event.**
   1.1 Call event center to determine open dates.
   1.2 Check with department heads on scheduling conflicts.
   1.3 Arrange teleconferencing equipment so remote employees can participate.
2. **Find speakers.**
   2.1 Work on vision and goals for the event.
   2.2 Have president of company send global e-mail outlining conference goals.
   2.3 Call departments for speaker nominations and topics.
   2.4 Write short descriptions for internal advertisements and send back to departments for approval.
3. **Invite attendees and advertise internally.**
   3.1 Finalize schedule.
   3.2 Develop flyer.
   3.3 E-mail flyer to all employees.
   3.4 Leave global voice mail.
   3.5 Publish on internal Web site.
4. **Plan for day of event.**
   4.1 Determine equipment and room needs.
   4.2 Finalize with events center.
   4.3 Develop survey.
   4.4 Put together packets.

Identify the Sub-Subtasks

If there are additional steps for each of the subtasks, identify those. In the conference example, these might include:

2.1 Work on vision and goals for the event.

    2.11 Schedule brainstorming session with group.

    2.22 Finalize list of vision and goals.

    2.23 Present to president of company for approval.

3.2 Develop flyer.

    3.21 Write content.

    3.22 Place order with graphics department.

    3.23 Get approval.

After you have identified all of the tasks, subtasks, and sub-subtasks, you can assign time estimates for each. Project management software allows you to do this easily. You can also assign task dependencies (or predecessors) in the software, or tasks that must be completed before another task can begin. You can automatically enter this information as you go, and the software will keep track of the total time. The following figure shows how the time estimates might look for the project.

Task	Estimated Time	Predecessors
1. Decide on a location and date for the event.		
1.1 Call event center to determine open dates.	1 day	
1.2 Check with department heads on scheduling conflicts.	2 days	1.1
1.3 Arrange teleconferencing equipment so remote employees can participate.	1 day	1.2
2. Find speakers.		
2.1 Work on vision and goals for the event.		
2.11 Schedule brainstorming session with group.	1 day	
2.12 Finalize list of vision and goals.	1 day	2.11
2.13 Present to president of company for approval.	1 day	2.12
2.2 Have president of company send global e-mail outlining conference goals.	1 day	2.1
2.3 Call departments for speaker nominations and topics.	2 days	2.2
2.4 Write short descriptions for internal advertisements and send back to departments for approval.	3 days	2.3
3. Invite attendees and advertise internally.		
3.1 Finalize schedule.	2 days	2.4
3.2 Develop flyer.		
3.21 Write content.	1 day	3.1
3.22 Place order with graphics department.	1 day	3.21
3.23 Get approval.	1 day	3.22
3.3 E-mail flyer to all employees.	1 day	3.23
3.4 Leave global voice mail.	1 day	3.1
3.5 Publish on internal Web site.	1 day	3.23
4. Plan day of event.		
4.1 Determine equipment needs.	1 day	
4.2 Finalize with events center.	1 day	3.1
4.3 Develop survey.	1 day	
4.4 Put together packets.	2 days	3.23

Tasks can also be displayed as a diagram. A typical diagram might look as follows for this project:

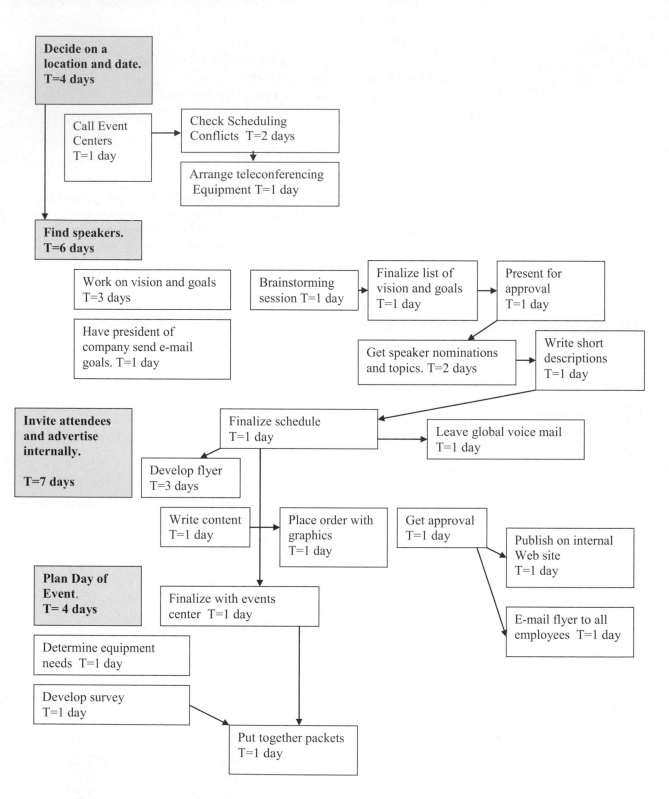

To complete a chart such as the one above, sometimes referred to as a pert chart, begin with all activities that have no predecessors. These can be started at the same time as soon as the project begins. Then continue filling in boxes with the activities that follow those you have already filled in. You can also write the time it takes to complete each of the activities within the boxes. Some will take longer than others.

If you are using project management software, these categories are built in, and you can fill them in as you go. Project management software also allows you to input all the resources you will need to complete a project, assign tasks to different people, and will visually show you how long each task will take in terms of the total project.

Yes You Can!

As organizations continue to adapt to technological changes, the nature of the organization itself is dramatically changing. Organizations are moving into more team-based, project-oriented structures where employees direct and discipline their own activities. Employees who are self-directed and who have project management skills are now in high demand. Developing these skills further, in addition to communication skills and knowledge of team dynamics, can greatly enhance your success as a technology professional.

and ITT Tech Can Help!

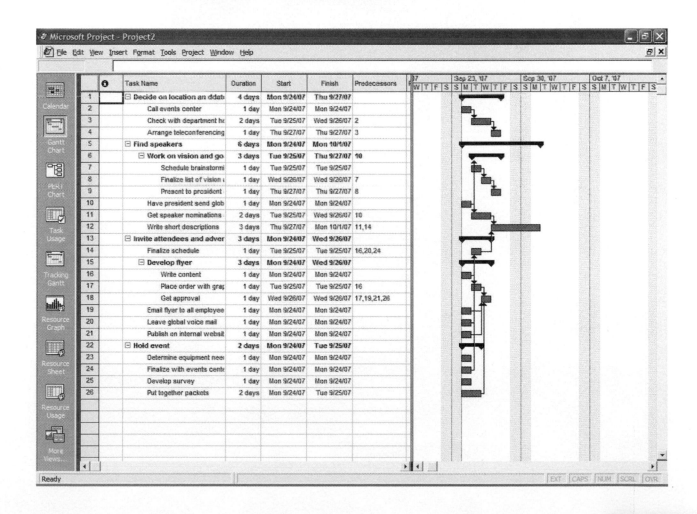

chapter 7 | Changes in the Workplace: Present and Future

Contents

Suggestions for video conferences include:

- Monitor your gestures and facial expressions.
- Don't interrupt.
- Dress for the camera. Don't wear white; avoid patterns, shiny jewelry, or other fashion accents.
- Become familiar with the technology beforehand.

Studies suggest that the benefit of video conferencing is not in the outcome of the immediate conversation but instead in the building of relationships.

What's Changing in the Workplace of the 21st Century

As the world changes we have to adjust, technologically as well as in other ways. Some of the changes that are likely to occur in this century are technical, of course. We'll see new technologies emerge and old ones subside. The nature of work is also going to change. Where the jobs are will change. Manufacturing used to be the mainstay of the U.S. economy, but we are increasingly becoming a service-based economy, in which the majority of workers provide services instead of commodities.

Manufacturing jobs are moving overseas to countries such as China and India. This trend is call *off-shoring* if a whole company is moved to another country and *out-sourcing* if only part of the firm's work—for example, the accounting—is sent to workers in another country. One important reason that companies are hiring abroad is that is where the fastest-growing markets exist. Companies such as Procter & Gamble, IBM, Caterpillar, and Coca-Cola get more than half of their sales and income from markets outside of the United States.

Due to the globalization of the workplace, many workers will find that they need to work shifts other than 8 A.M. to 5 P.M in order to reach and collaborate with coworkers in other countries at times when they are on duty. Global workplaces are made easier by the computer, which enables us to keep in touch with coworkers at all times of day and night. When someone sells an item in Detroit, for example, that order can be immediately transmitted to China, where the item is produced and then shipped to the buyer. This is called *supply-chaining*.

The United States has remained a powerful and strong economy due to constant innovation in products, services, and companies. Now we are competing with other nations that also are very good at innovating. Product innovation depends largely on engineers. Both China and India are graduating more engineers than is the United States. In fact, China and India together are graduating approximately three times more engineers than the United States does per year.

However, we shouldn't worry about change. Many of today's jobs did not exist 15 years ago. There are now more options for ways to perform your work, such as telecommuting or starting your own business. Today's worker faces fewer stigmas associated with changing jobs or changing careers. In fact, most workers will change their jobs up to 12 times in their careers and will make three to five career changes in their lifetime.

More job opportunities will be available at all hours of the day or night, any day of the week. Many workers will be required to use and adapt to new technology. Many will start as temporary employees and will need to prove their skills in order to be considered for long-term positions. More job opportunities will be available in the expanding service and information systems sectors. This is an exciting time to be entering into a new career, but it certainly requires that you understand the key trends that are shaping the workplace.

How could a student assistant position with a professor help your career?

The Need for Knowledge Workers

An employee becomes more valuable as he or she accumulates new skills. The challenge is to remain an outstanding contributor on the job while learning new skills. As organizations downsize or flatten, employees must possess multiple skills, such as the ability to learn, use new technology, or sell a product. These people have an edge. They may, for example, be able to transfer from the training division, if it is reduced in size, to the sales division and therefore remain employed.

There is good opportunity to move up within a company these days, though. A generation ago, the country shifted to a service-based economy in which fewer people produced industrial goods. Instead, more people provided services such as advertising or accounting or sold retail or wholesale products. Now we are in the midst of another shift, toward a knowledge-based economy in which employees will be expected to manage technology and information itself. The Bureau of Labor Statistics predicts in its occupational forecast for the year 2014 that the fastest-growing careers are in highly skilled professional, managerial, and technical areas. The fastest job growth will be in areas that involve the management and production of specialized knowledge.

Sometimes it is necessary to spend time after work taking classes and studying job-related materials to keep learning new skills. In years past, some employers took an active role in guiding employees toward new skills and often paid for training. In the current workplace, however, this responsibility almost entirely belongs to employees, who are expected to be proactive in learning new skills. Seek out training opportunities inside and outside of work and make sure your employer knows that you are interested in putting in the effort to learn.

The Importance of New Technology

Technology is so much a part of everyday life that most of us don't stop to think about how much we depend on it. Think about what you did today since you woke up. You will probably be able to name many activities that depend on technology. Just as it has affected our personal life, technology has revolutionized the kind of work we do, where we work, and how we complete our work. One in eight jobs is directly related to the field of high technology. Software engineer, CAD operator, computer programmer, and network administrator are some of these job titles. However, technology is used in almost all of today's jobs to some extent.

Technology has affected where and how we work. Thanks to telecommuting, some workers can work from a home office rather than a company site, using phones, fax machines, modems, e-mail, and other communication tools to stay in touch with coworkers and clients. Small businesses are being created and operated from home as well, with the aid of technology.

Think about technology and careers on a continuum. On one end are jobs that are directly related to technology such as computer programmer. These are the jobs that produce the technology we use daily. These are the jobs of the new economy. The fastest-expanding industries are those for which the main product or service is information. As you move along the continuum, jobs are less directly tied to technology. Somewhere in the middle of the continuum are the jobs of administrative assistants who use software packages for work processing as well as jobs that are influenced by technology. For example, teachers have vast amounts of information available for research over the Internet. Distance education technology teachers will be in increased demand as more people try to learn at any time and any place. Such a teacher must be able to adapt to the changes in teaching that require the use of technology. Many jobs will be affected by advances in technology, and those persons who are comfortable with and knowledgeable about computers may be the best job candidates regardless of where their jobs fall on the continuum.

At the opposite end of the continuum are the jobs that are least influenced by technology. These are the jobs of the old economy. Workers in construction, transportation, general manufacturing, and retail stores are furthest from the technology end of the job continuum and must deal with real-time issues that affect the bottom line. These industries take longer to lower costs, develop new products, and increase profits. In manufacturing, new technology that reduces costs may also reduce the need for some employees, resulting in layoffs. Furthermore, wages in these industries tend to rise with cost-of-living adjustments rather than through company profits.

The contrast between the new and old economy can be seen in the salaries offered to new college graduates. According to a report by the Office of Policy Development, Economics and Statistics Administration, average wages per worker in information technology industries are twice the national average. Information technology employment also provides self-employed and independent contractors the flexibility and mobility to work outside of a traditional organization. Although these temporary workers often earn less in wages and benefits and have less security than permanent workers, many prefer to be independent because they can command comparably high salaries and move from one employment situation to another with relative ease.

The Global Economy and the Changing Corporate Structure

A decade ago the United States was generating most of the world's technology; today that figure has diminished. The United States is striving to develop a more global economy by establishing trade agreements with other countries, such as the North American Free Trade Agreement (NAFTA). Global competition and multinational corporations will continue to influence the business world and our economy. Today it is not just the Fortune 500 companies, such as General Electric, IBM, and AT&T, that conduct business and have offices throughout the world. Employees wishing to advance in this new international economy must have the ability to speak more than one language and understand the cultural customs of other countries.

In today's global economy, NAFTA has created a need for multilingual talents, and Asian investments in Latin America and Mexico are expanding. Many of the border factories—in Tijuana, for example—are run by Japanese, Chinese, and Korean corporations. The ability to converse in two or more languages is an asset in the workplace.

Success in the global economy requires innovative, high-quality, timely, customized and efficiently produced products and flatter, leaner organizations. Successful companies these days tend to have the following traits:

- They have a flat management structure that has shifted away from management-directed systems toward team-directed systems that require knowledge workers on each team.
- They utilize a virtual corporation by spreading out their functions across the globe.
- They create production efficiencies through the use of technology.
- They move manufacturing plants to locations that offer good educational institutions and low labor costs.

- They recruit highly skilled workers.
- They are able to evolve and adapt as a company.
- They pursue e-commerce opportunities and customization of products to consumer demand.

In a global economy, an employee who helps the company remain competitive by being informed about technology, competition, and alternative ways to complete job requirements more effectively and efficiently will be recognized as extremely important to the company. Such employees will have the core jobs, whereas others will be hired as temporary employees. The more skills that you can demonstrate to an employer, the more valuable you will be. For example, a network technician who can communicate effectively with the various departments within a company and displays an aptitude for helping customers will be able to evolve with the expansions and changes that occur within the industry.

Lifelong Learning

The ability to adapt to the changing world of work is of the utmost importance. An estimated 40 percent of the jobs that will be available in 2010 have yet to be created. It is also possible that, due to advancing technology and other factors, you may advance in your career or change careers later in life. No matter how your career evolves, the need to continue educating yourself to keep up with technological change will be ever-present.

The Internet is bringing such education to people whenever they have time for it. Just 23 million Americans were enrolled in continuing education programs in 1984. That figure is predicted to be over 100 million by 2007, according to the National Center for Educational Statistics. There are also now over 2,000 corporate universities. More and more college classes are combining class attendance and Web-based instruction to maximize use of the research that can be found on the Internet.

To maintain currency in your career, you must get updated training throughout your life. To be able to do this, though, you must have good time-management skills and self-discipline.

As it gets easier to study anytime and anywhere, more people are earning college degrees, which is making the job market more competitive. Many of the best job opportunities during the next decade will demand that applicants have cross-functional training to broaden their qualifications. Today's career college graduates are finding that, to compete for the best jobs, they must commit to lifelong continuing education to bolster their job skills and prepare for career changes.

 Index

G

Gardner, Howard, 45
Generalizations, 93
Giving, 11
Global learning, 61, 63
Globalization, 134–135
Goals, 16–21
   attitude and, 12–13
   challenging, 18
   collective, 16
   conflicting, 17
   congruous, 19
   identification of, 17
   individual, 16
   key characteristics of, 18–20
   long-term, 16
   measurable, 18
   positive, 19
   prioritization of, 16–17
   self-esteem and, 20–21
   short-term, 16
   SMART, 127
   specific, 18
   time management and, 103,
      104–105
   time-sensitive, 18
   values and, 10, 19

H

Hall, Edward T., 106
Hardship, coping with, 14
Hearing, vs. listening, 69
Help for students, 34–36. *See also*
   Student resources
Honesty, 11

I

I vs. "you" statements, 119
In the Dance of Life: the Other
   Dimensions of Time (Hall), 106
Income, education and, 5
Independent study. *See* Online
   learning
Index card method, 99–100
Inside-out approach, 13
Instructional methods
   learning styles and, 54–55
   note-taking and, 79
Integrity, 12. *See also* Values
   personal, 12
Intelligence, multiple forms of, 44,
   45–48, 118
Internet resources. *See also*
   Technology
   evaluation of, 92

J

Judging vs. perceiving, 57, 59

K

Katzenberg, Jeffrey, 112
Keirsey Sorter, 49
Keirsey, David, 49
Key words and phrases, listening
   for, 71–72
Knowledge workers, demand for, 135

L

Lag-time response, 81
Learning Resource Center, 36
Learning Style Assessment, 61
Learning styles, 44
   active vs. reflective, 61–62,
      63, 65–66
   cognitive, 65–66
   effective learning and, 62–64
   intuition vs. sensing, 57–58, 59,
      61–62, 64
   job performance and, 55
   self-assessment for, 61
   sequential vs. global, 61, 63
   study methods and, 48, 54
   teaching styles and, 54
   theorist, 65, 66
   visual vs. verbal, 62, 64
Learning, 45
   accommodative, 65
   assimilation, 65
   convergent, 65
   cooperative, 40–42
   distance. *See* Online learning
   divergent, 65
   experiential, 65
   individual differences in, 44
   lifelong, 137
   multiple intelligences and, 44, 45–48
   personality traits and, 49–53
   pragmatic, 65
Lectures
   note-taking during, 73–79.
      See also Note-taking
   online. *See* Online learning
Library, virtual, 35–36
Lifelong learning, 137
Lincoln, Abraham, 15
Listening, 68–72
   constructive, 70
   cultural aspects of, 69, 70
   definition of, 69
   effective, 68–69
   emotions and, 71
   for key words and phrases, 71–72
   in L-STAR system, 73
   objective, 70
   obstacles to, 70–71
   prejudging and, 70–71
   with purpose, 70
   talking and, 70–71
   vs. hearing, 69
   as whole-body experience, 69–70

Listservs, 41
L-STAR system, 73–74

M

Mapping system, 77–79
Matching questions, 82, 84
Motivation, 14–16
   attitude and, 12–13
   external, 15
   fear and, 13–14
   internal, 15–16
   sources of, 15
   values and, 10
Multiculturalism. *See* Cultural
   diversity
Multinational corporations, 136–137
Multiple intelligences, 44, 45–48
   communication and, 118
   self-assessment for, 46–47
   skills associated with, 48
   Smart descriptors for, 47–48
   study techniques and, 48
Multiple-choice questions, 85–86
Myers, Isabel Briggs, 49, 56
Myers-Briggs Type Inventory, 49, 56

N

NAFTA, 136
Negative self-talk, 20
Netiquette, 40–41
Nonverbal communication, 117
North American Free Trade Agreement
   (NAFTA), 136
Note-taking, 73–79
   in class, 67–68
   Cornell system for, 75–76, 77
   L-STAR system for, 73–74
   mapping system for, 77–79
   missed information in, 77
   for online courses, 39–40
   outline technique for, 74–75
   during reading, 66–67
   symbols for, 74
   teaching styles and, 79
   vs. taping, 77–79

O

Objectivity, in critical thinking, 93
Off-shoring, 134
Online learning, 37–42
   asynchronous vs. synchronous,
      37–38
   collaborative, 40–42
   e-mail in, 40–41
   note-taking in, 39–40
   readings in, 39
   receiving instructional materials
      in, 42
   sending assignments in, 39, 42
   skills needed in, 39

Thinking
creative, 95, 106
critical, 95. *See also* Critical thinking
definition of, 90
levels of, 90, 91
outcome, 104
vs. feeling, 57–58, 59
Time diary, 110
Time management
definition of, 102
delegation in, 104
goals and, 103, 104–105
at home, 112–113
overcommitment and, 102–103
prioritization in, 103–105
procrastination and, 106–109
for relaxation and recreation,
105–106, 110
scheduling in, 104–106, 109
for school, 110–111
steps in, 102–105

television and, 109–110
time bandits and, 109
time diary in, 110
tools of, 109
for work, 111–112
To-do lists, 109, 111
Tradition, appeals to, 94
True-false questions,
84–85
Turner, Tina, 119

Values
congruence of, 12
in critical thinking, 94–95
goals and, 10, 20
identification of, 10–12
impact of, 10
integrity and, 12

motivation and, 10
self-esteem and, 10
Verbal learning, 62, 64
Victory wall/file, 21
Video conferences, 134
Virtual Library, 35–36
Vocabulary for ESL students, 72

Web sites. *See also* Technology
evaluation of, 92
Wheel of Life, 11
Word processing programs, 39–40.
See also Technology
Writing, 99
index card method for, 99–100
paraphrasing in, 100
process of, 100
reference citations in, 99–100

Part II

Power Up: A Practical Student's Guide to Online Learning

Taken from:

Power Up: A Practical Student's Guide to Online Learning
by Stacey Barrett, Catrina Poe, and Carrie Spagnola-Doyle

CONTENTS

Note: Every effort has been made to provide accurate and current Internet information in this book. However, the Internet and information on it are constantly changing, so it is inevitable that some of the Internet addresses listed in this textbook will change.

PREFACE

Mission of the Book

Some research indicates that as many as 80% of online students do not persist in their programs. They may drop out because they have misconceptions and/or misunderstandings regarding the realities of online learning including the expectations, the potential obstacles, and the necessary preparation required to succeed in the virtual classroom.

As an online student, you are embarking on a dream, making an investment in yourself and reaching for success. This book is designed to support you as a student new to online learning, giving you practical tips and information to help you achieve your goals in the online environment efficiently and effectively.

Elements to Support You

In this helpful guidebook, you will explore the realities of taking classes online. The material covers standard topics with an online spin, as well as these specific topics particularly relevant to online learners:

- Motivation
- Time management
- Self-knowledge, including learning styles
- The online classroom and community
- Working in the online classroom
- Communicating online
- Strategies for successful online learning
- Critical thinking and online research
- Computer concerns
- Creating a personalized study environment
- Maintaining online success

To help you focus your learning, a *Power Up* section begins each chapter, summarizing the important concepts. To expand your knowledge, a *More Power to You* section closes each chapter, listing websites that feature further information or ideas related to the material discussed in the chapter.

Elements Teachers Will Find Helpful

This book is a resource to help students acclimate to the online classroom faster and more confidently than they would otherwise. As an added plus, instructors will find the information useful when conducting the online class. The available PowerPoint slides summarize the course concepts and provide an easy way for instructors to integrate concepts from the text into their classrooms. Please check your courseware documents for location of and access to the PowerPoint slides.

Acknowledgments

We would like to acknowledge first and foremost our families, for allowing us to dedicate the time to write this book.

Each of us would like to thank the other two for the opportunity to work as an author on this team.

We also would like to offer special recognition to the following individuals who helped us with various aspects of the book: Joe Spagnola, Lorenzo Sierra, danielle Couch, Dr. Nancy Forrester, Dr. James Wood, Dr. Pam Lawhead and the IAEGS Team, and Jesse Ong from Hallmark Institute of Technology.

And, our sincere thanks to the following reviewers: Dr. Jamie Morley, Apollo College; Carole Suihkonen; James M. Wood, University of Phoenix/Green Mountain College; Katie Rosenthal, Ashford University; Angela Oleson, independent online instructor; Mac Adkins, DECADE Consulting/Troy University; Pamela Lawhead, The University of Mississippi; Elaine Gray, Appalachian State University; and Nancy G. Forrester.

INTRODUCTION

Looking at Online Learning

Many students begin an online program and wonder if they made the best decision. Some call this "buyer's remorse"; others may say they suffer from "cognitive dissonance." The bottom line: It is a scary new adventure and you may have a lot of questions. You have taken the plunge. You are an online learner! This book will help you through the experience. We answer many of the questions that being an online learner present— answers to questions that may have occurred to you as well as answers to questions you may not have thought to ask yet. We also provide tips for success based on our own experiences and the experiences of our students.

Students are often faced with questions like these: "Is your school a real university?" "How can you learn online?" "Are you sure your degree will be worth anything?" or the famous "Do employers hire people with an online education?" Of course companies hire people with degrees received from an online institution, and, yes, your degree can be a worthwhile investment. There is a misconception that online education is the "easy route" and degrees garnered in this modality are really not "earned," but we assure you, (and we know students who have been through an online program will attest to this, too) nothing could be further from the truth.

In this book, we identify, discuss, and dispel these and numerous other myths regarding online education. However, to begin, we want to arm you with some knowledge that will help you right now to address these questions and any doubts you may have about online education.

The number of students enrolled in online education programs is growing rapidly. The Sloan Consortium study in 2004 reported an approximate 23% increase in students taking classes online. In 2005, the increase in students obtaining an online education was about the same; however, the number of students entering the postsecondary market was only 18.2%. According to the Sloan Consortium, this statistic supports the point that growth in online enrollment exceeds the growth in enrollment in higher education as a whole. In addition, many high schools are now moving toward offering online options. At least two states currently are considering making the completion of an online class a requirement for high school graduation. Initiatives like these tell the true story: Online education is the wave of the future.

Although some people still question the validity of online education, the number of postsecondary schools offering online classes has grown to approximately 70% (National Center for Education Statistics, n.d.). Determining the exact number is sometimes difficult because schools report online education differently, and at this time no set reporting guidelines have been established. Some schools offer entire programs online; others may only offer individual classes or some parts of a particular class online. If every school that offered some type of online component were counted, the estimated number would be close to 98%, quite an impressive statistic. The research indicates that going to school online represents the present as well as the future.

Although some people are still very concerned with what employers think, the latest research indicates that half of all hiring managers say they would give equal consideration to both types of degrees. "In fact, many employers who are familiar with online education often like the attributes of typical online learners. These students [tend to be] independent, self-motivated, and well organized" (Carnevale, 2005). We explore these qualities of successful online learners in more detail later in the book.

In the past, employers hired people with educational backgrounds to which they could relate—applicants with traditional degrees. As more and more hiring managers themselves earn degrees from online universities, however, expectations will change. Degrees from online institutions are becoming more the norm. The wave has started and is gaining momentum. As increasing numbers of people earn degrees from online schools, the online learner will be the employee of choice for some employers. You are on the leading edge.

So how does your online degree stack up? An online program is probably not going to be as acceptable to some as a degree from Harvard or Yale. But for those with that mindset, neither is a degree from a state on-ground school. And realistically, were you going to be able to attend Harvard or Yale anyway? We must compare apples to apples. If you obtain a degree from an online school that is accredited (see Appendix B), for all practical purposes, your online degree is equivalent to a degree from a state institution or any other school in your area you opted not to attend.

The Impact of a College Degree on Your Career Success

The boss of two of the authors once said he was so proud when he finished his doctorate that the next morning he woke up, opened his door, and was ready to let all the employers in. After all, he was "Dr. Romine!" Of course no one was at his door.

We go to school with the idea that an education will better our standard of living, which is true in most cases. But you still have to work hard and keep pursuing your goals. Most likely, you are not going to finish your degree and the next day have employers begging you to come to work, but your education can lead to greater opportunities and the ability to negotiate some job situations more easily. You will have the opportunity to change your standard of living.

Let's consider for a moment what acquiring a college education means. How does it change you, and why do you need to complete a degree program?

According to the Bureau of Labor Statistics (1999, 2004), over the next decade the upward trend of companies wanting to hire college-prepared employees will continue. As more and more of the lower-level jobs are outsourced, there will be a need for educated and trained people to fill the gaps. And as the baby boomers prepare to retire, not enough people will be available to fill these positions. Skilled, educated people will be needed to catapult the workforce forward, in areas such as management, engineering, education, and accounting, as well as many trade and technical positions.

LEVEL OF SCHOOL OBTAINED	WEEKLY EARNINGS (IN DOLLARS)
Less than a high school diploma	401
4 years of high school; no diploma	456
High school graduates; no college	574
Some college; no degree	642
Associate's degree	694
Occupational program	677
Academic program	714
College graduates	986
Bachelor's degree	916
Master's degree	1,102
Professional degree	1,377
Doctoral degree	1,398

Median usual weekly earnings of employed full-time wage and salary workers 25 years and over by educational attainment and sex (2004 annual averages)

Source: Bureau of Labor Statistics, 1999, 2004

On average, a worker with a high school diploma or less will earn poverty wages. Of course, there are exceptions, but, in general, education pays. The difference in total life earnings between a high school diploma and a college degree is estimated to be $1 million (see table above).

Moneymaking aside, though, what do you gain from a college degree? A degree obviously will give you the skills and knowledge to do your job more effectively. But in addition to that, it can give you greater self-confidence and self-esteem. A degree gives you the absolute knowledge that you were able to succeed at this endeavor—to persevere and take your education to the next level. This knowledge should give you the confidence that you can achieve anything to which you set your mind.

Finally, earning a degree is an achievement no one can ever take away from you. When one of the authors finished her degree, she told her kids, "Look what I did. Now, no matter what, I will always have this. No one can ever take an education or experience away from you." What else can you say that about in your life?

We hope we have confirmed your desire to attend school online and perhaps even made it stronger. Going to school is a privilege. It is the opportunity of a lifetime, so enjoy and embrace it. You deserve this experience! Lastly, focus on enjoying this opportunity to learn, worry less about the destination, and bask in the journey of education.

The Authors

We are extremely passionate about online education and student success and have taught, taken part in, developed, and been exposed to online education for more than 10 years. We are educators who deal with online success every day. Here we share our wealth of experience to bring you inside information on how to succeed as an online student. Adopting the proven and practiced tips in this book will increase the chances of your success.

Please know that we stand behind you as you embark on becoming a successful online student. We have been there. We made it through, and so can you.

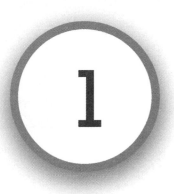

Becoming an Online Learner

1

Online education is where it is at. As an online student, I have control of when I learn, how I learn, and what extra I learn. I gain only as much as I put in; this is what distinguishes the online learning environment. Online education is moving toward a user driven, just-in-time model, and as an adult learner this is exactly what I want from my education.

— Dan Record, instructional designer and online PhD student

Power Up by:

- Examining your motives ahead of time for wanting to take an online class/program.
- Acknowledging the many myths circulating about online education. Know the difference between the myths and the facts.
- Recognizing that being an online student is not easier than being a student in a traditional classroom. It is just different.
- Understanding that time commitment, open-mindedness, autonomy, and self-motivation are expected of a successful online student.
- Understanding expectations for time on task: For every hour in class, students should spend 3 hours studying or reading outside of class. You will need to factor in the necessary time for your learning.
- Making sure you have the necessary technical equipment and skills before you start your online class.
- Understanding that most endeavors are generally not smooth at the beginning. Give this one a little extra time, effort, and positive energy, and you *can* be a successful online student.

Taking on the new identity of "student" for the duration of your class or program is undeniably a *huge* undertaking. Committing to completing a degree takes deep dedication and desire. You will have to become accustomed to a brand-new mindset. The decision to become an online student should tie heavily into your own goals and dreams because everything you are about to embark on comes down to *you*.

Because online education is still fairly new, many misconceptions are still connected to it. The number-one fact to remember as an online student is that this mode of education *is not* easier than being a student in a traditional classroom. It is just different.

- You have a lot more flexibility regarding time spent in and around class, but
- Online learning still takes as much if not more time compared with a traditional classroom experience.

Online Learning: Hybrid or All Online

You may choose to attend one or more online courses or you may select a program that is offered entirely online. Maybe you never planned to be an online learner, but during your available time frame a required course is only offered online, making you an online learner by default. Whatever the situation, you will find that online courses are both similar to and different from classes in the on-ground classroom. These similarities and differences may not be what you expect, so remember to keep an open mind!

In general, university courses are categorized by modality in four ways:

1. *On-ground, or traditional courses.* These are the courses that many of us grew up with. We go to a designated classroom at a particular time, and a teacher guides us through the course material. Homework is assigned for the times between classes, and it is generally due from one class meeting period to the next. Some assignments, and most tests, take place during designated class time.

2. *Online courses.* These are courses in which the entire class is staged online. For the most part, students and instructors never meet each other face to face.

3. *Blended, or hybrid courses.* These courses are sometimes difficult to distinguish. A blended course has some online components and some on-ground components. How this occurs, though, can vary greatly:

   a. One hybrid course may have students attend a local classroom once a week but offer all other instruction online.

   b. Another may meet only for the first week and the last week of class in a classroom, and the interim of the course occurs online.

   As long as the course combines online learning and traditional classroom time in some way, it is considered blended.

4. *Web enhanced courses.* *Web enhanced* is a newer term in online learning. For example, for a web-enhanced course, you retrieve your materials online. You do

not actually attend class online, but your book, grade postings, and other course materials may be available online. Most schools have some type of web enhancement already, but surprisingly, many do not. Sometimes, schools begin with a web-enhanced approach before they launch a full online program.

None of the course modalities outlined is better than the others in terms of quality. For any course, many factors make the difference in whether it is "good," including the quality of the instruction, the teacher, and the organization of the class. You will have to decide what makes a class "better" for you based on your own goals and priorities. Which of the modalities of learning outlined sounds like it might work best for you?

What Is Expected of a Student?

To begin with, you must truly understand what you can expect to encounter in this new role as an online learner. You have the power to create your own success. Here are some of the issues that are important for an online learner to understand.

The Importance of Time Commitment

1. *You* are your own self-regulator in an online environment and to succeed you must plan and manage your time correctly.
2. Although there most likely will be a designated *day*, online courses often do not have a designated class time. So you will need to determine how much time your class responsibilities will take and establish your own schedule for how to integrate coursework into your life.
3. Attending school online will take *the same if not more time* than a traditional class; what's different is how you allot the time and when you expend the time.

The Importance of Open-Mindedness

Online is both similar to and different from a traditional classroom. Manage your expectations!

1. Have an open mind when you start online courses, and be willing to explore and become familiar with the medium.
2. Discover what the differences are, and learn how to take advantage of them instead of letting them intimidate you.
3. Remember, only an open mind can be educated.

The Importance of Autonomy and Self-Motivation

1. In an online environment, there is no need to make yourself presentable, drive to campus, locate parking, and find the classroom. But although you may be able to participate in class while in your pajamas, you will still have to engage fully in the online environment.

2. You will have to make time for class and homework, be responsive to your instructor and fellow students, and you will have to do a lot of reading and writing.

Everyone takes a different amount of time to acclimate to the online environment. It may be confusing and overwhelming at the start, but you may be surprised at how quickly you become comfortable. Give yourself a chance to adjust and get up to speed.

Myths and Facts About Learning Online

If you are new to online learning, you may have some misconceptions or you may not be aware of some facts regarding this medium. Take a look at the following table that lists myths and facts, and see how your own knowledge and experience with online measures up.

MYTH	FACT
Online courses are less rigorous than on-ground courses.	Not necessarily. Online learning varies by course just like the traditional classroom, but, overall, you will probably be expected to do more writing, and you will need to participate more actively than you might have in a traditional classroom.
Instructors in an online environment are more aloof.	It depends on the instructor, but, in many cases, online instructors are extremely responsive to student contact, and you may find it even easier to initiate contact in the online environment
Online courses cost more than on-ground courses.	Tuition can be considerably higher, but you should also factor in such expenses as gas, parking, and child care that online students do not have to pay for.
It is harder to interact and make friends with your classmates online.	Not necessarily. Although an online classroom is different from a traditional classroom, you may have just as much opportunity for interaction. Once you become accustomed to interacting mainly through writing, you will find plenty of opportunities to seek out others and bond with your classmates. Online courses often have a chat room or lounge area in the course where students are encouraged to go and virtually "hang out" and interact with each other. Our experience has been that students are more communicative and self-revealing in an online environment.
Online classes fit easily into a busy schedule.	Perhaps. Online courses are more flexible, but just because you do not have go to the classroom at a certain time doesn't mean you do not need to dedicate time to your class work.

(continued)

(continued)

Homework in the online environment is not the same.	Not necessarily. Actually, most of the assignments you will find online are similar, if not the same, as in a traditional classroom and consist of papers, exams, presentations, and so on.
Online education is lower quality.	Not so. The same accrediting bodies that work with traditional schools approve online education. Online courses frequently use the same instructors and curriculum as their traditional counterparts. The bottom line is that, just as with the traditional classroom, the online classroom is what you make of it.
Online instructors are always online and available.	Not so. Some online instructors have established office hours when they are available. At other institutions, there might be a 24- or 48-hour guaranteed response time. The policy varies with the instructor and the institution. It is your responsibility to find out what the policy is.
It is impossible to work in virtual teams.	Not so. Virtual teams are the reality, not only in many classroom situations but also in the workplace. A good team is a good team whether it is virtual or face to face.
There are no support systems for online learners.	Not necessarily. Online schools vary, but often they have virtual incarnations of the same resources that traditional schools have, such as labs, tutors, and libraries.

Online classrooms provide a level of interaction and give-and-take that is not always possible in a traditional classroom. Both the breadth and the depth of student engagement can be increased.

In terms of breadth, it is common for all students in the class to see each other's assignments. That can be a little hard to accept at first and you may feel intimidated, but keep in mind, the other students feel the same way!

In terms of depth, there is greater time and opportunity to review the work of others, as well as your own thoughts. You will have time to really review one another's messages and assignments because these will be posted and remain in the newsgroups for the duration of the class. This differs from the need to respond immediately that is typical of face-to-face classroom discussions. Assuming it is not a scheduled discussion, an online student who needs time to process information can read the material, go for a walk while formulating a response, and then return and respond.

Are You Ready to Be an Online Student?

Readiness means many things. We discuss these issues in more depth later in the book, but for now, consider the following.

Time Available

You recognize you will need to schedule time for your online course. Keep in mind that for traditional students, the expectation is that for every hour in class, they will spend 3 hours studying or reading outside of class. The same formula is generally applied for online courses. A student taking a 3-credit class for 16 weeks spends about 9 hours a week out of class on assignments. It is quite possible an online student will have a compressed class that may last only for 5 to 8 weeks, so factor in the necessary time for your learning.

Technical Equipment

Do you have access to a computer? Do you have an Internet connection? Have you satisfied the requirements of your institution regarding platform and speed of connection?

The school generally does not care what kind of computer you use. But they do have specifications for the platform you use (e.g., Windows, Mac).

1. At the very least you will need to have a word-processing application, an Internet browser, and a slide presentation application.
2. Your Internet connection speed will also need to be at a certain level. And you will want to make sure you have, or can download, certain relevant plug-ins and support programs such as Java or Adobe Acrobat.

Technical Skills

You will need to rely on your technical skills as much as your study skills in the online environment. Ask yourself these questions:

1. Do you know how to type?
2. Do you know how to format a document?
3. Do you know how to send an e-mail with an attachment?
4. Are you a competent reader?

You will find numerous resources to help you attain these skills: friends and neighbors, online tutorials, outside training courses, and maybe even training labs offered by your institution.

Your Motives

Consider why you have chosen to further your education. Ask yourself these questions:

- How serious are you?
- Why are you doing this? You might be doing it to obtain a promotion at work or to expand your career opportunities or just because you love to learn. Take time to understand fully the reason you are doing it. Own it.

- What goal will this degree help you achieve? Or is it the goal in itself? Only you can truly answer this question. Are you doing it for your own reasons or to please others?
- Do you really have the time for it?
- Do you really want to dedicate the time that will be necessary?
- Are you looking forward to what you will learn about?

Really take the time to explore your own thoughts and feelings about the details of this degree and decide whether the timing and the focus are right for you. Knowing the answer to *why* you are motivated can help you *stay* motivated.

Adapt Your Attitude and Prepare for Success

We said this before: Do not begin this online learning endeavor expecting it to be easy, but don't anticipate failure either. Cultivate your self-confidence and be willing to change the way you think about school and your own abilities.

Do not become distraught the minute something goes wrong. You will have assignments where you will not score as highly as you thought you would or wish you would. Everyone has those! Do not immediately think of this as failing, but try to look at it as an opportunity for improvement. Think positively: You will succeed.

The first time you do anything can be very challenging. Recall the first time you rode a bike or your first day on the job. Most things are generally not smooth at the beginning, but give it time, effort, and positive energy, and you *can* be a successful online student.

Here is an analogy: Look at your introduction to online learning as you would your first visit to a foreign country. You will need time to learn the language, the lay of the land, and how to interact with the local people, but, given sufficient time and effort, it will soon become second nature. Give yourself time to adapt to online learning.

→ MORE POWER TO YOU

Now is your chance to explore the topics of Chapter 1 further. For each of the chapters in this book, we have selected a few specific websites that can be helpful resources for you. Check out the sites listed here. Enjoy expanding your knowledge, and *more power to you*!

Preparing Yourself for Online Learning
http://www.studygs.net/online/index.htm

Is Distance Learning Right for You?
http://distancelearn.about.com/od/isitforyou/a/considering.htm

The 7 Mistakes That Distance Learners Make
http://distancelearn.about.com/od/distancelearning101/a/7mistakes.htm

For Online Students: Resources, Guides, Tips & Tutorials
http://www.ibritt.com/resources/stu_forstudents.htm

Note: As we all know, the Internet is dynamic and ever evolving. If any of these websites are not available or you wish to seek out additional information, we encourage you to do your own online search. Consider the concepts covered in the chapter that are most important to you, and think of various terms that could be used to describe them. For this chapter, some potential keywords include:

> *successful online learner*
> *preparing online student*
> *online readiness*

When searching online, consider different ways to express ideas. Remember to use synonyms and related words. Try phrasing things in different ways. And always review more than the first few pages of the search results.

For more specific information on searching online, refer to Chapter 9.

Know Thyself: Self-Discovery for the Online Learner

2

Power Up by:

- Completing an honest appraisal of your skills. Ask yourself, as well as coworkers, classmates, and friends, for unbiased information on your strengths and weaknesses. Use that information to become a more well-rounded person.

- Becoming aware of your strengths. This allows you to identify what tasks will be easy for you and take less time.

- Becoming aware of your weaknesses. This allows you to identify what tasks will be more difficult for you and therefore take more time, and it also enables you to pinpoint areas where you need to improve.

- Learning how to predict how much time you need for a task. This will help you plan your study time and give others honest input in team situations regarding what you can contribute.

- Becoming aware of your intelligences and learning styles. Find ways to take advantage of them and use your strengths.

- Identifying the peak times when you are at your best and the valley times when you are not. Try to plan your work around these times.

- Understanding that personality tests are simply indicators to help you know yourself better. Think about how the results relate to being a student, specifically an online student.

In Chapter 1, we mentioned how self-analysis can be an important tool for your online education. But introspection is only one small part of the self-examination that can be helpful to you as a learner. Another important step is to look honestly at yourself and determine what comes easily for you and where you struggle, especially in terms of schoolwork and self-management.

"Know thyself," said the ancient oracle at Delphi. Knowing yourself can be helpful for everyone but especially online learners. The better you know your own preferences, skill levels, and strengths and weaknesses, the better you will be able to adapt to and take advantage of the online environment.

Why Explore Your Strengths and Weaknesses?

Although it may not be obvious, knowing your own strengths and weaknesses does matter. It can save you time and energy. Being aware of your strengths allows you to be aware of what will be easy for you and take less time. Being able to predict how much time you need for a task will help you to plan your study time and offer honest input regarding what you can contribute to team situations.

Your *strengths* are areas where you can mentor others who are not as skilled and help them grow.

Your *weaknesses* are those areas where you will need to have patience with yourself and dedicate extra time to polishing your skills. They are also areas where you may want to look to others for help. Being aware of your weaknesses allows you to be aware of the things that will be more difficult for you and therefore take more time. If you know your weaknesses you can recognize and plan for the things that will take more time and effort for you to complete, and you can pinpoint areas where you need to try to improve.

A positive quality of online education is that it allows you to be more in control of your time, so you can nurture and develop those weak areas and change them into strengths. You can also obtain feedback and help from others who are stronger than you in those areas.

You will need to be honest with team members about your skill levels. The best team assignments are produced by those teams that take advantage of all their members' skills.

Assessing yourself realistically is tough to do! Do not be afraid to ask coworkers, classmates, and friends for unbiased information on what they see as your strengths and weaknesses. You might be surprised at what you will find, and this whole process can be an excellent opportunity for growth.

Keep in mind: Knowing your strengths and weaknesses should not lead you to depend solely on what you are good at and avoid the areas where you tend to do poorly. You will not always have the choice of focusing on your strong areas, so it is important to develop your skills in areas where you are not as strong. Your goal should be to complete an honest appraisal of your skills and then use it to become a more well-rounded person. With time and perseverance, you may even develop new talents!

Tools for Self-Assessment

We've discussed the value of asking other people for input on your strengths and weaknesses. What about other ways of assessing yourself?

A multitude of resources are available, both in print and online, that can furnish insight into your personality and preferences. Keep in mind that these tools can vary in their ease of use as well as their accuracy. Further, you will find some of the more trusted tools cost money. It will be up to you to determine whether such an investment is a smart move for you.

A clear, comprehensive self-assessment is important whether you are an online or an on-ground student. However, self-knowledge can benefit you considerably as an online student.

Personality

We are talking about personality not in reference to whether you laugh at jokes or like to have fun but rather in terms of understanding your own mindset and attitudes when it comes to studying and learning.

Do you know your personality type? You can learn about different personality types through a web search or by reading a book on the subject. A typical search on the web using the queries "personality test" or "personality profile" will yield many free tests, and you will find numerous references to the most popular personality test, the Myers-Briggs Type Indicator (MBTI; Myers & Briggs Foundations, n.d.).

Isabel Myers Briggs and her mother developed the MBTI over 50 years ago. One of the most trusted assessments in the world, it is grounded in the work of the psychologist C. G. Jung. This assessment evaluates your personality by looking at 16 different indicators, resulting in a scaled differentiation between sensing and intuition, thinking and feeling, introversion and extroversion, and judging and perceiving.

When taking personality assessments, remember they are simply indicators to help you know yourself better. Do not pigeonhole yourself. Rather, think about what the results mean, whether you like what they represent, and if you want to change anything. For example, you may find you are very introverted, and you would like to be more extroverted. You might create a goal of becoming more social by putting yourself in situations where you will have to interact with others. Or perhaps you like being introverted and do not wish to change. Think about how the results relate to being a student, specifically an online student.

Multiple Intelligences

Many theorists suggest that humans have multiple intelligences, which indicates that certain components of intelligence align with preferred learning styles: mathematical, visual, physical, musical, verbal, naturist, extroverted, and introverted frames of reference. You may find you are stronger in some areas than in others, and thus this would be your intelligence area. The ideas behind multiple intelligences are grounded in the theories of Howard Gardner (Gardner, 1983).

You have heard people say, "I am not that good at math." According to these theories, such individuals may not have a high mathematical intelligence. Similarly, if someone can pick up a guitar and immediately play a song, he or she would be said to have a high musical intelligence. What do you enjoy? Do you sing when the radio comes on? Do you like karaoke? Do you prefer to be outdoors hiking?

All of these preferred activities could be pointing to your intelligences. Becoming aware of your intelligences and finding ways to take advantage of them is a way to leverage your strengths.

For example, if you are a nature lover, and you like to be outside, you might find that if you were to purchase a laptop and do your work by the lake, your writing would be much easier and your thought process much more defined. It's yet another beautiful aspect of online learning.

What about music? How can you incorporate this into studying? Think about how you learned your "ABCs." It was most likely through singing. You may find if you have musical intelligence, you want to listen to soft music while you work. Or perhaps you can put some complicated material into the lyrics of your favorite song. Determine where your intelligences lie, and then consider how you can use them to be successful in an online environment.

The goal of this section was to make you aware of these assessments and the impact they can have on you. If you are interested in learning more, search on the Internet using keywords such as *multiple intelligences*, *intelligences*, and *Howard Gardner*.

Peak/Valley Times

Peak times are when you are at your best and valley times are when you are not. We believe one of the most positive factors in online learning may be just this: the ability to focus your studies during your own peak times.

Certainly there are times you are more productive throughout the day. Pay attention and figure out when those times occur. You can explore the peak/valley concept by completing an exercise and then evaluating whether it was easy for you. If you determine it was more difficult than it should have been, perhaps it was the wrong time of day. The next day, try another exercise at another time of day and see what happens. Were you able to complete the work more easily? It will take some time to track your patterns, but once you figure them out, you will be able to work so much more efficiently. This is another benefit of online learning. You can login to class and study during your peak time, not your valley time.

Peak and valley times can be changeable within the day, month, or year. For example, if you are a morning person, then during the winter your peak time may be much later than in the summer.

Some people characterize peak/valley times as being a "lark" (i.e., alert and productive in the early in the day) or being an "owl" (i.e., alert and productive more in the evening and at night), but that description may be too simplistic. Maybe during the week, when you drink coffee, your peak times are in the morning, but on the weekend, when you sleep in, your peak times are late in the afternoon. Pay attention to these details and know what works best for you, and then capitalize on these times. That is when you will be the best learner possible and thus the most successful student. Being able to take advantage of your peak times fits right into the flexible structure of the online environment.

Ronald Gross is well known for contributing to the concept of peak and valley learning (Gross, 1999). To find more information, search on the Internet using the phrase *Gross and peak learning.*

Learning Styles

The idea of learning styles relates to the way you take in and process information. Some of the most notable learning styles include visual, auditory, and tactile-kinesthetic.

- *Visual learners* learn best by seeing the teacher, concepts, diagrams, and so on. Visual learners often like to take detailed notes.
- *Auditory learners* learn best by listening. They like to talk things through and listen to others' opinions and ideas.
- *Tactile-kinesthetic learners* learn best by doing, moving, and touching. They learn via using their hands or by incorporating movement into their thinking and study.

You may want to sit back now and think which way you learn best and then consider how this will work in an online environment. If you are a *visual* learner, how could you best learn online? Perhaps you could print more material and have it available to review.

As an auditory learner, you might read books and messages aloud. You may even consider buying software that will change text to auditory CDs so you could listen to someone reading your book.

As a tactile-kinesthetic learner, you might take ideas and map them on a piece of paper or build constructs of ideas.

Stringers and Groupers

Another learning style that relates to the way you process information is that of the stringer versus the grouper (Hill, 2001). Are you someone who likes to look at the big picture only? Do you tend to see the 40,000-foot view? Or do you like to see all of the details and work your way up?

A person who likes to look at the big picture first and then looks at the details is called a *grouper.* This type of person may begin a class by thinking about all of the assignments from a global perspective and then may consider each minute detail. Notice we say "may." Groupers sometimes don't see as many of the details as they should.

A *stringer* is a person who looks at each detail and does not see the bigger picture until the end. This type of person looks at each detail of each assignment and may not see how they all fit together. Notice we say "may." Stringers may never see the bigger picture.

Either style can take you where you want to go. And you can learn how to make your style work the best way for you. But to be a successful student, you need to be a little of both. You are going to have to stretch yourself and leave your comfort zone. If you are a grouper, you must learn to look at each detail or you may miss something of great importance. If you are a stringer, you want to look at the big picture to assure you understand how the assignments fit together. Curriculum is often constructed in such a way that the concepts build on one another. It will be helpful to you to notice and understand this structure.

It can be useful to find out the learning styles of your friends. You may find that you know several people with different styles from yours. They do say opposites attract! You can help each other along the way.

Applying Self-Assessment Information

Self-assessments can be fun and interesting, but they are most helpful if you listen to the feedback and use it to plan how you can become a more efficient and effective learner.

Remember, you do not want to pigeonhole yourself or to become frustrated with what you discover from these assessments. When you feel discouraged, realize you may be out of the comfort zone that is your learning style or your personality paradigm. Keep in mind that experiencing this discomfort can be the start of the process of learning and changing, if you choose to take advantage of it.

You will need to continue to evaluate what you can do to help enable your own success.

→ MORE POWER TO YOU

Now is your chance to explore this chapter's topics further. Check out the sites listed here. Enjoy expanding your knowledge and *more power to you*!

Know Your Type
http://www.knowyourtype.com/google.html

Advice for Enhancing 3 Basic Learning Styles
http://www.sdc.uwo.ca/learning/index.html?styles

Advice on Bringing Your Learning Styles Into Balance
http://www.mindtools.com/mnemlsty.html

Thinking and Learning Skills Course
http://www.ldrc.ca/projects/projects.php?id=26%20

Successful Learning: Cycle through Learning Styles
http://www.cdtl.nus.edu.sg/success/s127.htm

If any of these websites are not available or you wish to seek out additional information,

we encourage you to do your own online search. Consider the concepts covered in the chapter that are most important to you, and think of various terms that could be used to describe them. For this chapter, some potential keywords to search include:

personality profile
learning styles
peak learning times

When searching online, consider different ways to express ideas. Remember to use synonyms and related words. Try phrasing things in different ways. And always review more than the first few pages of search results.

For more specific information on searching online, refer to Chapter 9.

Motivation and Goal Setting: Overcoming Obstacles

3

Power Up by:

- Understanding that new online learners often share common obstacles. Don't let them discourage you.

- Planning for the cost of an online education, which may mean you have to develop a new budget and/or make some financial sacrifices.

- Balancing your own needs with those of others. Reassure people close to you of their importance to you even though you are focused elsewhere. Know when to put yourself first.

- Acknowledging conflicting priorities (family, work, etc.) and taking action. Organize your schedule, set your priorities, and be ready to revisit them occasionally.

- Planning your time wisely to help you manage stress. Take it one day or one project at a time. Avoid procrastination and overcommitting.

- Focusing on celebrating small successes, such as the submission of your first assignment or a compliment from a classmate.

- Making reasonable goals. Do your best, but admit that you do not have to be best at everything.

- Following the SMART model when setting a goal: *S*pecific, *M*easurable, *A*ttainable, *R*ealistic, and *T*imely.

- Recognizing that journaling can be an important tool for you throughout your career as a student and beyond. It can serve as a recording method, a tool for problem solving, and a stress-management strategy.

D eciding to become an online learner or any type of student, for that matter, can be very rewarding. However, there may be obstacles to overcome on the way to those rewards. Inevitably, hindrances come along with new endeavors; it is how you deal with these stumbling blocks that makes the difference. Let's take a look at some of the common challenges that new online learners often share.

Financial Concerns

The dreaded financial commitments that come along with enrolling in a program or a class at an institution can really put a damper on your plans. But you do have many options.

Accommodating the cost of online education may mean you have to develop a new budget and/or make some financial sacrifices. We realize everyone is in a different situation, but here is one simple example. What if you give up buying your lunch every day and brown-bag it instead? Do the calculations to see how much you could save over a year. This might help you feel better about your financial commitments.

Lunch out = $7.00

52 weeks in a year times 5 days a week = 260 days

$7.00 × 260 = a savings of $1,820 dollars a year! This will pay for one or more 3-credit classes.

Maybe you already take your lunch. If so, try analyzing where you are spending your money and think about how you might be able to pinch a penny.

Do you smoke?

Do you buy lottery tickets?

Do you stop for coffee every day?

Do you drive to the store when you could walk? With the price of gas, consider using less as much as possible. Another great feature of online classes is that you do not have to drive to class.

Further, do not forget about the financial aid and scholarships that are available (see Appendix A). The negative aspect of financial aid is that you have to pay it back, which can be quite difficult in some cases.

Statistically, many individuals graduate from college so deep in debt that even with a good paying job, small raises make little difference because all the extra money is simply going to pay for the loans. Thus it is wise to pay for your education as you go, if at all possible. The sacrifices you make now will mean an easier time later. Also, remind yourself that eventually the debt will be cleared and you will still have the earning power of the degree. Try to be creative in looking for ways to make more money and cut expenses. You can find a way.

Conflicts with Family, Friends, and Self

Besides the worrisome financial concerns, family and friends may be envious, fearful, or negative when they hear you are going back to school or taking some online classes. Our advice is simply to give them time.

A Lack of Support

Although we all hope the people we care about in our lives will be understanding and encourage our choices, that is not always the case. Consider, though, what those around you may be feeling. People close to you may be fearful of losing you, of being left behind. Reassure them of their importance even though you are focused on other things right now. Some people may not understand your reasons for attending school online. Let them know why it matters to you, or share what you are doing in school and include them when possible. Certain individuals may be unwilling to listen to your reasons or be consoled by your words of reassurance. In these cases, you may have to make the decision to put yourself first.

You may suffer some guilt over the time you spend on school. Realize that you need to adjust your priorities for the situation but you will not be in these circumstances forever. Remind yourself that sometimes you must put yourself first.

Spreading Yourself Too Thin

Between family and work you may have so many conflicting priorities, you are in danger of spreading yourself too thin. The best option is to organize your schedule, set your priorities, and be ready to revisit them occasionally. Be aware that you might well have to give some things up while you are pursuing your degree. But the sacrifices will be worth it. In just 2 to 4 years you can go back to your old routine but with a diploma on the wall!

You will probably feel overwhelmed sometimes. Most adults have busy, full lives before they ever add school to the equation. Just remember to take it one day or one project at a time. Do not facilitate your own stress. Recognize the need to plan your time wisely. Explore what might be easy, or sensible, for you to give up. Do your best, but admit that you cannot be perfect at everything.

Keep Your Spirits Up

You may have a hard time just envisioning that you will ever succeed at this new endeavor. But you can change this negative self-perception. If you lack confidence, focus on celebrating small successes: the submission of your first assignment or a compliment from a classmate or instructor. Use a journal to track your incremental improvements and successes.

Be sure not to set yourself up for failure. Make reasonable goals, do not procrastinate, manage your stress, and beware of taking too many classes at once. If you are haunted by the past, you have to move beyond it. For instance, if you dropped out of school or failed a course before, give yourself permission to try again now. Do your best to live in the present.

Michael Jordan once said, "I missed 100% of the shots I never took." This is a new situation, and you are different. Give yourself a chance to change and grow.

Reaching Goals Means Setting Goals

The most successful people are those who set goals—for their career, for their self-development, and for their personal life. Goals are established first for the future 3 years or more, and then broken into smaller chunks.

Studies show that articulating significant goals leads to an increase in a person's effort and thus success (Hamner & Harnet, 1974; Locke, 1968). Further, this success leads to higher self-esteem, which contributes to future success!

Setting goals is critical, and here are some questions to consider: First, why are you setting a goal? Is your goal a personal one, a performance goal for the course, or a long-term goal, such as completing your degree?

Think about a day when you woke up and had no idea of what you wanted to accomplish. Did you accomplish anything? More often than not, the answer to that question is no. Explore what you want: Is it earning an A, reaching for a better work/life balance, or just improving your participation in class? Then divide each goal into smaller, more immediately manageable parts and plan how you will attain each one. You may feel more comfortable setting mostly short-term goals or you may prefer to take the long view, but whatever you do, have goals.

Have you ever ended a day after completing all your goals and felt fantastic and invigorated? If the answer is yes, it is probably because you accomplished your goals that you felt successful.

Steps in Goal Setting

When setting a goal, follow the SMART model: *S*pecific, *M*easurable, *A*ttainable, *R*ealistic, and *T*imely. For example, you have set the goal of *acquiring an education* or you would not be in school.

Let's apply the SMART model to that goal:

Goal:	Acquiring an education
Specific:	Gaining an associate's degree within 2 years of beginning a program
Measurable:	Will be measured if within 2 years the degree is complete
Attainable:	Do you have the resources in place to pursue this goal?
Realistic:	Is this a realistic goal at this time in your life, given what you have going on?
Timely:	Two years is normally what would be required to complete an associate's degree, so this is a realistic time frame.

The preceding list outlined a long-term goal. Now break the goal into smaller parts:

Goal: Finish 30 credits my first year (you fill in the following sections)
Specific:
Measurable:
Attainable:
Realistic:
Timely:

Now let's break the goal into smaller sections:

Goal: Finish my first class within 3 months
Specific:
Measurable:
Attainable:
Realistic:
Timely:

Finally, *even more* specifically:

Goal: Finish my first class within 3 months with a grade of no less than a B.
Specific:
Measurable:
Attainable:
Realistic:
Timely:

Here's the bottom line: You know how you eat an elephant; one bite at a time. Set your goals, determine the reasons for them, and then establish manageable subgoals.

When each of us started our academic programs, we had no idea if we could complete them. But we were motivated and we set goals. Each of us decided we would complete one class at a time. And here we are, finished with the programs.

For more information on setting goals, do an online search for *SMART* and *goal setting.* Many wonderful resources are available to you.

Journaling as a Tool for Success

Journaling has a long history. People from generations ago recorded their experiences and thoughts over time. Archived journals have made it possible for us to tap into the experiences of others and learn firsthand about the past. The literature is convincing about the many advantages to journaling as a personal strategy for success

(Baikie & Wilhelm, 2005) as well as an educational strategy for success (Kerka, 1996). Many schools have even made journaling a requirement of the curriculum.

Journaling can be an important tool for you throughout your career as a student and beyond. Remember, there is no right or wrong way to journal, no particular format or style.

Although many people associate a pen and paper with journaling, you can record your voice on a tape recorder as your journal or type a document on your computer. Find the method that is most comfortable for you. The more at ease you feel with the way you have chosen to journal, the simpler it will be to express your thoughts, feelings, and opinions freely.

We do recommend some type of system where thoughts are recorded somewhere tangible. Thinking is essential, of course, but exporting these thoughts to another format constitutes true journaling.

Reasons for Journaling

Journaling can be constructive in numerous ways.

1. *A method of recording your experiences for later reference.* As you continue through your online education, journaling can help you remember the highlights of your student experiences, so you can go back and reread them for motivation and encouragement.

    You can track what you did that worked best for you in your classes, so you can use those strategies again. Document what did not work out well for you too, so you can learn from those experiences and avoid them.

2. *A tool for problem solving.* You can use journaling as a strategy to problem-solve. You can explore your concerns regarding school by journaling, so you can become aware of, and possibly overcome, those obstacles.

3. *A stress-management strategy.* Lastly, journaling is an excellent tool for managing stress. Studies show that taking the time to express your thoughts and feelings in a journal not only makes it easier to process things that happen, but it also helps people deal more effectively with stressful situations.

So use journaling as a method to learn from your experiences and explore your thoughts, rather than merely as a way to track the bad things that happen to you or to express negative thoughts. Writing with a focused goal in mind will be more beneficial than just random jottings.

Another part of the whole concept of journaling is self-reflection. You may like to exercise and think, or drive and think, or ride a horse and think. In a sense, reflection is part of the journaling process, but you have to take it one step further and solidify these thoughts surging in your mind into a permanent format. One of your authors says she thinks things through while on her morning run. As her endorphins flow, her mind gets going. When she returns home, she quickly journals the ideas, thoughts, and revelations she had while she was jogging.

Simply put, journaling is a powerful tool that can help you take concepts, thoughts, and ideas and make them more tangible and thus more useful to you. Journaling is a great technique simply to learn more about yourself. It is one of the best ways to fully explore your new identity as a student, uncover the reasons you became a student, learn about your motivators as a student, and become a more efficient student.

For more in-depth information on types of journals and how journaling can help everyone from chronic pain sufferers to adult students, do an Internet search with the phrase *benefits journaling*, and peruse the results.

Freewriting

Freewriting is a form of journaling. There are many ways and reasons to freewrite; here we focus on freewriting as a way to relieve stress, encourage relaxation in your life, and find inspiration.

To use freewriting to help yourself de-stress, visualize a place that makes you feel relaxed. It can be anywhere. Paint a vivid picture in your mind of how this soothing place looks, smells, and sounds. Come back to this same place each time you freewrite. Once you have yourself in your tranquil place, begin to write, type, or draw anything that comes into your mind. Your writing does not have to be a complete sentence or picture. Grammar rules need not apply. Jot down anything that pops into your head, even if it is the phrase "I cannot think of what to write." When something new comes into your head, record it. Do not worry about the continuity of your thoughts. Just write, type, or draw. If your writing is too neat and coherent, you probably have not loosened up enough.

Freewriting relieves stress because it helps rid your mind of clutter. Many of the random thoughts that continually bombard you can be recorded during freewriting and unchained from your subconscious. Freewriting should not be forced. Use it to soothe and calm your mind whenever you need it. You will find a sample of a freewriting exercise used to relieve stress and anxiety below.

> Butterflies around the corner.
> Life is an adventure. Rabbits. Cotton
> candy and daffodils. Never ending Mist
> free. Penguins gliding on cherry Ice,
> incredible feelings and not sure what
> to say, rainbow, lasting impressions,
> Helmet, life lessons and papers stacked
> up, obtaining things done in time,
> clock wrench, paper dolls, books, what
> to say next. Harper, what am I doing?
> What is next? Vivid yellow lucid
> dreams and a summer breeze drifting
> with monumental moments—Fear,
> along with excitement!

Freewriting is also an excellent way to find inspiration for problem assignments. You may have been given an assignment you do not quite understand. A beginning step is just to process the information. Begin with a blank sheet of paper or computer screen and then just start writing or typing your thoughts around the subject. Next, do research, and as new ideas come to you, type or write them into the document. If you continue this practice, sooner or later you may have some great ideas available you can use to formulate your paper.

→ MORE POWER TO YOU

Now is your chance to explore this chapter's topics further. Check out the sites listed here. Enjoy expanding your knowledge and *more power to you*!

Goal Setting for Everyone
http://www.mygoals.com/

Study Guides and Strategies (Learning)
http://www.studygs.net/

Journaling for Stress Management
http://stress.about.com/od/generaltechniques/p/
profilejournal.htm

Freewriting
http://www.delmar.edu/engl/instruct/stomlin/
1301int/lessons/process/freewrit.htm

Motivating Yourself
http://www.studygs.net/motivation.htm

If any of these websites are not available or you wish to seek out additional information, we encourage you

to do your own online search. Consider the concepts covered in the chapter that are most important to you, and think of various terms that could be used to describe them. For this chapter, some potential keywords to search include:

staying motivated
setting academic goals
planning personal budget

When searching online, consider different ways to express ideas. Remember to use synonyms and related words. Try phrasing things in different ways. And always review more than the first few pages of search results.

For more specific information on searching online, refer to Chapter 9.

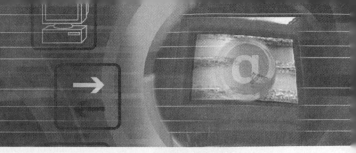

The Commitments of an Online Student: Managing Your Priorities

4

Power Up by:

- Making more time by using your available time wisely.
- Applying time-management techniques such as using a personal calendar, addressing all of your responsibilities, and saying no.
- Avoiding procrastination. Plan ahead, and be aware of how much time it will take to do something. Don't wait until the last minute.
- Knowing when to ask for help. Realize that sometimes the best option is to reach out to others.
- Recognizing the relationship between stress management and time management. Successfully managing one will help with managing the other.
- Taking responsibility for your own stress level. Recognize your stressors and how you respond, and be aware of the best ways for you to manage stress.
- Surrounding yourself with supportive people.
- Treating yourself as a priority.

At this point in your life, you probably have plenty to keep you busy and active: your family, job, friends, and hobbies. Being an online student will just add one more ingredient to that complicated mix. In the interest of being successful throughout your life, not just at your job or in school, we invite you to explore two concepts: time management and stress management. Having an understanding of both will make it much easier to meet all your commitments and stay sane while doing it!

Time management is a common term, but what does it actually mean? For our purposes, time management means

- Knowing how much time you have.
- Knowing how much time it takes to complete different tasks.
- Knowing how to manipulate circumstances to fit your obligations into the time you have.

Overall, it means making *more* time by using the time you have wisely. You can adjust your schedule in different ways. For instance, you can use time in waiting rooms and while commuting. You can get up earlier or go to bed later.

Procrastination is another common term, but it means more than just waiting until the last minute. It also implies not planning ahead and not recognizing how much time it will take to do something. Do not wait until Saturday to start a paper due Monday. If you have a question but your instructor does not have weekend office hours, you will be stuck! Time management and procrastination are not just relevant to school. They can impact all aspects of your life. To be efficient and effective in anything you do, *avoid procrastination and practice good time management.*

The tendency to procrastinate is magnified even more in an online environment because you do not have to go to class and run the risk of being humiliated if your work is not done. You can just not submit a paper and, although your faculty member may contact you, no one else will know. This situation can also occur when it comes to participation. If you delay participating, no one will notice but you and your instructor. Imagine a snowball rolling downhill, however. It becomes bigger and more out of control the further downhill it goes. So avoid procrastination and set yourself up for success.

Avoiding Procrastination

How to avoid procrastination is fairly simple to summarize but a bit harder to actually do. Here are some steps to take:

- Plan ahead.
- Be aware of how you are actually spending your time.
- Recognize of how long things take to complete in real time.
- Do not put obligations off until the last minute.

Knowing your strengths and weaknesses can also be constructive in fighting procrastination. You may want to review that section now, with an eye toward how your preferences and strong and weak areas affect the way you plan your time.

Managing Your Time Successfully

Time management is a bit more complex because there are many considerations and no specific formula exists. Everyone has to evaluate his or her personal situation and abilities and figure out what works best.

Answering All of Your Responsibilities

Most everyone today has to juggle commitments. Ideally, you can make a single schedule for how your day or week or month will go and stick to it, but, in reality, new commitments arise and events are cancelled or reprioritized. The picture is constantly changing.

Not everything is within your control, which can make it difficult to stick to your initial plan. So you will need to constantly prioritize and reprioritize to adapt to the changing nature of your obligations over time. For instance, if you have a big work project due one week, you should anticipate not having as much time to devote to school during that period. You will also need to take responsibility for those decisions.

Using a Personal Calendar

Creating your own personalized calendar can be a helpful tool for tracking and managing your responsibilities, showing you how your personal, professional, and school life overlap. The most successful person has one calendar that shows *all* of his or her obligations and plans. This technique can enable you to manage your life much more effectively. You can use a day planner, a wall or desk calendar, Microsoft Outlook, your PDA, or whatever works for you. The important thing is not *how* you track the demands on your time but that you *do* track them.

To find more information and tools on time management, do a Web search on *time management* and *time management tools*.

Saying No

People often have a problem saying no to others, but it is OK to say no gracefully and for a good reason. No one wins when you accept a responsibility you know you cannot fulfill or when you realize you will not be able to meet an obligation but you do not speak up. Saying no is not about being cruel, unresponsive, or a slacker; rather it is about being honest and effective. Now that you are in school, the need to say no may arise more frequently than before because you have more commitments.

When It Is Necessary

When you are beginning to feel out of control or overwhelmed or when you *know* you will not be able to perform a task, it may be time to consider saying no. Be realistic about your abilities and your obligations! Tune in to your own feelings and be aware of your commitments, as well as your stress levels, and try to judge your capabilities fairly.

Realize that sometimes, even when you might want to say no, it is just not possible. Distinguish between those times when it is a viable option and when it is not.

How to Say It

Saying no is not about making excuses, throwing fits, or avoiding guilt. Do not beat around the bush. Say no gracefully and succinctly. Do not list all the reasons for your refusal. Be brief, reasonable, and calm, and realize your refusal will not make the world crumble. Be direct and apologetic. If you can suggest alternative solutions that might help the situation, that's even better. Do your best to make the situation as painless as possible for those affected by your actions.

Be Confident in Deciding to Say *No*

If you determine that saying no is justified, do not second-guess yourself. Own your no! Don't agonize over whether it was the right decision after it is done. Your refusal to do something might not be painless, but it should free you to address other, more important obligations with a clear mind and conscience. It is easier to make decisions and move forward if people are honest about what they can and cannot do. Saying no is not about getting you off the hook or shirking responsibility. The goal in being honest about when you need to say no is to help improve efficiency, to avoid letting yourself or others down.

Like so many of the concepts discussed in this book, knowing when and how to say no can benefit you as much out of school as in class. With regard to the online classroom, knowing when to say no can be an essential skill for working in project teams. For instance, if you will be unable to complete part of a team project, you should speak up as soon as you realize it, so the team can make other arrangements. Perhaps you can trade with another team member to work on a part that is due later.

Conversely, outside the classroom, if you have overscheduled yourself and you find you must cancel lunch with a friend in order to complete an assignment, tell the person as soon as you realize it. Be forthright and apologetic, but honest. Try to reschedule for a more suitable time. If money is an issue, perhaps you can offer to cook dinner. If you can come up with an attractive trade-off for those you would otherwise be letting down, then do so.

The Frequency of Saying *No*

Knowing when and how to say no is key, and it is also important to recognize how often you are making refusals. If you find yourself doing it a lot, there is a bigger problem. Step back and take stock of what is going on. Are you overscheduling yourself? Are you being unrealistic about how long tasks really take to complete? Are you procrastinating? Are you a people pleaser who says yes to everything and then realizes you cannot possibly do it all? Be honest. You can save yourself a lot of trouble by saying no at the beginning, rather than saying yes and then changing your mind.

Look at your schedule and consider your true feelings about your obligations. It is acceptable to back out of a commitment or opt to say no occasionally for a good reason, but if you are making a habit of it, watch out! Respect others and yourself by being realistic and honest about your responsibilities and capabilities.

Asking for Help

Sometimes the online environment can be confusing. Instructors don't always consider what it is like to be a student, and so they may not always supply the right information or adequate instructions to guide you through assigned tasks. Or maybe you just need more details on what is expected. Asking for help can often move you past a hurdle, so you can continue to accomplish all the goals on your learning path. Asking for help has much in common with saying no. You need to consider the following factors.

When It Is Appropriate

Of course, you never want to abuse help by asking for it all the time without trying to think a challenge through on your own first. But if you have struggled with the problem and repeatedly hit a wall, it is time to ask for someone else's input or guidance.

You also want to make sure you do not wait until the last minute to ask for help because other people have tight schedules too. You do not know how long it will take someone to respond to your request, so poor planning ahead of time may really put you behind. This is another reason it is always wise to avoid procrastination and start on your assignments right away. Then if you run up against any roadblocks and need to ask for help, there will be adequate time.

Make the Request the Right Way

As with saying no, be polite but also detailed and direct. Ask nicely and let the other person know you have tried to figure it out on your own first. If someone is going to help you, he or she needs to know exactly where you are stuck and what solutions you have already tried.

Also remember that asking for help is often reciprocal. Consider people studying together. It is often at the request of one person who needs help understanding course concepts, but when two people study together they usually both end up with a clearer understanding of the subject matter. If you ask someone for help, it can often mean you may be *giving* help to that person some other time.

Be Comfortable Asking

The largest mistake people make is equating asking for help with weakness. Your commitment to education is a huge obligation, and you are working hard. Sometimes you have exhausted all avenues and the best option is to reach out for some help. So equate being able to request help in appropriate situations with strength.

Analyze Your Requests for Help

Like saying no, monitor how often and why you ask for help. Why do you need help? Did you do all the reading and follow all directions before you asked for help, or are you just looking to others to get you through the hard parts? Learn to rely on yourself and try diverse approaches to solving problems. Are you totally lost in the class? Make sure you enroll in courses that are appropriate for your learning level rather than trying to skip out of lower-level courses. Are there certain subjects where you always have trouble and know you will need help? You might want to let your instructor know beforehand, so he or she can suggest any relevant resources or supports that the school provides.

Stress Management

Some stress can be productive. It motivates you and makes you sharp. Stress only becomes a problem when it starts impacting your performance negatively.

How is stress management related to time management? Successfully managing your time can help you eliminate stress, and successfully managing your stress can aid you in the effective use of your time. Just as there are lots of methods for managing time, many strategies for managing stress are available too.

We have already mentioned that journaling can be a great reliever of stress. Here are some additional ideas to keep in mind regarding stress management.

Taking Responsibility

Many times we are powerless over the factors that cause stress in our lives, of course, but how we respond to them *is* completely in our control. These three steps will help you take responsibility for your stress:

1. **Recognize *what* stresses you out.** Rush-hour traffic? Having too many commitments at the same time? A screaming child? People who do not listen? Computer problems? There are too many potential stressors in the world to list here. But it would behoove you to pay attention and determine your so-called hot buttons. Just knowing them sometimes decreases their ability to affect you.

2. **Recognize *how* you respond.** What happens when you are stressed? Do you become short-tempered? Tired? Depressed? Do you react similarly to all stressors or differently every time? Know how stress affects you so you can prepare yourself and respond appropriately.

3. **Be aware of the best ways for *you* to manage stress.** What relaxes you? How do you take your mind off your troubles? Exercise, hobbies, spending time alone, journaling, spending time with family/friends, talking it out? Know what helps you release stress. Experiment with new ways occasionally; you might find it helpful to have a variety of methods at your disposal. Know how to fit those therapeutic activities into your schedule. And do it before your stress levels reach the point of desperation!

Surrounding Yourself with Supportive People

Accepting the support of people around you, whether they are friends, relatives, or class-mates, can help you deal with negative experiences. Supportive people can remind you to keep perspective on whatever is bothering you. If you do not already have a strong social network of friends and relations, never fear. Interactions in the online classroom can result in friendships that will last a lifetime. Your classmates are some of your best resources. They can support and commiserate with you, and they know what you are going through like no one else does.

Treating Yourself as a Priority

Part of managing your stress is taking time for yourself so you will be better able to meet your responsibilities. In today's busy world, it is easy to devote every spare moment to work, school, family, and friends. But remember that making yourself a priority can benefit all those other activities as well by helping you become a more relaxed, focused, and productive person.

For those of you who have difficulty finding personal time, review the previous section on saying no. Remember, if you are in a positive state of mind, you are more likely to be productive as well as receptive to learning.

→ MORE POWER TO YOU

Now is your chance to explore this chapter's topics further. Check out the sites listed here. Enjoy expanding your knowledge and *more power to you!*

Developing a Schedule
http://www.studygs.net/schedule/

Avoiding Procrastination
http://www.studygs.net/attmot3.htm

Home-Work Life Balance
http://www.organizedassistant.com/article/Article/
Reclaiming-Self—Making-Time-For-Yourself/66

Learning to Say No and Mean It
http://www.confidenceworld.com/members2/work7.htm

If any of these websites are not available or you wish to seek out additional information, we encourage you to do your own online search. Consider the concepts covered in the chapter that are most important to you, and think of various terms that could be used to describe them. For this chapter, some potential keywords to search include:

avoid procrastination

time management

stress management

When searching online, consider different ways to express ideas. Remember to use synonyms and related words. Try phrasing things in different ways. And always review more than the first few pages of search results.

For more specific information on searching online, refer to Chapter 9.

The Online Classroom and Community

5

Power Up by:

- Knowing your instructor is the subject-matter expert. Contact your instructor for issues directly related to the specific class.

- Recognizing that online learning can mean exposure to a wide range of people from all over the world, from every age group, gender, and background. You can potentially learn as much from your classmates as you do from the instructor.

- Recognizing that it is worthwhile to read other people's postings. It will enable you to learn what their personalities are like and what you might have in common.

- Knowing what venue is appropriate for various types of communication in your classroom.

- Acknowledging that you will probably be assigned to project teams quite often during the course of your online education.

- Initiating contact with your team members and clarifying the roles, responsibilities, and expectations right away.

- Understanding you should contact your advisor for any concerns relevant to your program, schedule, or faculty member.

- Identifying the role and contact information for the tech support department, and understanding you should contact tech support only for specific problems involving the online system of the course.

- Taking the time to explore your institution's website, or virtual campus, and see what it offers.

When we say the "online classroom and community," who exactly are we talking about? The foremost members of your online classroom are obvious: you, your fellow classmates, and your instructor. In some cases there may also be a teaching assistant or other types of specialized positions such as peer tutors or course assistants. The members of your online classroom include anyone who is in your first line of contact for the course.

What exactly your online community is may be a bit hazier. The members of this community can include all those individuals just mentioned in addition to the dedicated resources available from your school but outside your classroom. People such as advisors, program chairs, and librarians, as well as individuals and groups from the wide world of the Internet, can be resources for you.

For each of these groups, let's look at who they are, what you might expect from them, and when it is appropriate to contact them.

Your Instructor

Instructor, teacher, professor, facilitator—whatever term is used to identify him or her, this person is the subject-matter expert who will lead you through the course material and give you direction regarding what is expected and what resources are available to you.

Depending on the requirements of the school, your instructor probably has at least a master's degree in a subject relevant to the teaching topic, if not a PhD or other type of doctorate/terminal degree (EdD, DBA, DM, JD). In the online environment, instructors generally post a brief biography, as well as virtual office hours when they are available for communication, and their specific course policies. Information about instructor availability and other resources should be clearly stated. You will need to explore your online classroom thoroughly. Do not be afraid to ask questions prior to enrolling in an institution, and if you do not like the answers, consider looking for another school.

Beware of coming to your online classroom with the expectation that the instructor's role will mirror what you have experienced in other classrooms, online or on-ground. Instructor roles can vary quite a lot in the online environment, by individual instructor as well as by institution. Some instructors see themselves more as guides and mentors, willing to converse with you at length. Others are only available to students for specific, limited concerns, and depending on the school, there may be other people whose role it is to respond to your questions or problems, such as learning assistants, preceptors, or course coordinators.

When to Contact Your Instructor

Communication with your instructor depends on the boundaries he or she sets. In general, it is safe to assume that, unless otherwise stated, you can contact your instructor for any of your questions regarding the course content, assignments, and activities. Whenever you do not understand a concept in the reading or discussion, or expectations are not clear regarding assignments, grading standards, or due dates, do not hesitate to contact your instructor. If you are having a problem on your project team or having personal problems that affect your class performance, contact your instructor as soon as possible to minimize misunderstandings.

For course scheduling, graduation requirements, or computer problems, your instructor is *not* the appropriate resource. Who is depends on how the school organizes its online academic and administrative departments. You might be able to ask your instructor where you can turn in these situations, but do not expect the instructor to address them.

You are responsible for exploring those other resources. It's a good practice to find out ahead of time, so you are not caught in a bind. While you are exploring the online class, put together a course contact list and keep it close at hand.

Response Time

How quickly should you expect your instructors to respond to your questions? It can vary per institution, but find out by asking them what to expect or by posing an actual question. Some instructors adhere very strictly to their scheduled office hours; others are more flexible. Some respond immediately to every message, whereas others may take hours or even days to get in touch with you. Be willing to follow up; never be satisfied with not receiving a response. If your instructor does not respond or does not show up to class, contact an advisor or administrator at the school and apprise them of the situation.

Finally, know what venue is appropriate for various types of communication in your classroom. Many instructors have a space in the online course specifically for posting questions about the class, so all students will see their answers. If your classroom does not have such a space, e-mail may be the most viable option. Explore your online classroom to figure it out.

Do not ask about grades in a public forum.

Your Classmates

Your classmates are an obvious and easy resource for you to consult. Do not be afraid to lean on them for support.

When you have a question you believe is too foolish or obvious to pose to your instructor, or if you just need minor clarification, or even if you are just curious to know what others think, turning to your fellow students is the simple solution. And if you need someone to commiserate with you over the difficulty of an assignment, no one is more appropriate than one of your classmates. You may end up learning almost as much from your classmates as you do from your instructor. Your classmates come from different backgrounds and can provide a wealth of resources and knowledge. Their varying perspectives and learning styles can give you insight into the course content that you might not otherwise discover.

Do not be intimidated by the variety of people in your classes; online learning can mean a wide range of people from all over the world share your classroom. Engaging with your classmates can lead to lifelong friendships.

Read other people's postings to become acquainted with their personalities and see what you might have in common. You will probably be able to tell from the way people introduce themselves and respond to the discussion questions who will be the best ones to ask particular questions. You will discover who is serious and knowledgeable, who is more lighthearted and relaxed. What type of question you have or interaction you are looking for will determine which one of your classmates you wish to engage. There also may be times when you want to pose a query to the entire class to gain a wide variety of answers.

The rules and regulations for contacting your fellow students are in no way as structured and definite as those for other parties in the online community, so do talk to your classmates when you feel the urge. Of more concern is the *where/how* of the communication. Do not start personal conversations in class areas dedicated to specific tasks or questions. Usually there will be a lounge or other chat area set aside in the online classroom where students can communicate more casually with one another. E-mail is always an option too.

Your Project Teams

Because project teams are a subset of your classmates, the same information just described applies to them, just within a narrower scope. Project teams are typically formed to address larger assignments, so students can share expertise and abilities, support each other in their learning, and produce synergy through the collaboration. Some research suggests that depending on the individual and the group situation, people may learn more when they work in groups (Rowland, Lederhouse, & Satterfield, 2004). They learn more about the subject matter, as well as gaining team skills. Virtual teams are also commonplace in the working world, so working in this way in the classroom will help you be effective under similar circumstances at your job. You will probably be assigned to project teams quite often during the course of your online education.

The question that always arises regarding project teams is "How is it possible to work in teams online?" But there is every reason for it to work! You have classmates who are your potential team members. You have virtual meeting rooms. You have many ways in which to dialogue, such as chat rooms, Instant Messenger, and e-mail. You are offered even more flexibility to meet with your team than in a face-to-face environment. All of these options make team interaction not only possible but equally as productive as it is in the on-ground environment.

Project teams are usually created by breaking a class into several subgroups. The number of people on a team may vary. Sometimes an instructor takes care to ensure that teams include members of differing experience or expertise or that members are in close time zones, to facilitate working together. You will be responsible for helping your team run smoothly and succeed.

If you are on a project team, a percentage of your grade will be based on the team's work, and sometimes that may be significant. You may be graded on a project as a whole, and sometimes team members grade one another anonymously on their group participation. So be proactive whenever you are assigned to a team. Take the following steps:

1. Initiate contact with your team members as soon as they are identified.
2. Make sure you all have a common understanding of the requirements for the project.

3. Start clarifying individual roles, responsibilities, and expectations right away.

4. Set up a timeline for achieving the project milestones that allows you to progress reasonably toward the final due date.

Communication is key for virtual teamwork. We will say it again: Be sure to contact your team members as soon as you are grouped together, and keep up communication throughout the project. Because you have a designated reason to be in contact with them, and you have built rapport, often team members can be great resources for other questions you have about the course. As with the rest of your education, the difference between a successful team experience and a miserable one is often in the planning and preparation. Be sure to spend adequate time early on to clarify roles and expectations.

Your Advisor

Your instructor is there to help you with issues relevant to the course, and your classmates can provide personal support. However, your advisor is the one to consult for questions on scheduling classes, financial aid, or issues with a faculty member.

Do not ask your instructor about your next start date, and do not ask your advisor how to gain extra credit. Determine whose job it is to address which specific concerns (in the case of the example noted here, the answers are the opposites). You will gather answers more easily, and the various people who are your resources will thank you for not wasting their time. Because your advisor is a resource outside the classroom, you will ordinarily communicate by e-mail.

Tech Support

Tech support is the general term for the department of people dedicated to keeping the computer systems for the school up and running smoothly. You will most likely communicate with tech support personnel by e-mail or phone.

Take note of the telephone number for tech support and their hours of operation. Not all schools have technical experts available 24/7, so find out exactly when you can contact them. You might find it helpful to know their busiest times (e.g., Sunday afternoons, before classes start up on a Monday). Service will probably be delayed during those periods.

Recognize when it is appropriate to contact tech support and when it is not. Call tech support if you cannot access your course, if links or buttons in your course are not functioning, or if there seem to be technical problems with the course system.

Tech support is generally *not* there to help you format a document, understand a software application, or solve your hard drive problems. In most cases, tech support should never be used as an excuse for why you didn't submit an assignment. If downtimes are scheduled for certain systems, students are generally informed ahead of time, and you will be expected to take that into consideration and work around it.

Other School Resources

Just as you would explore the traditional campus of your school if you were there, take the time to check out your institution's website, or virtual campus, and see what it offers. Here are some initial areas to investigate:

- Does the school have an online bookstore? If so, what are the policies regarding ordering and shipping books? If not, where should you acquire course materials?

- What kind of learning support is available? Are there tutorials, learning labs, or a writing center? Are live tutors available for any subject?

- Is there a school library? How do you access it, and what type of assets and aid does it offer?

An online institution often has numerous other virtual resources. Take the time to explore your school and the resources available for each course you take.

→ MORE POWER TO YOU

Now is your chance to explore this chapter's topics further. Check out the sites listed here. Enjoy expanding your knowledge and *more power to you*!

Instructional Strategies for Online Courses
http://www.ion.uillinois.edu/resources/tutorials/pedagogy/instructionalstrategies.asp

Tools, Tips, and Software Online
http://www.librarysupportstaff.com/ed4you.html#usetools

Back to School
http://adulted.about.com/cs/backtoschool/a/reentry_tips_2.htm

Six Ways to Work More Effectively with a Virtual Team
http://www.microsoft.com/atwork/worktogether/virtual.mspx

Cooperative Learning
http://www.studygs.net/cooplearn.htm

If any of these websites are not available or you wish to seek out additional information, we encourage you to do your own online search. Consider the concepts covered in the chapter that are most important to you, and think of various terms that could be used to describe them. For this chapter, some potential keywords to search include:

virtual work teams
building successful teams

When searching online, consider different ways to express ideas. Remember to use synonyms and related words. Try phrasing things in different ways. And always review more than the first few pages of search results.

For more specific information on searching online, refer to Chapter 9.

online

hybrid

on-ground

Types of Online Classrooms

6

 Power Up by:

- Knowing that the term LMS (learning management systems) refers to software programs that organize and provide access to online learning services for students, teachers, and administrators.

- Recognizing that most LMSs share many of the same elements, although they may be organized differently.

- Understanding that your school may have its own proprietary LMS specifically designed for the faculty and students at your institution.

- Identifying the common areas of all online classrooms.

- Taking the time to explore and navigate your school's LMS before your class starts.

All the content created for you as an online student has to be stored and delivered. *Learning management systems (LMSs)* are software programs that organize and provide access to onlinelearning services for students, teachers, and administrators. Typically, an LMS provides an instructor or other school agent with a way to create and deliver content, monitor student participation, and track student performance. An LMS may also give students the ability to use interactive features such as threaded discussions, video conferencing, and discussion forums. Although LMSs differ in presentation and programming, the Advanced Distance Learning Group, sponsored by the U.S. Department of Defense, has created a set of specifications called Shareable Content Object Reference Model (SCORM) to encourage the standardization of learning management systems (www.bytepile.com/definitions-l.php). As a result, many of the mainstream LMSs for the postsecondary (college) market are SCORM compliant.

Some institutions create their own proprietary LMSs, but most take advantage of the range of products on the market. The most common LMSs that universities and colleges use today are Blackboard, eCollege®, Moodle, and ANGEL®. Your school's LMS is probably one of these.

This chapter describes the most common LMSs and offers some tips on using them successfully. Even if your school has created its own LMS, many of the same organizational principles and properties still apply.

What to Expect in Your Online Classroom

Regardless of the LMS used, the online classroom usually contains the following basic areas:

- Classroom announcements
- Academic discussion, where discussion questions are posted
- Course content materials and information are available
- Assignments and assessments
- A chat room, lounge, or other virtual location for socializing with classmates
- Resources related to the course content, such as web links and articles

When you take a course using any of the LMSs mentioned, you might be asked to view multimedia material. So before you start, check with your school and/or instructor to find out what software to install on your computer. Examples of this software may include, but are not limited to, the following:

- Adobe Reader (free download at http://www.adobe.com/products/acrobat/readstep2.html)
- Adobe FlashPlayer (free download at http://www.adobe.com/shockwave/download)
- Quicktime Player (free download at http://www.apple.com/quicktime/download/win.html)

- Real Player (free download at http://www.real.com/)
- Microsoft Office
- Corel WordPerfect Office
- Open Office (free download at http://www.openoffice.org/; this software reads, writes, and converts Microsoft Office documents)

Common Platforms for Online Classes

Next we describe the most common LMSs, along with their features and some screen shots. Take this opportunity to familiarize yourself ahead of time with the LMS you will be using. It will make your orientation with the class and its landscape that much easier. The information here is only preliminary, so visit the website for your LMS and read more or complete a tutorial on the program.

Moodle

The Moodle LMS supports the following features (for more detailed information, you may want to visit www.moodle.org):

- Assignments
- Chat (supports images)
- Quiz
- Gradebook
- News
- Calendar
- Resources (external links, etc.)
- Syllabus
- Announcements
- Discussion forum
- Course evaluations
- Journal
- Survey
- Glossary
- Wiki (shared, modifiable content page)
- Blogs (unedited news or comments)
- RSS feeds (frequently updated digital content)
- LMS Support (Moodle Help Desk)

Before you start a course, always check to see what features are available in *your* Moodle LMS.

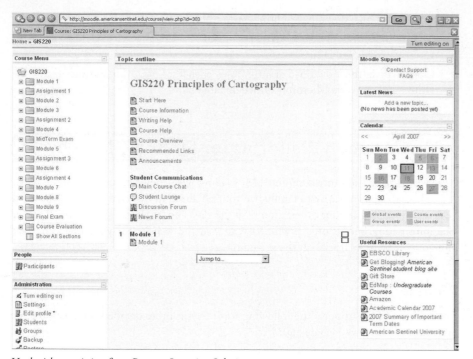

Used with permission from Pearson Learning Solutions.

The image above represents a sample course home page in Moodle. The course you take may look a little different. This course home page includes a navigation block, a link to th.abus, instructor notes, course announcements, and a course calendar.

Moodle is distributed to schools as "open source" software, which means there is no standard student interface. It is completely customizable for a school and its faculty members, so this snapshot of Moodle serves as a model of what a course *can* look like, but the course you take might vary.

Because Moodle is customizable, all the features available are not necessarily used for every class, so be aware of the possible features available.

Moodle provides three standard options for the setup of the course: activities arranged by week, activities arranged by topic, or a discussion-focused social format. Your course will probably be organized in one of these three ways.

You can view discussions by date, by thread, or by author. Your posts in the classroom can include attachments, an image, or a URL. The discussion tool includes a formatting text editor. Posts may be peer-reviewed by your fellow students. A student may receive posts to the discussion forums as daily digests of subject lines or whole posts as e-mail. You can subscribe to forum RSS (Really Simple Syndication) feeds, chunks of information based on preferences you submit.

The hardware requirements for Moodle include a basic personal computer running a standard operating system and a stable Internet connection. Moodle requires a browser supporting HTML 3.0 or higher (Microsoft Internet Explorer, Netscape 7.1 or higher, Mozilla Firefox 1.5 or higher).

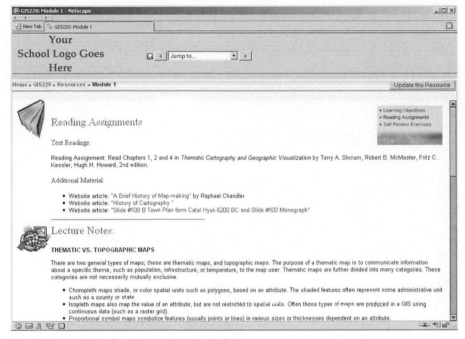

Used with permission from Pearson Learning Solutions.

The image above illustrates a sample Moodle lesson page. A lesson is called a *topic* or *weekly* in Moodle. Because Moodle is open source, the format of the lesson pages varies widely. You can expect to find within a lesson an overview, lesson objectives, reading assignments, lecture notes, and review exercises. Assignments and tests are handled separately. Whether or not a final proctored exam is required depends on the school offering the course. Always check before you start a course to see if a proctored exam is required and, if so, where it will be administered.

Take a few hours to explore all the parts of the course, including lessons, assignments, and lectures. Spending the time up front to figure out what is in the course and where it is located will pay off later on.

ANGEL®

The next image represents a sample course home page in ANGEL®. The content in each course you take will be slightly different, but the basic layout of the ANGEL® interface is relatively standard. The screen shot shows what you will see after you log on.

The ANGEL® LMS supports the following features (for more detailed information, you may want to visit www.angellearning.com):

- Assignments
- Student lounge (chat)
- Quizzes
- Gradebook

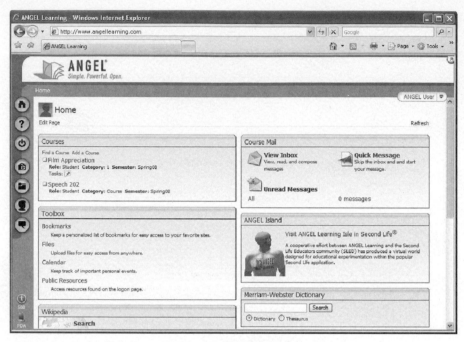

Used with permission from Dr. Pamela Lawhead and ANGEL®.

- News
- Calendar
- Internal e-mail
- File exchange (with virus detection technology)
- Whiteboard
- Bookmarks
- Search (course content or classmates)
- Ability to work offline
- Group work
- Community networking
- Student portfolio
- Resources (external links, etc.)
- Syllabus
- Announcements
- Discussion forum
- Journal
- Glossary
- External links
- Polls

- Dictionary/thesaurus
- Student personal setting
- Multiple display options (frames/no frames/PDA)

The hardware requirements to run ANGEL® include a basic personal computer running a standard Windows or Macintosh operating system and a stable Internet connection. ANGEL® requires a standard browser (Microsoft Internet Explorer 6.0 or higher, Netscape 7.0 or higher, Mozilla Firefox 1.0 or higher).

ANGEL® allows offline work, allowing the instructor to put the course on CD-ROM for students who may not have regular access to the Internet. The course can be accessed and then viewed offline, or students have the option of downloading it.

Students and instructors have their own personal folders in ANGEL® where they store all of their class work. The folders can be edited using a browser. Assignments are submitted using drop boxes. You can upload files to a shared course or group folder and download all the contents of a folder at one time. You can share the contents of your personal folders with other students and the instructor. A virus detection technology can be used throughout the file upload/download process, which protects files within the program.

The image below illustrates a sample ANGEL® lesson page. Within a lesson you can expect to find an overview, lesson objectives, reading assignments, lecture notes, and review exercises. In ANGEL® the lesson often might be a link to a multimedia presentation such as PowerPoint slides, video, or audio. The content and delivery of the instructional presentation is left entirely to the instructor creating the course.

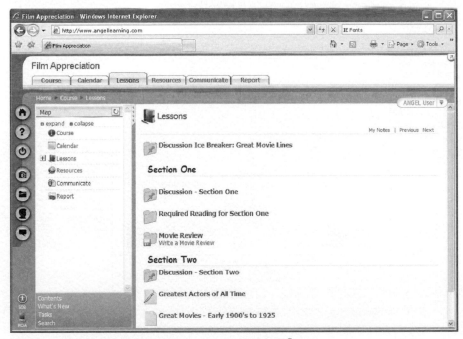

Used with permission from Dr. Pamela Lawhead and ANGEL®.

Assignments and tests may be handled separately. Whether or not a proctored exam is required depends on the school offering the course. Always check before you start a course to see if a proctored exam is required and, if so, where it will be administered.

Note: The instructor for this course has placed links to all materials necessary for the completion of the lesson in the Lessons tab. The tabs at the top of the lesson remain fixed for all lessons in all courses. Navigation through the course is available in the left-most frame of the screen, which can be toggled into or out of view.

eCollege®

The next image represents a sample course home page in eCollege®. The type of content in each course is proprietary LMS content delivered through eCollege.com. Like other proprietary LMS packages, the user interface is standardized across installations. The course you take may have different graphic elements with various selectable color schemes, but navigation through the course is standard.

The eCollege® LMS supports the following features (for more detailed information, you may want to visit www.ecollege.com):

■ Announcements

■ Assignments

■ Calendar

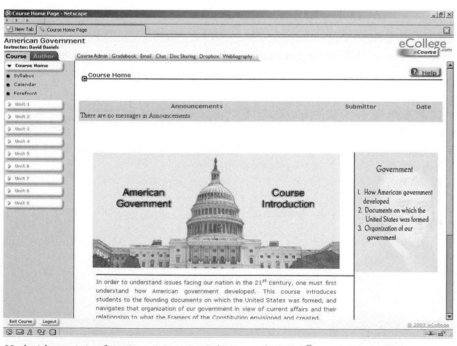

Used with permission from Pearson Learning Solutions and eCollege®.

- Chat
- ClassLive (synchronous communication interaction with whiteboard/chat/audio)
- Document sharing (with virus detection technology)
- Drop box (for assignment delivery and grading)
- E-mail
- Glossary
- Gradebook
- Group work
- Internal e-mail
- Journal
- Lecture (course content)
- Quizzes
- Review
- Syllabus
- Tasks
- Threaded discussion
- Webliography (possible external links)

Students can download discussion group content into a format that can be printed or stored locally, as well as synchronize their address book and calendar events with a PDA (personal digital assistant). Instructors can publish course content on a CD-ROM for students who do not have Internet access. Instructors can also publish course content on a CD-ROM that can be linked dynamically from within the online course. Instructors can record synchronous sessions so students can review them asynchronously at a later time.

ECollege® has an internal e-mail option. Students can use the e-mail feature to e-mail individuals and groups. Students can attach files and spell-check outgoing messages. They can also use a searchable address book to e-mail individuals and groups.

The chat tool supports private rooms and private messages. The system creates archive logs for all chat rooms. Instructors can schedule chats using the course calendar. The chat tool supports unlimited simultaneous group discussions.

In an eCollege® course, students have access to personal online calendars where they can track all their assignments, deadlines, and due dates. Students can view their grades on completed assignments and any instructor feedback, including total points earned, total points possible and percentages per unit, and overall course grade.

The software includes support for discussion forums. Discussions can be viewed by date, by thread, by author, by group, and by topics defined by the instructor. Instructors can associate a discussion with any course content. Instructors may create separate discussion environments for small groups. Instructors can limit discussions to specific time periods. Only the instructor may delete posts, which can include attachments, images, or URLs. The entire discussion can be saved or printed for offline reading. Discussion threads are expandable and collapsible to view an entire conversation on one screen.

Students can submit assignments using drop boxes and can upload files to a shared course or group folder. Students can share the contents of their personal folders with their instructors. Instructors can upload files to the personal folder of a student. Virus detection technology is used throughout the file upload/download process.

The hardware requirements to run eCollege® include a basic personal computer running a standard Windows or Macintosh operating system and a stable Internet connection. ECollege® requires Microsoft Internet Explorer 5.5 or greater or Netscape 6.2 or higher. For Macintosh, Microsoft Internet Explorer 5.1 or higher, Netscape 7.1 or higher, or Safari 1.2 is required.

In the process of taking a course in eCollege®, you might be asked to view material written in a word processor format (MS Word, WordPerfect, etc.). You also might be asked to submit materials in this format. So, before you start, make sure you have this type of software installed on your computer.

Whether or not a proctored exam is required depends on the school offering the course. Always check before you start a course to see if a proctored exam is required and where it will be administered.

Blackboard

Before you delve into the details of Blackboard, it is interesting to note how this particular system evolved. Blackboard was initially designed to manage courses in a traditional/ on-ground college environment. It was intended as a tool to replace the massive amount of paper used to teach a face-to-face class and to provide students with constant feedback regarding their progress in the class, rather than being initially designed to serve as a wholly online course method like most LMSs.

The next image represents a sample course home page in Blackboard. The type of content in each course differs, but the basic layout of the Blackboard interface is relatively standard across implementations. The screen shot here is what you see after you log on.

The Blackboard LMS supports the following (for more detailed information, you may want to visit www.blackboard.com):

- Address book
- Announcements
- Assignments
- Calendar
- Collaboration
- Digital drop box (student upload)
- Discussion board
- Electric blackboard
- Glossary
- Gradebook

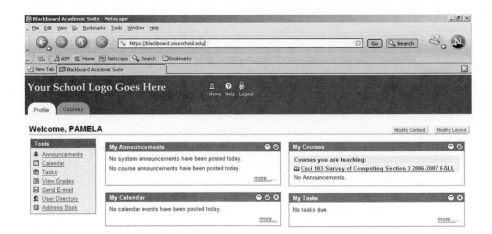

Used with permission from Dr. Pamela Lawhead and Blackboard.

- Group pages
- Messages (internal e-mail)
- Quizzes
- Resources (external links, etc.)
- Roster
- Student home page
- Surveys
- Syllabus
- Tasks

The Java-based chat tool supports unlimited simultaneous group discussions and private messages. Instructors may moderate chats and suspend students from the chat rooms. The system creates archive logs for all chat rooms. Instructors can view chat logs and share these with students.

Discussions can be viewed by date and by thread. Instructors can associate a discussion with any course content. They can enable or disable anonymous postings and determine whether student posts are re-editable after they are first posted. Posts can contain URLs and file attachments, and they may contain HTML. The threaded discussion software includes a formatting text editor that can create mathematic equations.

Instructors may create separate discussion environments for small groups of students and teaching assistants.

Students have a private folder where they can upload and download files, and instructors can upload files to the personal folder of a student. Students can upload files to a shared group folder, as well as submit assignments using drop boxes.

The hardware requirements to run Blackboard include a basic personal computer running a standard Windows or Macintosh operating system and a stable Internet connection. Blackboard requires a standard browser (Windows 2000/Windows XP, Internet Explorer 5.5 or 5.6, or Netscape 6.0 or 7.0; Macintosh OS 9.x/OS X, Internet Explorer 5.0 or 5.1, Netscape 6 or 7, or Safari (Macintosh OS X).

The final image in this chapter illustrates a sample Blackboard assignment page. Within a lesson, you can expect to find an overview, lesson objectives, reading assignments, lecture notes, and review exercises. The content/layout of a lesson can include any activity that is Web viewable. Hence lesson presentation in Blackboard is nonstandard. Access to the content, however, is standard and available only through the "Content" link.

The Blackboard layout is uniform across courses and educational institutions, as are most proprietary LMSs. Whether or not a final proctored exam is required depends on the school offering the course. Always check before you start a course to see if a proctored exam is required and where it will be administered.

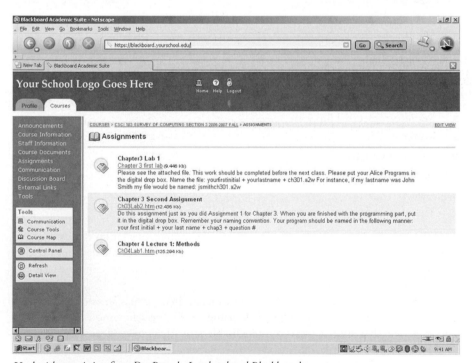

Used with permission from Dr. Pamela Lawhead and Blackboard.

Proprietary Systems

If your school has its own proprietary LMS, take the time to explore and navigate through the LMS *before* your class starts. We recommend at least a few hours to examine the course and all its associated pieces. Find out if there is electronic or printed literature about the school's LMS or if any online tutorials are available. Doing this research ahead of time will help you concentrate on the content of the course itself once class begins.

→ MORE POWER TO YOU

Now is your chance to explore this chapter's topics further. Check out the sites listed here. Enjoy expanding your knowledge and *more power to you*!

Moodle
www.moodle.org

ANGEL®
www.angellearning.com

eCollege®
www.ecollege.com

Blackboard
www.blackboard.com

Example and explanation of navigation in an online course
http://www.letu.edu/opencms/opencms/future-students/SGPS/orientation/navigatingcourse.html

If any of these websites are not available or you wish to seek out additional information, we encourage you to do your own online search. Consider the concepts covered in the chapter that are most important to you, and think of various terms that could be used to describe them. For this chapter, some potential keywords to search include:

> (Insert your school's LMS in the blank.)
> _____*tips*
> _____*tutorial*
> *working in*_____

When searching online, consider different ways to express ideas. Remember to use synonyms and related words. Try phrasing things in different ways. And always review more than the first few pages of search results.

For more specific information on searching online, refer to Chapter 9.

Communicating Online: Who, What, When, How, and Why

7

Power Up by:

- Understanding that synchronized communication occurs when we all talk and listen to each other at the same time.

- Understanding that asynchronized communication occurs when participation in a conversation is spaced out over time.

- Becoming aware and following basic e-mail communication guidelines.

- Addressing various online communication concerns such as language, listening, and appropriateness.

- Following appropriate guidelines for responding to messages in the online classroom.

- Differentiating the various forms of online communication, including forums, newsgroups, chat rooms, wikis, and blogs.

Because everyone must be involved, the online learning environment offers a rich and diverse experience. Unlike on-ground classrooms, one or two people cannot easily dominate an online class. Everyone is expected to respond to every question, and thus participation is much more equitable.

In an online course, you have the opportunity to make connections with other students in various states and time zones, maybe even different countries. Communication in the online environment puts few limits on time and place. The classroom environment is also considered far less intimidating than a face-to-face classroom because almost all communication takes place from your own computer in your own comfortable space.

You can communicate online by using a variety of tools and avenues. Following are the more common ones you will probably be exposed to as you begin and continue your online adventure:

E-mail

Forums/newsgroups

Chat rooms

Wikis and blogs

E-mail

Almost everyone uses electronic mail these days. Proper computer etiquette is essential to communicate well online. Use these strategies when you are communicating in your virtual classroom.

E-mail Communication Guidelines

Even if you do not consider yourself a writer, as an online student, you will be. And there are certain conventions and considerations to keep in mind to make your writing clear, readable, and inoffensive.

Wallpaper

Avoid background wallpaper or setting your messages up to look like electronic stationery for online messages and e-mails. Although it may look fancy, it can make messages hard to read and actually slows things down between systems because wallpaper takes up more space in the computer's memory.

Fonts

Although you have many options, there are certainly more acceptable fonts when sending messages. Avoid using an offbeat or unusual font, even if you think it is expressive of your personality. It may be difficult for others to read. If all reading is done on screen, stick with sans serif fonts (like this). Serif fonts (like this) are easier to read on a hard-copy page.

Make sure your font size is in the middle and readable range, generally 12 point. Large or small fonts may make reading more difficult for others, depending on their screen size and the keenness of their eyesight.

Color

Although it can be fun and interesting to use different font and background colors, resist the temptation. Some color combinations work better than others: A dark font on a light background is always easier to read and more professional.

Avoid high-contrast colors. For instance, stay away from blue text on an orange background. Colors should have medium tone or brightness so they show up but are not overwhelming on the screen.

As people age, the color red becomes harder to distinguish, so avoid using red for large sections of text.

All Caps

Do not use all caps. In an online environment, using capital letters conveys YELLING LOUDLY. In addition, depending on the length of your message, writing in all caps makes your message difficult to read on screen.

Emoticons

Emoticons are emotional graphics used to enhance your message visually. They are best used to be sure you clearly convey your intentions whenever you use humor, anger, or a subtle emotion in a message or posting.

Some people use the winking emoticon to denote humor :).

Another popular emoticon is the unhappy face to denote something sad in a message: ☹.

Do not overuse emoticons because they can make your messages seem silly or shallow. However, when used sparingly, you can put your point across and express the appropriate tone.

Note: For any of the word-processing functions just discussed, if you do not know how to manipulate fonts, colors, and the rest, ask a classmate or friend, use the tutorials included in the program, or do a search online for information on formatting documents specific to your word-processing program.

Spelling and Punctuation

Spelling and punctuation are just as crucial in an online environment as in a hard-copy business letter. You want to come across as an educated person. Although you may not be graded on your grammar and spelling in online discussion, it will certainly affect people's perceptions of you. Poor spelling and grammar skills lead others to lower expectations regarding your intelligence and professionalism. Further, your intended message may be misconstrued, at the very least. Use the tools available in your LMS.

Abbreviations

Any of you who send text messages know there are many common abbreviations. (ttfn = ta-ta for now; ttyl = talk to you later, etc.). But for classroom communication, you need to be more formal and avoid slang abbreviations.

Also, clarity is important, and not everyone is familiar with these abbreviations. It is best to write out terms in the more conventional way. In the end, though, your instructor will set the tone for the class, so pay attention and follow his or her lead about the level of formality of language. In using more traditional abbreviations or acronyms, present the full word or phrase at least once before using the abbreviation or acronym.

In your online communication, be courteous, concise, and positive, but try to express your personality in your writing. You do not want to sound dry or like a robot. It may take you a while to find your voice online, but try to reach a level where your online communication is similar in tone to your voice communication in an on-ground classroom.

Other Online Communication Concerns

Reading Between the Lines. Communication is complex, whether written or spoken. When you do not have visual and auditory cues, you can easily misconstrue people's comments. You do not have the same nonverbal cues to reference in an online environment as you do face to face, but you can still gain insight into people's communication.

Different people have different styles. Pay attention to how people express themselves, and you will begin to have a sense of their thoughts beyond just their words as you get to know them. But be cautious in your interpretations. Your own moods and preconceived notions can influence the way you interpret other people's communication. Usually, we can assume all messages are intended in a friendly, professional way, unless strong indicators within the message itself point in another direction.

Learning to Listen Online. In a classroom setting, you wouldn't have the TV on or children running around. If you are working in the online classroom, though, there may be numerous distracters in the environment. Try to limit the background noise in the area where you are working and really focus so you can read online content accurately.

For some people, listening to music is not a distracter; for others, any noise disrupts their attention. Do what you need to make your environment work for you so you can focus and process the online content. Consider this: If all you have to add to a discussion is "I agree," maybe you didn't listen or process well enough.

Quality of Responses. Keep in mind that the online communications in your class may be archived for a long time. Any time you misspell a word or say something foolish, your words may live on to haunt you. Take the opportunity to think before you post a message to the class. One good approach is to create all your responses in a separate document and take the time to reread and fine-tune them before you upload them for all of the world to see.

However, we do encourage you not to avoid responding because you are intimidated. Too much thought might mean you decide not to post a piece that would lead to a great discussion. Again, there is a fine line. Here is an example:

Let's say a fellow student made a comment about his boss that made you think the student was the problem, not the boss. You would want to respond. So do not talk yourself out of it, but think how you can get your point across without contributing to the problem or hurting feelings.

E-mail Addresses: Keep It Professional. During your program, you will need an e-mail account. Most of the time, your e-mail account is school sponsored. Be careful about the names you use because others will see them. Do you really want your e-mail to be sexymama@schoolname.edu? Choose your e-mail address name wisely and make it simple and tasteful. We recommend "your first name your last name@schoolname.edu." It is easy to remember and, most importantly, clear and professional.

Knowing What Not to Share: Personal Information. Surprisingly, in an online environment, people tend to share more, rather than less, information. Sometimes people share too much, disclosing inappropriate details regarding intimate personal subjects in the guise of responding to course questions or assignments. Perhaps this problem relates to the anonymity factor, or perhaps people just get carried away. So keep in mind: Monitor your own communication and try to keep your communication appropriate. Steer away from private disclosure unless personal revelations are the specific focus of an assignment. Your instructor and classmates are wonderful resources, but they are not personal counselors.

Be aware that although you may want to talk about your employer and your job experiences, you should be careful about the information you divulge. Many companies have policies regarding disclosing proprietary information. Lastly, consider what contact information is appropriate. Some students create a signature line and include their phone number. Do you really want your phone number available on every single message you send? Your communication in the online classroom should be professional and courteous rather than soul-baring.

Review of Synchronized and Asynchronized Communication. Synchronized communication occurs when we are all talking and listening to each other at the same time, whether in a classroom, or over the phone, or through a virtual meeting. Everyone is engaged and participating in the communication at the same time.

Asynchronized communication occurs when we are not all engaged in the conversation at the same time, even though we are all participating. For instance,

- The old-fashioned exchange of letters among pen pals
- E-mail
- Exchanging voice mails

■ Participating in an online discussion in which one person responds at 8 A.M. and is offline by 9 P.M., and someone else doesn't respond until he comes online from 11 P.M. until 2 A.M.

Whether your course interactions are synchronized or asynchronized depends on the institution and the instructor. Be aware of the nature of any specific communication situation. If it is asynchronized, you probably have more time to review your responses. Consider giving others a chance to respond to your initial postings before you come back for more. The point of online discussions is to hear more than one voice, and the input of others may give you more food for thought.

Threading Responses in the Classroom. You must deal with a large number of messages every day in the online classroom. You can help others manage the sometimes overwhelming number of messages by creating messages considerately. Here are some examples.

   1. **Use an appropriate subject line.** During the course of a conversation, the topic often changes. Therefore, if the subject line reads "Week Two-DQ1" and the conversation has evolved to a discussion on time management, change the subject line. You should be able to maintain the thread with a new subject line without a problem.

   2. **Place your message first when replying to someone's message.** The newest addition to the conversation needs to be the first thing read. Then be sure and include the relevant sections of the previous message, or even the entire previous message, so people can follow the conversation. Readers can then elect to read further if they need a reminder about what has gone on before. If the older messages are placed first and the newest at the bottom, readers are forced not only to scroll down to read the latest comment but also they must skim the notes previously read.

   3. **Be attentive to the appearance of your notes.** As mentioned earlier, avoid fonts that are difficult to read because of style, color, or size. The format should not be more important than the content. Keep in mind when reading on the computer screen that long paragraphs are difficult to follow. As a general rule, limit each paragraph in an e-mail message to five to seven lines if possible.

   4. **Reduce confusion by considering a variety of methods of replying.** Although most often a straightforward reply is appropriate, sometimes you can intersperse comments on each point in the original message, increasing the readability of your response.

   5. **Exercise good editing techniques.** In threaded discussions, editing of notes refers to removing those portions of the message to which you are replying that are unnecessary to understand your comments. Although it is important to include enough of the previous message(s) to place the note in context, you will seldom need to include the entire message. It is frustrating to download lengthy messages that include dozens of messages already read, and it is equally annoying to download a message that mentions research but contains no references whatsoever.

Forums/Newsgroups

Forums and newsgroups are essentially worldwide bulletin systems, made up of individuals chatting virtually about a particular topic in synchronous time. Forums and newsgroups can be about any topic.

For instance, if you are having a particularly hard time with a final paper, you can create a forum. Perhaps call it "final paper discussion." This will be a place where students are able to talk about their challenges regarding the final paper and strategies to make the paper easier to write, as well as inviting general comments on the final paper. The positive brainstorming and synergy that can come out of forums and newsgroups is substantial and a great resource for online students.

Chat Rooms

Chat rooms are virtual rooms where casual conversations with your peers can take place. They are for two or more people to have a text-based dialogue. Most major course management systems, such as the ones outlined in Chapter 6, have chat room capabilities. Chat rooms are not only used educationally, but they are also available on many popular Internet portal sites.

For instructional purposes, chat rooms can be used for the following: small groups meetings, brainstorming with your classmates, virtual office hours with your professor, and study review sessions.

Pros for Chat Rooms

- Chats can be recorded, archived, and posted for future viewing.
- Chats can allow real-time communication, which can be faster than e-mail or posted discussion in the classroom.
- Chat rooms are an excellent way to connect with your classmates outside of the classroom.

Cons for Chat Rooms

- The fast environment can make some people feel uncomfortable and overwhelmed.
- Individuals with limited English proficiency or below-average typing skills may not adjust well to the fast-paced environment.
- Chat room conversation can be hard to follow when everyone is chatting at once. Just like any conversation in person, if you are being interrupted it may be difficult to finish your thought.

Wikis and Blogs

The term *wiki* is derived from a Hawaiian term for "fast." A wiki is a collaborative online database in the form of a website that allows visitors to join in the adding, removing, and editing of content.

Wikis are an extremely democratic way of presenting information because anyone can participate. However, this same open access means that wikis are not always reliable sources. The people who post information may be experts in the field or they may not. They may have the best intentions of presenting the truth on a topic or they may not. Be wary of the content of wikis, and always look for corroboration on wiki content from more reputable sources.

Blog is short for "web log." A blog is a running chronological journal of personal thoughts posted online. A blog may include proprietary multimedia content such as pictures, video, or audio, as well as links to information and other sites available on the Internet. Blogs exist on any and every topic, and they are generally updated regularly. Some people use blogs in the same way as diaries or personal journals; others use them more as editorials or forums to express their opinions on specific topics such as politics or music. Blogs may have restricted or limited access to outsiders, or they may be public sites. Some public blogs even provide a source of income for their authors, through posted advertisements.

→ MORE POWER TO YOU

Now is your chance to explore this chapter's topics further. Check out the sites listed here. Enjoy expanding your knowledge and *more power to you*!

Virtual Communication
http://hbswk.hbs.edu/archive/2122.html

Netiquette
http://www.studygs.net/netiquette.htm

Blog
http://www.marketingterms.com/dictionary/blog/

Got Something to Say?
http://www.livingdot.com/

Wikipedia
http://www.wikipedia.org/

If any of these websites are not available or you wish to seek out additional information, we encourage you to do your own online search. Consider the concepts covered in the chapter that are most important to you, and think of various terms that could be used to describe them. For this chapter, some potential terms to search by include:

netiquette

document formatting basics

e-mail guidelines

When searching online, consider different ways to express ideas. Remember to use synonyms and related words. Try phrasing things in different ways. And always review more than the first few pages of search results.

For more specific information on searching online, refer to Chapter 9.

Working in the Online Classroom

8

Power Up by:

- Recognizing that most people find it more difficult to read from a computer monitor than hard copy. Be careful and focused when you read text on-screen.

- Understanding that being a good reader doesn't mean you read fast. A good reader is one who understands and processes the information being presented.

- Knowing that typing will be the medium for all your communication in an online environment. Evaluate your typing skills. If you are at all weak, seek to improve.

- Being aware that poor writing skills will impact your grade, regardless of the course subject. If your writing skills are weak, seek to improve.

- Identifying the qualities of good writing. Improve your own writing through increasing your reading, obtaining feedback, and doing more writing.

Although the online learning environment shares many similarities with the traditional on-ground classroom environment, numerous factors set online learning apart from other instructional mediums. Some of the differences are not obvious; others are plain to see. In this chapter, we review the factors you need to consider when working in the online classroom.

Reading in an Online Environment

Although it may not be obvious, there is a difference between reading text on a computer screen and reading text on paper. Reading on-screen is generally harder on your eyes and can result in blurring, eyestrain, and visual fatigue (Rhodes, 1998).

Most people do not read as quickly or efficiently from a computer monitor as they do when reading hard copy. Evaluate your own skill level. If you are not a strong reader, you might print out any important text so you can read it on paper. Having the hard copy gives you the opportunity to make notes or highlight within the document, which can be very helpful to your learning and retention. Some software has this capability too, which is worth exploring.

Do not make the mistake of thinking that a good reader equates to being a fast reader. Reading effectively means you understand and process the information presented, however much time it takes.

Online reading requires scrolling down the page to follow the text, which can irritate your eyes as you track the moving text. In addition, it is quite easy to miss whole passages of text if you are not careful as you scroll down a web page.

Some schools take this into consideration and try to minimize the need for scrolling in their materials. But even if you are fortunate enough to be in a class where only short passages are placed on-screen, you are bound to run across overlong. There will probably always be the need for some scrolling.

Thus you must be careful and focused when you read text on-screen. Pay close attention to where you are on the page, as well as what the text is actually saying.

Printing out every bit of information can result in lots of paper waste. If this concerns you or, if printing everything out is not an option, consider reading pertinent passages on the computer more than one time to ensure you process the information. Good reading skills are one of the keys to your success as an online student, so do all you can to optimize and improve your skills.

Typing Skills: A Necessity

Whether you are a good or a poor typist, you *will* be a typist if you are an online student. Typing skills are almost as important as reading skills for an online learner. In a traditional classroom, you might be able to get away with typing only when you have an assignment due. But in an online environment, you are typing all of the time. Typing will be the medium for *all* your communication, so you need to polish your skills if you are at all weak. Being a reasonably fast, accurate typist can make a real difference in the time it takes you to respond to questions and complete assignments, both on the initial writing and on the editing and correcting of errors.

Even today when typing on the computer keyboard is common, many people still type with the hunt-and-peck or two-finger method. What matters is not whether you have had formal training in typing, but whether you are efficient and effective. Some people who hunt and peck are faster than others who type in the traditional manner. Determine whether your typing skills could be improved, and consider the following options: online typing programs, software packages, library books, or typing courses at local schools and colleges.

Good typing skills will contribute to making you a successful online student.

Writing Skills: Practice Makes Perfect

How well do you write? Undoubtedly, you will write a great deal during your academic career. You will have essays, papers, maybe even poems to create. If you are a strong writer, congratulations! If you are not, now is the time to improve your skills. You may have the most revolutionary new idea that ever occurred to anyone, but if you cannot express it competently and concisely in writing, it will not be recognized.

Poor writing skills will impact your grade, regardless of the course subject. There are as many ways to describe the qualities necessary for good writing as there are writers, but in general, good writing has the following qualities:

- *Correct spelling.* If you are a poor speller, you know it by now. Take advantage of the spell checker. Ask someone who is a good speller to check your work if you can.

- *Proper grammar and punctuation.* Know and apply the rules for grammar and punctuation. If you need help, refer to the style guide for your school or invest in a grammar handbook.

- *Appropriate word choice.* If you have a good vocabulary, use it. If you do not, start developing it. Avoid slang. Strive for clarity and conciseness. Use language that is correct for the audience, the subject, and the circumstances.

- *Variable sentence structure.* Sentences should vary in length and structure between simple and complex. Use various techniques to help the text flow.

- *Logical organization.* Good writing sets up ideas in a logical, understandable order. The point of the writing is clear, and relevant details and examples obviously support the main idea. A particular format is followed as required.

- *A unique style.* Good writers are professional while still letting their own distinct personality come through into their writing.

Always be sure to proofread your work so you can catch any errors in the areas just outlined. One simple, yet effective, proofreading technique is to read your work aloud slowly and listen carefully for awkward phrases or transitions. You can also find numerous resources in the library, the bookstore, and online, with advice and practice exercises for polishing your writing skills. If you know your writing skills are weak, start to work on them now.

Improve Your Writing by Reading

The more you read, the better writer you will become. Try to read more and to read more diverse types of material. Challenge yourself in the areas of vocabulary and subject matter, and you will see your own thinking processes and vocabulary improve. If you do not read, it is likely you are not a great writer, and you will stay that way until you increase your reading. No matter what your interests, books and periodicals are available that address them.

Find motivation, and start reading more. It will expand your mind and improve your writing skills.

Improve Your Writing by Practicing

Of course, the more you write, the better writer you will become. Here are some ways to improve:

- Keep a journal. It is a great way to practice your writing skills and find your voice.
- Find someone who is a good writer to review your work and give you feedback.
- Keep in mind that good writers seldom finish anything in one draft. It takes multiple drafts to arrive at a well-written product. Expect to go through consecutive drafts of any writing assignment. Each draft will be an improvement over the last. And the more time you spend, the better your final product is likely to be.

Your instructors will probably vary in how much they emphasize writing skills. Keep in mind that, just like students, instructor skill levels vary. Those instructors who are not strong writers are unlikely to give you much constructive feedback. Those who have high-level writing skills will be the most critical when it comes to evaluating student writing. If you are fortunate to have an instructor who offers constructive criticism, take advantage of it. Learn as much as you can. You might even ask if he or she would be willing to review your papers for other classes. The instructor might not have the time, but it never hurts to ask.

Improving your reading, writing, and typing skills will serve you well for all your online courses. Plus, the added bonus is that polishing these skills will also benefit you in your career.

→ MORE POWER TO YOU

Now is your chance to explore this chapter's topics further. Check out the sites listed here. Enjoy expanding your knowledge and *more power to you*!

Reading Speed Test & Improvement Techniques
http://www.jcu.edu.au/studying/services/studyskills/effreading/

Reading Comprehension Lessons
http://www.readingcomprehensionconnection.com/

The Art of Close Reading: Parts 1–3
http://www.criticalthinking.org/articles/sts-ct-art-close-reading-p1.cfm

http://www.criticalthinking.org/articles/sts-ct-art-close-reading-p2.cfm

http://www.criticalthinking.org/articles/sts-ct-art-close-reading-p3.cfm

Typing Practice
http://www.learn2type.com

Typing Games to Help You
http://www.berkeleyprep.org/lower/llinks/typing%20games.htm

If any of these websites are not available or you wish to seek out additional information, we encourage you to do your own online search. Consider the concepts covered in the chapter that are most important to you, and think of various terms that could be used to describe them. For this chapter, some potential keywords to search include:

> *online reading skills*
> *typing tutorial*
> *writing skills*

When searching online, consider different ways to express ideas. Remember to use synonyms and related words. Try phrasing things in different ways. And always review more than the first few pages of search results.

For more specific information on searching online, refer to Chapter 9.

Who
What
Where
When
Why
How

Thinking and Researching Online

9

Power Up by:

- Examining your thinking process. Pay attention. Try to think more deeply about the information presented in class by translating it into your own words, making connections, and asking questions.

- Being aware that the basis of critical thinking is questioning. Ask thoughtful questions. Remember not to take information at face value. Consider other perspectives.

- Understanding what search engines are and how to use them.

- Being a critical researcher. Don't assume everything you find on the Web is accurate. Dig deeper.

- Understanding the serious offense of plagiarism. Avoid plagiarizing by always citing your sources correctly and completely.

Although you have undoubtedly had experiences in which you had to research and think things through in your lifetime, researching online requires particular strategies and methods. This chapter covers the most important techniques.

Thinking About Course Content

Thinking is internally processing the information presented to you. Here are some ways to help you really think about the concepts presented in your class:

- Relate the new information to your own experiences or what you've already learned.

- Translate the concepts into your own words. What related ideas and information does the new content bring to mind? Be sure to take note of any questions that occur to you regarding the ideas presented in class.

- *Do not* parrot the text or the responses of your classmates. Use your own background knowledge and experiences to contribute to what you are reading and learning. How might the concepts being discussed in class apply to you? Keep an open mind.

- Try to have a holistic as well as a personal view. How do these ideas impact your life as well as the greater world?

- Pay attention to your thought process. Try to communicate in your writing *how* your ideas progress from one point to the other. Think of working out a math problem. It is helpful for you and others to be able to see the process. This approach not only shows your instructor how you are thinking through the concepts, but it can be helpful to your classmates as an example of a way to approach their learning.

- Ask questions. Seek clarity about the goals of individual assignments and activities, and try to ensure that what you take away from an assignment matches the learning objective.

- We all learn from one another. Pay attention to the comments and insights of your instructor, as well as your classmates. Use their diverse knowledge and perspectives to round out and contribute to your own. Don't forget to give credit to others for their ideas!

Critical Thinking

The basis of critical thinking is questioning, which can help you achieve clarity regarding what is being said, as well as why and how. Here are some questions to consider:

- Is this correct?
- Who is saying it and why?

- Who is the intended audience for this information?
- What perspective is being put forward?
- What other perspectives are there that might be relevant?
- What sounds right about this to you and what sounds wrong, and why?
- Why would someone want you to believe this?
- What other questions does this information provoke?

Try to remember not to just take information at face value.

Ask Questions

Don't be afraid to ask questions, even if you do not obtain sufficient answers. Just the asking can help you gain clarity about the important concepts. Questioning is also a valuable way to decipher your own views about the information presented in class.

Remember, asking questions does not mean just interrogating your instructor and classmates. It also means being open to letting others question you. It even means questioning your own opinions and preconceived notions, trying to determine their origins truthfully. Responding thoughtfully to others' questions can also clarify your own reasoning.

Internet Research

Critical thinking is especially important with regard to Internet research. Thinking about an idea and approaching it from different angles will aid you in doing online searches. Also, being critical of the information presented will help you sift through the vast amount of data on the Web and determine which online sources are relevant and reliable for your purposes.

Search Engines

Search engines are the tools you use on the Web to lead you to information. You are probably already familiar with a few of them. If you have online access you may already use Google, Alta Vista, Ask.com, or Yahoo!

A search engine typically features a page with a box where you to type in words to describe the information you want. Type in the word(s), hit return, and the 'engine' searches the Internet for mentions of those particular word(s). If you are unfamiliar with search engines, go to Google.com and experiment with searching. Use any tutorials or help information offered.

How and where a particular engine searches can vary. Some search engines look for specific forms of information, such as scholarly materials, while others are more general.

Technically, search engines can be categorized into two types: individual search engines and metasearch engines.

- Individual search engines are the most basic ones. They search the whole Web.
- Metasearch engines are those that search, and usually organize, the results from other search engines.

Decide what type of search engine is right for your purposes before you begin your research.

Types of Online Searches

You can do a basic, uncomplicated Web search using an engine such as Google just by directly typing in the relevant terms. There are two tricks to effective searching of this type: language options and persistence.

You need to think critically about your topic and come at it from various angles, using different words and giving yourself language options. Putting together a successful online search is a little like note taking. The best way to do it is not just to copy out exact words from the lecture or text but to grasp the main ideas and restate them in your own language. It is a game in word association, and it helps to have a wide vocabulary, a creative thought process, and a knowledge of synonyms. For instance, say you are searching for information regarding "online learning." Of course, your obvious initial search terms are those words. But try varying the words. What other terms would express the same concept or something closely related? For "online" you might consider *computer*, or *distance*, or even *virtual*. For "learning" you might try *learner*, or *classroom*, or *student*. Mixing up and recombining all these different, but similar terms, will give you some more interesting and diverse search results than just the basic concept you started with. And if you can't think of various terms right away, do that initial search using "online learning," and see what other related terms are included in the results list from that search to give you additional ideas.

The element of persistence comes into the equation in two ways. Try numerous different word combinations before being satisfied with your results. And do not limit yourself to finding information in the first few pages of results that come up. Skim through three to five pages of the results, especially if nothing really relevant seems to have come from the search. Sometimes the good stuff is buried further down the list.

Although you can always do a search as just described by typing any terms into the engine that are relevant to what you want to find, the Internet does offer more complex options. You might need to use a specific type of search method. Two basic types of online searches are "Boolean" and "Wild Card."

Boolean Searches

A Boolean search uses the terms *and*, *or*, and/or *not* to set particular limits on the information being searched. Boolean is the type of logic used in these searches. It defines the relationship among the terms used in the search. Boolean logic takes its name from the British-born Irish mathematician and philosopher George Boole.

The easiest way to envision what you are doing when you use a Boolean search is to show it through Venn diagrams. Observe the following examples:

Using the term **OR** in a Boolean search

Goal: I would like information about college.

Query: college OR university

In this search, you will retrieve records in which *at least one* of the search terms is present. You are searching on the terms *college* and also *university* because documents containing either of these words might be relevant. Look at the accompanying figure.

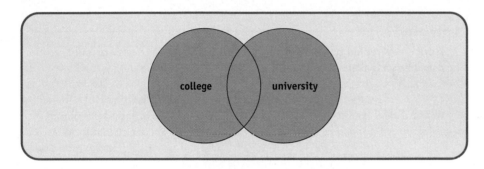

The shaded circle with the word *college* represents all the records that contain the word "college." The shaded circle with the word *university* represents all the records that contain the word "university." The shaded overlap area represents all the records that contain both "college" and "university."

OR logic is most commonly used to search for synonymous terms or concepts. The corresponding table is an example of how OR logic works.

OR logic collates the results to retrieve all the unique records containing one term, the other, or both. The more terms or concepts you combine in a search with OR logic, the more records you will retrieve.

SEARCH TERMS	RESULTS
college	396,482
university	590,791
college OR university	819,214

Using the term **AND** in a Boolean search

Goal: I'm interested in the relationship between poverty and crime.

Query: poverty AND crime

In this search, you retrieve records in which *both* of the search terms are present. This is illustrated by the shaded area overlapping the two circles representing all the records that contain both the word *poverty* and the word *crime* in the corresponding graphic.

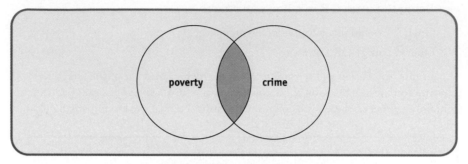

Notice how we do not retrieve any records with only "poverty" or only "crime." The corresponding table is an example of how AND logic works.

SEARCH TERMS	RESULTS
poverty	76,342
crime	348,252
poverty AND crime	12,998

The more terms or concepts we combine in a search with AND logic, the fewer records we will retrieve.

Using the term **NOT** in a Boolean search

Goal: I want information about cats, but I want to avoid anything about dogs.

Query: cats NOT dogs

In this search, we retrieve records in which *only one* of the terms is present. This is illustrated in the nearby graphic by the shaded area with the word *cats* representing all the records containing the word "cats."

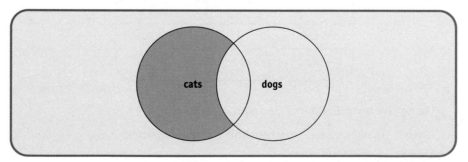

No records are retrieved in which the word *dogs* appears, even if the word *cats* appears there too. The accompanying table shows how NOT logic works.

SEARCH TERMS	RESULTS
cats	86,747
dogs	130,424
cats NOT dogs	65,223

NOT logic excludes records from your search results. Be cautious when you use NOT: The term you *do* want may be present in an important way in documents that also contain the word you wish to avoid.

Wild Card Searches

In a wild card search, you use a specific character among your search terms in a particular way, to expand the boundaries of your search. The two most common characters used are the question mark and the asterisk (the "?" and the "*").

The question mark ("?") can represent a single alphanumeric character in a search expression. For example, searching for the term "ho?se" would yield results that contain such words as "house" and "horse."

The asterisk ("*") can specify zero or more alphanumeric characters. It can be used in the middle or, more commonly, at the end of a word. Depending on where you place the asterisk, it can signify different words or just different forms of a single word.

For example, searching for the term "h*s" would yield results that contain such words as "his," "homes," "houses," "horses," "horticulturalists," and "herbaceous." Searching for the term "boat*" would yield results such as "boats," "boating," and "boaters." It is usually best to avoid using the asterisk as the first character in a search string.

A search term consisting of a lone asterisk and no other alphanumeric characters will retrieve every record from the database.

The Credibility of Information Online

When you do online research, keep in mind that finding current, accurate information is better than finding lots of information. Just because something is posted online does not mean it is accurate and valid.

Do not take everything you find on the Web at face value. Be critical of the websites you encounter in your research. Plagiarism is rampant on the Web. Many times you can do a search and find numerous sites that contain exactly the same information. You can usually figure out on which site the information originated: the site set up the most professionally, listed as created by a qualified individual that cites references for the information. In general, websites that end in *.gov, .edu,* and *.org* tend to be more reliable than just *.com* and *.net* sites.

Beware of sites that do not account for their sources or have not been updated recently. Be especially critical of wikis, where anyone, regardless of knowledge or qualifications, can contribute to the so-called truth about a subject. Wikis can result in some very well-rounded information, but the information may be inaccurate. When qualified editors do not oversee a website, it may perpetuate inconsistencies, fallacies, and flat-out untruths about the topics discussed.

Primary and Secondary Sources

The safest source for any information is the *primary source*, the place where the information was first expressed or put into print. In terms of technical research, a primary source is the study itself. If you are looking for information on music therapy, find a journal article describing an actual study on music therapy and the results. This would be your primary source.

Alternately, if you use a book, magazine, or Internet article that summarizes the findings of a number of music therapy research studies, you are using a *secondary source*, one that just restates information from its first occurrence. In general, the further you are from the primary source of information, the more likely there may be errors or oversights in the information.

The more often something is interpreted, the more chance there is of losing some meaning in translation. Never assume the first site to come up in search results is correct and adequate for your needs. Read through as many of the search results as you can. It will help you round out your perspective, as well as identify which sites stand out in terms of quality, readability, and scope of information.

Try the search again using terms that are synonyms. This can be a way to fine-tune your results and maybe find information that is not as obvious.

Do your best to gain a well-rounded view of the information available. Try to find sites that come at the information from different angles.

You may find that after you look at several sites, you can see mistakes in some of them. But you only caught those mistakes because you looked at the big picture instead of just trying to take advantage of the fastest, easiest view.

Academic Integrity and Plagiarism

Doing research puts you in a position to present views relevant to your topic other than your own. You will discover many interesting ideas. But be sure you keep track of which ideas are your own and which come from other people. You must cite your sources correctly and give credit to others where it is due. That honesty in dealings regarding your coursework is known as academic integrity.

Plagiarism can be defined as "the unauthorized use or close imitation of the language and thoughts of another author and the representation of them as one's own original work" (*Dictionary.com Unabridged*; http://dictionary.reference.com/browse/plagiarism).

In other words, you are plagiarizing when you copy the words or the thoughts of someone else and do not tell your audience that those words or thoughts were not originally your own.

Looking Closely at Plagiarism

The most important point to consider about plagiarism is not just that it isn't fair to others or can result in serious consequences. It is that if you plagiarize, you are passing up a chance for learning.

What's Wrong with Plagiarizing?

If plagiarism becomes a tempting option, maybe you need to rethink your priorities. Have you given up on school? If not, then the reason you are here is to *learn*. Doing research, thinking through ideas, and articulating your thoughts in writing are all a big part of that learning experience. You forsake that part when you plagiarize.

There is much more to consider with regard to plagiarism, however. What may seem like an insignificant act can be taken as an indicator of various character traits. For any given instance of plagiarism, any of these might apply:

- *You are a thief.* You couldn't be bothered to put in the required amount of work in terms of the research, thought, and writing the assignment required. So you used someone else's thought, research, and work, and stole the opportunity to learn from yourself!

- *You are unimaginative.* You used someone else's words and ideas, instead of paraphrasing or summarizing them, so you couldn't, or didn't bother to, think of new ways to express the information and ideas.

- *You are dishonest.* You didn't cite the ideas or information that you used properly, so, in effect, you tried to pass them off as your own.

- *You are disrespectful.* You didn't have enough respect for those who conceived the original ideas or did important research on the topic to give them the credit they are due. In addition, you didn't have enough respect for the readers of your work to give them the facts of the situation.

- *You are unprofessional.* Being professional entails extending a certain level of courtesy to others and following the guidelines for a task, as well as acting ethically. By plagiarizing, you broadcast the fact that you do not care about professional standards and are neither courteous nor ethical. Is that the way you want to present yourself? Probably not. So take care not to plagiarize.

What If You Plagiarize Accidentally?

Maybe you didn't deliberately plagiarize; maybe it was just an accident or an oversight, but ignorance or accident is really no excuse. You will be informed of the proper ways to cite information for your assignments, but if you aren't, it is your responsibility to ask about it. Because plagiarism in itself is dishonest and sneaky, it can be difficult to give people who plagiarize the benefit of the doubt that it was not intentional.

Although the penalties for plagiarism vary widely by instructor and institution, it is always regarded as a serious offense. Students who plagiarize may be asked to redo the assignment. They may receive a failing grade for the assignment or for the course. They may be put on academic probation, or they may even be expelled.

Common Instances of Plagiarism

Plagiarism occurs when students include a small part of another person's work in their own without giving credit to the source or when students submit an entire paper or project created by another person. It can also occur when a whole paper is made up of small parts of others' work.

There are websites where students can purchase complete papers written on a wide variety of subjects for common courses. Your instructor knows that, too. There are also websites instructors can visit, and just by putting in a small excerpt of text and doing a search, they can find out if a student has misrepresented a part or the whole of the work put forward as his or her own.

In this Internet age, where information is so easy to obtain, it is just as easy to track. So if you ever consider plagiarizing, do not forget it is just as easy for an instructor to run a search on your work as it was for you to commit your crime. But we hope that as a person who values learning—an honest, imaginative, careful, respectful person, with a good work ethic—you will avoid plagiarizing.

Citing Sources

The way to avoid plagiarizing is to always cite your sources correctly. Citations are brief notes describing what information sources you used, who originally wrote them and when, and where you found them. They can take the form of footnotes, endnotes, notes within the text, or even a separate resource page that lists all the sources you referred to in your research.

Your school will probably determine which format you must use to cite your sources. Many colleges adopt style guides to be used in all courses that not only illustrate the citation style but also describe the specific page format and organization of papers. In other cases, the particular program, or the instructor, may determine the style guide/citation requirements.

In rare cases, you may find you are given no guidelines regarding what is expected for citing your sources. Seek guidance from the instructor. If none is forthcoming, decide yourself how you will present the citations. Pick a style and apply it, rather than just skipping mention of sources altogether. Always give credit where it is due.

Some common sources for document and citation styles are the *Publication Manual of the American Psychological Association*, the *Chicago Manual of Style*, and the *MLA Handbook for Writers of Research Papers.* Numerous style guides are available though, so rather than going through any specific style and formatting rules here, we advise you to find out what guide is required in your course or for your school. Many of the guides have associated websites that can be quite useful, so do not hesitate to do a search for information on your school's preferred guide.

→ **MORE POWER TO YOU**

Now is your chance to explore this chapter's topics further. Check out the sites listed here. Enjoy expanding your knowledge and *more power to you*!

Search Engines
http://www.internettutorials.net/engines.html

Researching the Internet
http://www.studygs.net/research.htm

Thinking Like a Genius
http://www.studygs.net/genius.htm

Citing Websites
http://www.studygs.net/citation.htm

Thinking Critically
http://www.studygs.net/crtthk.htm

Wildcard Searches
http://apps.caes.uga.edu/impact/searchhelp.cfm

If any of these websites are not available or you wish to seek out additional information, we encourage you to do your own online search. Consider the concepts covered in the chapter that are most important to you, and think of various terms that could be used to describe them. For this chapter, some potential keywords to search include:

questioning techniques
critical thinking strategies
critical reading
online research
avoiding plagiarism

When searching online, consider different ways to express ideas. Remember to use synonyms and related words. Try phrasing things in different ways. And always review more than the first few pages of search results.

Strategies for Successful Online Learning

10

Power Up by:

- Monitoring your own openness and ability to give and receive feedback. Your opportunity to learn from your instructor and peers is directly related to these qualities.

- Giving feedback using appropriate guidelines.

- Being open and receptive to receiving feedback. Use it as a tool for self-improvement.

- Understanding that online learning takes just as much time, if not more, than face-to-face learning. The difference is in the flexibility.

- Knowing how to listen online. Focus, limit extraneous noise, read closely, and pay attention to content and tone.

- Identifying your own methods for effective note taking. Find the easiest way to gather and organize information so you can remember it.

- Recognizing the importance of test preparation. Remember to study the material, have ready access to resources, and pace yourself as you take the exam.

A n open mind is a mind that can be educated. It is a given that you will want to open your mind to new concepts and perspectives in your online program. But you also want to open your mind when it comes to accepting and giving feedback.

Feedback: Giving It and Accepting It Gracefully

Feedback is a necessary tool for helping anyone to improve, whether in an online or face-to-face environment. Accepting feedback may not always be easy. We all love positive feedback, but sometimes it is hard to swallow the negative feedback. Acknowledging and growing in our weak areas is how we can become more successful at anything.

Feedback does become a little trickier in the virtual environment. The lack of nonverbal communication signals makes it more difficult to understand a person's intentions. Without nonverbal cues, the giver of feedback has to concentrate on being succinct and careful with word choice.

We Love Feedback

For most online students, seeing feedback means the instructor is paying close attention to them and their online journey. Feedback can be taken as an indication that our work is of value. If you just spent several hours working on a major final paper, of course you want it to be read and appreciated.

Do remember, however, that many online classes today are not as teacher centered as they were in the past. Teacher-centered feedback is based on the premise that the instructor lectures, with little interaction from the students except their occasional questions. Many classes today are focused less on the lecture itself and more on the experiences and opinions the students can add to enhance the lecture. Teachers are not only leaders but also skilled facilitators in the classroom. This approach to learning means you will have an opportunity to learn from your classmates as well as your instructor. In fact, even as instructors, we were always learning new things from our students. Your ability to learn from your instructor and your peers is directly related to your openness and ability to give and receive feedback.

Giving Feedback

To give feedback, you must be honest and constructive. "Go for the ball and not the player." Try to be tactful. If you can find something positive, say it, but if you can't, try to be as diplomatic as possible in your comments while still being constructive.

Here are some strategies to help you offer appropriate feedback in the online environment:

1. Be clear and succinct about what you want to say. Reread your message before you send it for clarity, punctuation, and grammar. The more error free your message, the easier it will be to understand its intent. The more concise you are with your written communication, the less chance there will be of misinterpreting the goal of the feedback.

2. Emphasize the positive aspects of the feedback in the opening of your message, and always end the message with a positive and motivating tone. In the body of the message, provide the feedback and any constructive criticism you think is necessary.

3. Be descriptive in your feedback, rather than evaluative or judgmental.

4. Do not make any generalizations or assumptions when giving feedback, so avoid words like *all, never, always, everyone, only,* and *you.*

5. Limit your advice on how to fix the work. Often the most useful feedback is helping the person to recognize or better understand the area(s) that need improvement.

Receiving Feedback

As a receiver of feedback in the online environment, be aware of the restrictions on the person giving the feedback. Try not to make any assumptions, and go only by what is clearly stated. View the feedback with the understanding that whether it is positive or negative, feedback is meant to be constructive, not derogatory. Keep an open mind and try your best not to be defensive.

Feedback is a tool to help you improve, not an insult. Look at it as a quality improvement process. If you already knew everything, there would be no reason for you to be in school. You are in class to learn, and receiving feedback is part of that process. Here are some tips for focusing on the helpful messages in the feedback:

1. Divorce yourself from your emotions and try just to hear the criticism. Do not make excuses or evaluate whether it is right or wrong. Just listen.

2. Look for the practical advice within the feedback. *Yadda, yadda, nice job on this but <u>what you can do to improve is X</u>, yadda yadda.* Pick out the really constructive part of the message that you need to keep in mind for the future.

3. If the feedback was mostly criticism without any constructive advice, and you really do not know how to address the issue, go back to the person who gave it. If that is not an option, find someone else who would understand. Try to discover what steps you might reasonably take to make an improvement.

4. Try to see the big picture. Have you gotten feedback with similar comments before? Are there common areas that people always bring up? Clue in, and realize that if you are hearing it often or from multiple sources, the chances are it is accurate. Do something about it.

5. Realize that people who give you feedback often have your best interests at heart.

One of your authors recalls receiving a paper back from an instructor that puzzled her: He gave her an A, but he also wrote a few notes on how she could have made the paper better. She was confused. If it was an A paper, then why all the criticism and advice on how to improve it? She asked him about it, and he told her that although it was an excellent paper, it was not perfect. There is always room for improvement, and he thought she could do an even better job next time. She never looked at feedback the same way again.

Part of the reason you are taking classes is to better yourself. So be open and receptive to feedback, and use it as a tool for self-improvement.

Keeping Time in Mind

One of the largest misconceptions about online learning revolves around time. Many people who have never taken an online class make the assumption that online learning takes less time then learning in a traditional classroom.

In truth, as we said before, online learning takes just as much, if not more, time. The difference comes in the flexibility of your time.

With time such an important variable in the online environment, we next discuss some tactics that relate to time management in the virtual classroom.

Time on Task

Keep in mind that if you were in an on-ground class, you would probably spend about 3 hours per credit per week. Thus you would be expected to spend roughly 9 hours per week reading, studying, and completing assignments. This expectation applies to both online and face-to-face classes. The exact amount of time will vary depending on you and on the particular course.

Because of the flexibility in an online class, people may get carried away in either direction, dedicating too much or too little time to a course. Remember that the point of the course is not for you to post the most messages to the class. Neither is it for you to squeak through by doing as little as possible. If you want to succeed and actually learn in class, you need to put in the effort.

As you gain more experience in online learning, you will figure out how much time you need to spend to do well. If you pay attention and pace yourself, you will learn what it takes to meet your desired goals.

Every class may be a little different in the amount of time you allot for your studies. Much of this will depend on your previous base of knowledge regarding the curriculum and how quickly you are able to catch on, retain, and apply the information you need from the class.

Pacing Yourself

There are two basic and very different ways to approach how you will spend your time in the online classroom. The first is not to worry about exactly how much time you are spending on each item in advance. Jump into each topic with an open mind, and simply spend as much time as you need to absorb the information. This approach is ideal for students who do not have large time restrictions.

However, the majority of students, especially those who have chosen to take online classes, generally have time constraints. The second method is to develop formulas for how much time you are willing to commit to various aspects of the class.

For instance, a common formula might be to look at the time you want to spend on an assignment and correlate it directly to how many points the assignment is worth. Is a 5-point paper really worth 20 hours of your time?

For some people, it is easy to drown in a project, spending an inordinate amount of time (say 20 hours) on a project that is only worth 5 points out of a class total of 100 points. Consider that it might be logical to put the most time into the projects worth the most points. The assumption, after all, is that those projects that are worth more will take more time and research and thought than the ones worth not as much.

In contrast, there are other people who start a project and then immediately become frustrated with it before spending any major amount of time or making any progress. These people tend to radically overestimate the amount of time they spend. Before you give up on something, or decide it is not worth more of your time, estimate realistically the time you have actually put into it.

Consider how much time it takes you to do something and how much time a project actually warrants. For instance, when one of your authors was in her online program, she created a formula for how much time to spend on homework. It went something like this: 5 hours = a paper worth 10% of my grade and 10 hours = a paper worth 20% of my grade.

She used that formula as a guideline to make sure she was not spending too much or too little time on an assignment. You will have to work out your own formula if you are a person who likes that approach. But even if you do not use a formula, assigning a reasonable amount of time to spend on a project is a good one.

Study Skills

The basic skills that will help you be a successful student in an online course are the same as those in an on-ground course: paying attention, taking notes, and studying for tests. However, you might want to consider them from a slightly different angle in this new environment.

Paying Attention

You need to be focused when you are reading in the classroom, so you fully grasp all levels of the message. Being fully focusing means the following:

- Not trying to multitask while reading the message.
- Making sure noises around you are not interfering with your concentration, like television or other people trying to talk to you.
- Not rushing through because you are tired or you have time constraints.

It is essential for you to know what the sender of the message is saying (content), how he or she is saying it (tone), and finally the motive behind the message (intent). Rephrase messages you are unclear on and pose them back to the sender as questions (e.g., "So, what I hear you saying is ———; is that correct?"), to be sure you understand the message.

Without knowing the meaning of a message, you cannot respond to the message accurately and appropriately. Keep in mind, if you were in an on-ground class, you would not have a lot of noise around you. You would be in class focusing on what was going on.

Taking Notes

Do you need to take notes online? The answer really depends on you. Do not feel you have to take notes a certain way, because the most effective way for you to take notes (if any) is through your own note-taking preference.

Everyone has a personal learning style. Applying your learning style can help you process information more effectively. The most effective note-taking method for you will depend on your learning style. Listed here are some different techniques. Consider trying some or all of them to see what works best for you:

- Print out course content. Make notes in the margin or highlight pertinent sections.
- Copy and paste relevant sections of reading or lecture into a new document.
- Rewrite important information in your own language.
- Summarize the main ideas from the content.
- Use a fishbone diagram to denote cause and effect.
- Use mind mapping to make connections visually.

Effective note taking means finding the easiest way to gather and organize the information so you can remember it.

Testing in the Online Environment

You may not take very many tests online; in fact, you may not take any. Depending on your course/program, you may not be assessed through tests but only through alternative types of assignments like papers and projects. If you do have to take a test in an online course, it will likely be an open-book exam or you may have to do it in a proctored environment.

Regardless of the type of test you are taking, you need to study the same way you would for an on-ground class test. That is, *you need to know the material.* Many students fail an online test, even if it is open book, because they do not plan properly. There are three principles we recommend:

1. *Prepare.* Take the time to study before the test and have all your resources immediately available within reach when you actually take the test. Do what you can to increase your efficiency, such as tabbing the chapter summaries and having all your notes organized by topic.

2. *Take advantage of the resources available to you as an online student.* Know what tools and resources are available and allowed for you to use when you take the test. Be resourceful in the online environment. Be aware that when the instructors designed these tests, they knew you would have access to a multitude of resources. They factored that into the design of their assessment, so do not expect that just because an online test is open book it will be easy.

3. *Pace yourself.* Know how much time you have to spend on the test. In some cases, online tests are only available for a limited window of time, so be ready to focus on it completely when you choose to start.

For more information on note-taking methods or test preparation, we recommend you do a search online.

➤ MORE POWER TO YOU

Now is your chance to explore this chapter's topics further. Check out the sites listed here. Enjoy expanding your knowledge and *more power to you*!

Using Feedback
http://www.studygs.net/feedback.htm

How to Study
http://www.howtostudy.org

How to Study and Learn: Parts 1–4
http://www.criticalthinking.org/articles/sts-ct-teaching-students-study-learn-p1.cfm

http://www.criticalthinking.org/articles/sts-ct-teaching-students-study-learn-p2.cfm

http://www.criticalthinking.org/articles/sts-ct-teaching-students-study-learn-p3.cfm

http://www.criticalthinking.org/articles/sts-ct-teaching-students-study-learn-p4.cfm

Note-Taking Skills
http://www.arc.sbc.edu/notes.html

Note-Taking Methods
http://sas.calpoly.edu/asc/ssl/notetaking.systems.html

Study Skills Help Information
http://www.ucc.vt.edu/stdysk/stdyhlp.html

If any of these websites are not available or you wish to seek out additional information, we encourage you to do your own online search. Consider the concepts covered in the chapter that are most important to you, and think of various terms that could be used to describe them. For this chapter, some potential keywords to search include:

giving receiving feedback
online student study tips
note taking strategies
test taking

When searching online, consider different ways to express ideas. Remember to use synonyms and related words. Try phrasing things in different ways. And always review more than the first few pages of search results.

For more specific information on searching online, refer to Chapter 9.

Computer
Concerns

11

 Power Up by:

- Recognizing your computer as the primary tool you will use in the online environment. Make sure both the hardware and software are set up for ease of use.

- Being aware of how to work to with documents on the computer. Familiarize yourself with the capabilities of the main computer programs.

- Knowing the options available within your e-mail program for organizing and sending messages.

Computer skills are a necessity in this day and age. In fact, it is doubtful that the younger generations in elementary school today will ever have to upgrade their computer skills. Computers are a part of our everyday life and have changed the culture in which we live in many ways.

Your computer is the primary tool you will use in the online environment. It provides not only your access to the course, but also all the other tools that will enable you to communicate with people in the online environment and complete your assignments. Thus, you must have at least a rudimentary understanding of the main parts and programs of your computer and how to use them.

You may already know most of the information in this chapter. But if you are unfamiliar with these terms and concepts, you may find it helpful to do additional research on your own to fully develop your knowledge and technical expertise. Refining your computer skills will pay off in the long run.

Computer Issues

Probably your most important tools as an online student are the right computer and hardware. This hardware should include a monitor, keyboard, mouse/touch pad, and memory.

Some of you may already have a computer, but for those who do not, choosing a computer can be complicated. First, calculate your budget. Then decide what you are going to do with the computer. If you are going to check e-mail, surf the Web, and write letters, in addition to taking your online class, you want a different configuration than if you are going to play games or manipulate photos. We assume here that you are probably looking for the activities listed in the first example. You should also know that, just like when you buy a car, almost as soon as you purchase a machine it becomes outdated. Bigger, better, newer, and faster happens about every 6 months in the world of computers!

Hardware

Hardware is the term used to describe the parts of your computer that are tangible and take up space on your desk or in the machine.

The *monitor* is the screen on which the computer projects images of your computer desktop or different software programs such as Word or Excel or Web pages. Look at a series of monitors. What size monitor do you really need to take an online class? Make sure the monitor is bright enough for you to see. The monitor should be comfortable for *your* eyes, not the salesperson. Currently, inexpensive monitors provide adequate resolutions for everyday use. Don't be distracted by the case or the color of the frame. Look at the screen. Look at a few different pictures. If they all look good to you, choose the one with the lowest price.

The *keyboard* contains the alphabetic, numeric, and other buttons you use to type messages and documents. There are different types of keyboards, such as standard and ergonomic. Keyboards also vary in the action of the keys, how hard or how easy it is to press them down. Find a keyboard that suits you.

The *mouse* or *touch pad* is the tool you use to move the cursor on the screen and select or "click" on certain areas. A mouse is a separate piece from your machine. It may be linked to the computer by a cord or it may be wireless. A touch pad performs the same actions as a mouse, but it is integrated into the keyboard of the computer on laptop models. Currently, an optical mouse is the easiest to use. It does not have a roller ball to get dirty. Do not buy a touch pad until you try it out. Make sure you know how to adjust its response levels. Choose the keyboard, mouse, and touch pad according to your personal comfort and taste.

The *memory* is the part of your computer that retains information for future retrieval. In general, the computer itself should have at least 1 gig of memory and a video card that supports the monitor you choose. You cannot see the memory of your computer. It is buried inside the machine, and it is probably not a part you will handle much yourself. We need to mention it, though, because you do not want to run out of memory. The memory on your machine can become full depending on these factors:

- How much memory your machine has
- How much information you tend to save
- How often you clean out your mailbox and how often you eliminate extraneous information, like browser cookies, temp files, and your computer's virtual trash basket

If you buy a fast central processing unit (CPU) and a large amount of memory, the machine will probably keep you satisfied for 5 or 6 years. If you do not know how to empty your trash, delete your cookies or temp files, or clean out your mailbox, research these topics online or else ask a computer-savvy friend to help you.

Even if you do know how to eliminate obsolete or extraneous information from your machine, you may find that in time, as you do more work and save it for future reference, the memory of your machine nears full. If you let it fill up, you will not be able to save anything new. So try to keep track of how much space you have left in memory, and when the free space becomes slim, consider adding memory to your machine. A computer store or tech-savvy friend can help you with this.

Operating Systems

To run other programs, a computer must have an operating system, which comes in many different forms. They all control the CPU and its devices. However, because CPUs are not all the same, they must be talked to differently. An operating system (OS) acts like a bridge between the user and the CPU.

Windows is an OS created by Microsoft and probably the most common one used today. Close behind Windows is Macintosh. Many people have strong preferences regarding one OS or another.

The important thing for you to know is which one(s) are allowed in your online program. Some programs are open to both of these systems. Some only allow Windows users. Before you purchase a new machine or sign on to an online program, make sure you find out the OS requirements for the school's online program.

Common Software Programs

The software for a computer is just another layer between the user and the operating system. Simply put, a computer program is a set of instructions that tells a computer what to do. Next we describe some of the more common software programs you will likely be using in your classes.

Word-Processing Software

Microsoft Word (http://www.office.microsoft.com)

Corel WordPerfect (http://corel.com)

Both Word and WordPerfect are word-processing programs. They are designed to create documents by combining a comprehensive set of writing tools with an easy-to-use interface. Whenever you write a paper, or take notes, or put together a simple table, you will probably be using one of these word-processing programs.

Presentation Software

Microsoft PowerPoint (http://office.microsoft.com/en-us/powerpoint/default.aspx)

PowerPoint is a presentation software. Using this program, you can create dynamic and high-impact presentations using text, images, and even animations arranged on slides. Although you are taking your classes online, you still may be required to create presentations, so you will probably need to become familiar with this program.

Spreadsheet Software

Microsoft Excel (http://office.microsoft.com/en-us/excel/default.aspx)

Excel is a spreadsheet program. It sets up data as worksheets and workbooks, similar to an accounting ledger. You can use formulas within Excel to perform mathematical operations on the data. Excel lets you arrange data into rows, columns, and tables to manage, share, and analyze the information.

A multitude of other software programs are available for such activities as playing or composing music, creating web pages, diagrams, and art, and for many other functions. But these three programs are the main ones you will use as an online student. For each of them, you can easily discover a variety of online tutorials simply by doing a web search.

Internet Connections

In addition to the proper interface and software, another necessity for taking part in online learning is an Internet connection. Your course will be posted somewhere on the World Wide Web, and the Web will also probably be your main resource for research and information. To connect to the Web, you will need one of the types of connections shown in the following table.

TYPE OF CONNECTION	SPEED	COST
Phone line (dial-up)	~ 56 kb/sec	Varies, but usually lowest
DSL (T1 or T3)	~ 1–3 mb/sec	Varies, but higher than dial-up
Cable	~ 5–10 mb/sec	Varies, but higher than dial-up

In addition to the types included in the chart, there are also two other categories of connection: LAN (local area connection) and wireless (wireless modem). You might have a T1 LAN connection at work and wireless cable access at home.

As you can see, there tends to be a direct correlation between the cost of the connection and the speed it offers. The speed, or bits per second, of an online connection is the main factor in how long it will take you to download or upload information from the Internet. If you have a fast connection, loading can happen almost instantaneously. If you have a slow connection, uploads and downloads can be tedious and sometimes incomplete.

You may want to shop around for the right connection package for your needs. Cost can be affected by the competition among your local Internet service providers. Speed can be affected not only by your connection type, but also by the reliability of your service provider, how many other people are using your same connection (e.g., on a LAN), or by how many people are accessing a particular site at the same time. The time of day can impact the latter two factors.

A vast majority of online students use a dial-up connection. These students get by but not without struggles that may be unnecessary. The lower cost of a dial-up connection is paid for in the slower speed for downloads. That time could be saved with a digital subscriber line (DSL) or a faster moving Internet connection. This may not be an option for everyone, but if you can manage it, it is preferable.

Besides price and speed, connections can vary in accessibility and reliability. Certain types of connection may not be available in the area where you live. Depending on the newness and robustness of the connection materials, some connection types may be more reliable than others. One of your authors once had an underground phone connection that would often experience static during and after a rainstorm. The static meant she was frequently disconnected from the Internet whenever the ground was wet. Weather can be a major factor in the quality of your connection. High wind, lightning, and rain can all impact your connection, so be aware and try to plan ahead if possible.

Working with Computer Documents

As an online learner, most of the assignments you complete will be in the form of documents. You will spend a lot of time creating, editing, and uploading documents on the computer. There are a few tasks with which you should be familiar.

Creating, Formatting, and Saving Documents

The three most basic actions you will need to be proficient at are creating a new document, setting up the document, and saving it for future reference.

Creating Documents

When you first open any word-processing program, it offers you a new blank page on which to start writing. Most programs have a "button" on the menu at the top of the page you can select to start another new document (in Word, it is a small white rectangle, a blank page).

How you start off any new document is up to you. You will need to determine whether it is with an outline, or freewriting, or a series of notes. Once you start any document, it is a good idea to insert page numbers.

Formatting Documents

Formatting refers to how you set up the document and organize the information it contains. It can cover everything from paper size and margins to the fonts used in the headings and body of a document. The description of any assignment should specify the formatting requirements. Pay attention to these requirements. Sometimes you can miss enough points to fail the assignment when you do not format a paper correctly.

Knowing how to use the formatting options will pay off when your papers look professional and meet formatting requirements. You need to know how to do the following:

- Set margins
- Select the font size and type
- Italicize, bold, and underline text
- Add page numbers
- Insert headers and footers
- Cut/copy and paste within a document and from one document to another
- Use bullets and numbering
- Create tables
- Insert page and section breaks
- Create a new folder
- Save a document

Options for most all of these actions are available through buttons or menu options within the program.

If you are not familiar with how to perform any of these functions, take the time to learn. Explore the program on your own, or use the Help or Assistant options that are provided. You might ask for some basic document formatting lessons from a computer-savvy friend or find an online tutorial to complete. You can also purchase one of the many guides to common software programs carried by bookstores or the local library. Becoming proficient in using your software will help you succeed in the online classroom.

Working with E-mail

Not only do you need to master your word-processing program, you also need to be skillful in handling e-mail.

Here are some of the actions that we recommend you know:

- Adjusting the font size, color, and type of messages
- Attaching documents to e-mail messages
- Using CC (courtesy copy) and BCC (blind courtesy copy)
- Setting up preferences in your system for such options as the spell checker and the format of replies
- Creating a signature line

The same advice applies to learning all these tasks as we stated previously. Explore the program on your own, or use the Help or Assistant options provided. Ask for some basic e-mail formatting lessons from a computer-savvy friend. Find an online tutorial to complete. Purchase one of the many guides to common software programs sold at bookstores, or check it out from your local library.

Becoming proficient at all these skills is in your own best interest. Do not forget to review the guidelines for online communication technique in Chapter 7.

→ MORE POWER TO YOU

Now is your chance to explore this chapter's topics further. Check out the sites listed here. Enjoy expanding your knowledge and *more power to you*!

Outline of Computer Literacy Skills
http://www.mcps.k12.md.us/departments/techlit/docs/Levels%20of%20Use.pdf

How Stuff Works (click on the Computer option on the left menu)
http://computer.howstuffworks.com/

5-Minute Tech Tutorials
http://adulted.about.com/gi/dynamic/offsite.htm?zi=1/XJ&sdn=adulted&zu=http%3A%2F%2Fwww.thirdage.com%2Ffeatures%2Ftech%2Fbooster%2F

Online Tutorials and Courses (on technical and other topics)
http://www.learnthat.com/computers/

Basic Computer Tutorial
http://www.comptechdoc.org/basic/basictut/

If any of these websites are not available or you wish to seek out additional information, we encourage you to do your own online search. Consider the concepts covered in the chapter that are most important to you, and think of various terms that could be used to describe them. For this chapter, some potential keywords to search include:

basic computer terms

computer literacy

computer tutorial

When searching online, consider different ways to express ideas. Remember to use synonyms and related words. Try phrasing things in different ways. And always review more than the first few pages of search results.

For more specific information on searching online, refer to Chapter 9.

Creating the Ideal Personalized Study Environment

12

 Power Up by:

- Understanding that a personalized work space will allow you to be more efficient. Set up your space for optimal working conditions in terms of light, seating, and desk height and organization. Keep your own position in mind while working.

- Recognizing that you can find wireless access in many places, including airports, libraries, and coffee shops. But pay attention to the level of access, power source, cost, and privacy concerns when working remotely.

- Guarding your privacy when online. Use a secure connection whenever possible. If that is not an option, work offline until you need to upload or download information.

- Being aware of other concerns regarding working remotely, including time available during travel, varying outlet types, different time zones, and the difficulties of toting a computer along on trips.

The Importance of a Personalized Work Space

A personalized work space allows you to be more efficient. Maybe you are a completely organized, clean-desk person. Or maybe you prefer to be surrounded by piles of papers. However you work best, try to set up a dedicated work space for doing your class work where you are comfortable both mentally and physically.

Ergonomics

Ergonomics focuses on designing and arranging equipment to accommodate the people who use it. Consider these questions: Is your chair comfortable to sit in for long periods of time? Is your desk at the right level for you to access your work easily from that chair? Is your computer screen bright enough to make reading possible but not so glaring that it strains your eyes? All of these questions are ergonomic concerns regarding your work space.

Ergonomics is a buzzword these days because we have realized the implications of long hours at the computer. Some people are suffering from carpal tunnel syndrome. Others complain of shoulder and neck aches. Perhaps you spend a lot of time on the computer at work, and then you come home to the computer to attend class online. Make sure the items in your work space fit you and are set up to afford you the least amount of strain.

Here are few aspects of your surroundings to consider in terms of the ergonomics of your work space:

- *Lighting.* You need proper lighting in your work space. You do not want to harm your eyes by putting unnecessary stress on them, so consider purchasing a lamp to sit on your desk. Be sure your office space is in a well-lit place in your home. Check to be sure the brightness of your computer screen is at an optimal level.

- *Seating.* Your chair should allow you to sit in a comfortable, upright position, close enough to your desk or computer to allow easy access. Of course the chair cannot control whether you sit up straight or slouch. We leave that to you.

- *Desk.* Set up the height, space, and organization of items on your desk to make your work easily accessible. You should be able to comfortably fit your legs under the desk while you work.

- *Yourself.* A big part of remaining comfortable and productive depends on your own habits and actions. Remember to sit up straight. Change position occasionally. Breathe! And stand up and stretch every so often.

To find out more about setting up your work space properly, we recommend you search online or at your local library.

The Ideal Study Environment

How often have you thought, "I can't wait to get home and snuggle up in my favorite chair or in my comfy bed." How does that make you feel? Warm, safe, comfortable, and cozy? Now imagine how exciting learning could be if you had that same thought when you were preparing to study: "I cannot wait to go to my learning space and learn." What if the thought of going to a place to study could conjure up real excitement?

It can happen if you make it that way. You can be much more successful if you approach learning with enthusiam. Your learning space can become a special place for you. Online students have more control over their learning environment because they do not have to go to a stuffy classroom with one-size-fits-all seats and tables. However, this benefit can change to a major drawback if you do not create a pleasant study environment. If set up correctly, your environment can help put you in the proper mood for completing your work.

Too often students comment that they have a laptop, so they can work anywhere. They sit in their comfy chair or take the laptop to bed to work where they fall asleep! Keep in mind that the comfy chair and bed are associated in your mind with relaxation. You do not want to be too relaxed when it comes time to study. Further, sitting and trying to work in an easy chair or the bed does not provide the appropriate ergonomic support.

One of your authors became particularly aware of the importance of a well-organized work space when she visited a friend. The friend's office was brightly lit, with a beautiful cherry desk, a comfortable chair, books, pens, a computer, and a printer. It made her think, "I want to sit down and go to work." It was there that she realized how important a perfect learning environment could be. The moment had a huge impact on her. She went home and began to create her own ideal work space.

We know many of you are on a budget so it may take a while to achieve that perfect space. But once you do, you might rather be in that little area of your home than any other.

Think about what your perfect work space might look like. Consider what you have seen in other people's homes or offices. Ask yourself what you liked and didn't like, and begin to plan where and how you can create your own space.

Study Space in Your Home

Try to avoid setting up your study space anywhere that you will need to vacate later. It is time consuming to move your materials, and then you have to take time to reorganize everything. Every time you move things, you risk losing track of your supplies. In such circumstances your classroom and your work space become transient. At a subconscious level, you might begin to view your education as unstable too.

We recommend you do not set up your study space in the kitchen, at the dining room table, or the coffee table. Try to find yourself a spot, even if it is a tiny corner in your house or apartment, and make it a permanent home for your schoolwork.

If possible, create your work space where you have a window and a view. Taking a moment to catch your breath and relax is important. Two definite benefits will come from this. First, you will be able to look out and relax; quite often this break will trigger new thoughts. Second, you can open the window and let in some fresh air, which works wonders on a tired brain.

Work-Space Tools

First, you need your computer and a printer if possible. You also must have your books, including the school-sanctioned writing guide, a dictionary, perhaps a thesaurus, in other words, your resource books. Next you will need writing utensils and papers. You may want a calculator. Paper clips, stapler, and tape are also great additions.

Keep in mind that this list is not exhaustive, and most of these items can be purchased locally for a minimal cost.

Furnishing your work space does not have to be expensive. You may find bargains at garage sales or at a dollar store. Decorate your area with items that motivate you. Perhaps you want some pictures of people you admire or some quotes that inspire you. Furnish the area with your personality in mind. As you can see, you can put together a nice work space for a very reasonable cost if you open your eyes to the alternatives.

Working Remotely

One of the perks of online learning is that you are not necessarily limited by location. Especially if you have a laptop computer, you can, for all practical purposes, take the classroom with you.

For some, traveling is not an option, it is a requirement for holding the job that allows them to stay in school. For these students, learning the ropes of going to school while traveling is a necessity. For others, traveling is not required but something that may come up on occasion, and being able to access your class while on the road is a wonderful advantage. However, there are many things to consider and many pitfalls to avoid. As glamorous as it may sound, you may not be at your best when you are crammed into an airport chair, surrounded by people and noise. In addition, not always having the ability to connect to the Internet can be a problem. To be successful, you must be able to connect to class.

If your job calls for travel, you may log in to class from various locations. Even if travel is not required, you still can enjoy the portability of online learning. Airports, libraries, and coffee shops are some of the many places that offer wireless access. To work in any of these off-site locations, be aware of access (open/private), power source, cost, and privacy.

Where to Connect

Knowing where you can obtain Internet access, and knowing it ahead of time, is crucial. Do not assume you are going to be able to obtain wireless access "somewhere" when you travel. In addition, do not count on open access as you travel because remote networks can be notoriously unreliable. Common locations that offer wireless Internet access include the following.

Hotels

Many hotels offer wireless access in the room or else a connection in their "corporate work center." It can be complimentary or for a fee. Some hotels charge up to $15 or more a night for a wireless connection. Numerous hotels, especially in smaller towns, do not offer any access at all.

Airports

Some airports have Internet access and others do not. The access may not be free, and even if it is, it may not be compatible with your system without doing some manipulating.

Restaurants

Occasionally you can find a restaurant that offers wireless access. It may be completely free, free with your meal purchase, or available only for a separate fee.

Libraries

Many libraries do offer free Internet access, either through their network or on their local computers. Keep in mind, however, that to access the network, you will usually need a library member card. And when you are not a local resident, it is unlikely you will be able to obtain one.

Coffee Shops

Free access is a possibility. At some places, you can buy a day pass for $10 or so that will allow you to connect in areas where the company who sold you the day pass has service. For example, at a Starbucks, usually you can buy a day pass from T-Mobile for $10, but it will not work at all locations.

A common theme you might notice here is that access can be, but is not always, free. If you can find a venue that offers *reliable* free wireless or other access, count yourself lucky.

To work in any of these off-site locations, there are a few additional points to keep in mind. Most places allow you to plug in and not pay for electricity; however, available outlets are usually limited in number and can be hard to locate. The more obvious and accessible they are, the more quickly, and regularly, they will be in use by someone who got there before you. This situation means that you need to have plenty of battery power, and you may want to buy a backup battery.

Aircards

Aircards are becoming more readily available. With an aircard, you really are able to connect just about anywhere, anytime. You simply plug the aircard into your USB port and connect to your provider's network. While this is a very exciting option for students to have, keep in mind it can be expensive. To purchase an aircard, you usually have to spend between $50 and $100 and sign a contract—just like a cell phone. You then have the additional monthly service fee of $50–$75 (prices can vary). You might want to consider checking to see if your company sponsors aircard purchases. An aircard can provide you with a lot of freedom while in school.

Privacy

Do not rely on open access as you travel. Remote networks can be notoriously unreliable. Although most of what you are doing is not private, you just never know who is looking in on what you are doing, so it is best to be safe. Most people are not apt to look into your class and steal any information, but you never know. Use a secure connection whenever possible. If that is not an option, work offline until you need to upload or download information.

Other Concerns

Carry, Do Not Check, Your Computer

Plan to carry your laptop with you while you travel. The rough handling it can suffer when loaded as luggage can often result in a crashed hard drive or other damage.

Working Offline Between Connections

Some learning platforms allow you to download your messages and work offline. Find out if this is the situation in your class. If you are taking a long plane or car ride, you can use that time to read through class messages you have downloaded. If you cannot download messages, copy and paste as much as possible into Word documents. Then when you are on the plane or in the car, work on those items. This technique makes for an efficient use of time and assures you have what you need to log into class.

Changing Time Zones

Another factor to consider when traveling is the time zone. What time zone is your class in and what time are assignments due? You may have to adjust so you can meet the requirements of class in the usual time zone.

Traveling Abroad

In addition to time zone concerns, traveling abroad brings up entirely different issues. You have to consider that your electrical cords may not work. Online accessibility may be shaky or nonexistent, depending on your destination. The complete unfamiliarity of your surroundings may throw you off in general. You will need to consider all of these possibilities before you leave.

Vacationing

If you think going on vacation and taking your class work with you is a good idea, you might want to reconsider. First, ask yourself if taking class while on vacation really puts you in the right frame of mind to do your best. Usually the point of a vacation is to relax and escape from your everyday concerns and obligations, rather than to focus on doing homework. If you think you will be able to motivate yourself, consider time and access, as well as space in your luggage for the necessary supplies.

Supplies for Working Offsite

When you prepare to travel with your portable classroom, be sure to pack all necessary items. First and foremost, you will need your power cord! And verify your battery is charged fully before you leave home.

Be sure you have your manual for your computer, at least for the first few trips. If possible, read it through ahead of time and understand if there are any idiosyncrasies about your computer of which you should be aware.

One of your authors remembers when she traveled with her new laptop for the first time. She could not access the Internet. She struggled with it for hours. She called the help line at the hotel, she contacted friends, and finally, she realized what she needed to do it: turn on her wireless signal. So simple, yet it took a long time to figure out.

What else might you need to pack? If you travel a lot, you might keep a bag packed with writing utensils, paper, sticky notes, paper clips, and so on. You may even consider buying two copies of the resource guides or style manuals.

If you only travel on rare occasions, you need to evaluate what you will want to take. This decision will depend on what is going on in your class. If you are traveling and have a term paper due, you will want to take all resource guides and texts associated with the paper.

Planning for Contingencies

Take a few precautions to ensure that your travel does not disrupt your class participation.

Complete as many assignments as you can before you ever leave home. Then you can participate or submit the work while you are in transit.

Be sure you have written down the school's telephone number and your instructor's telephone number, just in case you need it. If you reach your destination and your computer will not work or you cannot connect to the Internet, call the school and let the people who matter know what is going on. That usually means your faculty member, and possibly your advisor or team members. Keep the lines of communication open. You are probably not going to be out of commission for an extended period, but be prepared for contingencies.

Overall, the picture we have tried to paint here is this: Traveling while attending school is possible and sometimes necessary. But by no means is it easy, and honestly, we do not recommend it. We hear numerous complaints from students about the difficulties of trying to stay on top of class work while traveling:

- How they could not find the time to complete their schoolwork.
- How trying to connect to the Internet using alternative methods was difficult or impossible.
- How hard it is to know what you will need when you are away, until it is too late.

Think about how time pressured you are when you travel. The stress of putting yourself in this situation is usually not worth it. Of course, you will be in your program a long time, and traveling is probably inevitable at some point. So before you leave, arm yourself with our tips and, most importantly, have a backup plan.

Do not let this section alarm you. If you have to travel and study, you can do it, but it will require extra planning and negotiation.

➔ MORE POWER TO YOU

Now is your chance to explore this chapter's topics further. Check out the sites listed here. Enjoy expanding your knowledge and *more power to you*!

Library Ergonomics
http://www.lib.utexas.edu/ergonomics

Ergo Tips
http://ergo.human.cornell.edu/cuergotipsintro.html

The Study Spot
http://distancelearn.about.com/od/managingyourwork/a/studyspot.htm

How to Create a Comfortable Working Environment
http://vertigo.hsrl.rutgers.edu/ug/ergonomics.html

If any of these websites are not available or you wish to seek out additional information, we encourage you to do your own online search. Consider the concepts covered in the chapter that are most important to you, and think of various terms that could be used to describe them. For this chapter, some potential keywords to search include:

ergonomics
keyboard yoga
working remotely
wireless access tips

When searching online, consider different ways to express ideas. Remember to use synonyms and related words. Try phrasing things in different ways. And always review more than the first few pages of search results.

For more specific information on searching online, refer to Chapter 9.

Preparing for the First Day of Class

13

Power Up by:

- Enjoying the journey of education.

- Preparing for the first day of class, both mentally and physically. Use both your excitement and anxiety as motivators. Get involved in your classes. Record your feelings and/or share them with others.

- Being proactive the first day of class. Ensure that you have the required textbooks and materials. Check into your class and figure out what you need to do. Post a personal biography. Review the syllabus and assignments. Complete the initial readings and assignments.

- Printing out the syllabus. You will reference it throughout the course.

- Considering carefully which course documents it makes sense to print out, what makes sense to save to your computer, and what you can leave in the course system to reference later.

The first day of school has finally arrived. The apprehension and excitement that have led up to this day may have been overwhelming, but now it is here. It may seem strange for an online student because there is not a lot of formality. On the surface, life may not seem as though it has changed much, especially for those around you. You do not have to get in your car and drive to class. You do not have to be somewhere at a particular time. But the train has started, and you want to be on board and not get left behind.

In this chapter, we discuss how to prepare for the beginning of school. The main message we would like to communicate to you here is to *enjoy the journey of education*!

Riding the Wave of Emotion

One of the authors remembers when she first started her program: She was sitting in her chair drinking coffee and thinking, "It is the first day of school." To her, things felt different. It is hard to explain, but she knew things were changing. To her family, however, it was just a typical day. She did not leave and go to class. She just spent a bit more time on the computer that day. She still thinks about that feeling and loves it. She was so excited and scared, and she thought, "I just have to complete a class at a time and someday I will be finished."

As you begin school, you will have a lot of feelings. You may feel nervous, excited, intimidated, anxious, and probably proud most of all. To begin acquiring an education is a very important step. Your entire world is about to change.

At a college orientation, a professor said that a parent of a graduate mentioned her daughter had completely changed during the years in school. To that, the professor replied, "Good, that is what is supposed to happen." The professor went on to explain that, if the school had not changed the student, the school would not have met its requirements and obligations to the student and her family.

Your school has the same obligation to you. The classes you take should help you grow and develop as a person. Not only will you gain new knowledge, skills, and perspectives, but you will also develop new relationships.

Let's talk about your feelings. First, you will be nervous, which is normal. You do not know what to expect and you wonder if you can live up to the commitments. The answer is, *Yes, you can.* Keep in mind that everyone in the class, and possibly even the instructor, is feeling the same way. It is normal to be apprehensive. Try to use this anxiety positively. Let it motivate and inspire you to plan and get organized for class. Use it as an impetus to catapult yourself into success, rather than letting it be a negative influence.

You are probably excited, too. You may have thought about and dreamed about this undertaking for a long time. Now the time is here. Try to capture some of this excitement using a journal. It may benefit you to remember this feeling later in the program, if and when the going becomes rough. Excitement is wonderful, so enjoy it and share it with others. You may be surprised to find that your feelings about furthering your education can inspire others to take on the same challenges—perhaps your friends or your children. When they see how much you are looking forward to taking this step, it can lead them to think about their own educational choices.

You are probably intimidated as well. Everyone probably feels this way when they are in unknown territory. Do not think you are the only one. You can manage your intimidation by taking a deep breath and becoming more involved. Force yourself to engage and to put new ideas and thoughts out there. School should be a safe environment to try new things. Take advantage of it. Talk about your ideas and let others respond. You are here to grow. Part of that growth is learning how to manage all these feelings successfully.

Finally, as mentioned earlier, you are probably very proud. You are a student! You are on the way to earning your degree. Just to be taking on this challenge is a great achievement. Enjoy this time and bask in the joy of being a student.

Keep in mind what you are feeling is no different than the others in the class, so you all have this in common. You might want to share your feelings with the other students and the instructor.

Actual Preparations

You have sorted out your feelings, and now it is time to begin. You will want to plan for acquiring your books and orienting yourself in your online classroom(s).

Textbooks

First, you want to ensure you have the required textbooks for your classes. Most courses have one or two books, but on occasion you may take a class that requires more. Or you may have one that uses no books and only relies on research and online readings. Although more schools are turning to e-books all the time, it is still the norm in the majority of courses that hard-copy textbooks are the main instructional material. Even if your school is using an e-book, you can often opt for a hard-copy book if you prefer.

Obviously, you first need to find out what the required materials are and how you are expected to acquire them:

- Are the books for your course actual textbooks or more conventional fiction or nonfiction works that can be found at your local bookstore or on Amazon.com?

- Does the school have an online bookstore where you can order your materials?

- Will you need to open an account with the school bookstore for the duration of your program?

- Unless you are going to buy them from a local store, what is the average timeline for delivery? In other words, how soon can you expect to receive your books after you place the order?

Acting fast is wise because sometimes books can be back-ordered or there are delivery issues. By ordering your course materials as soon as possible, you can alleviate or avoid problems. Having the right books for your course, on time, will help you be successful.

If you do not have your books by the first day of class, you are not going to start off on the best foot. So acquire them as soon as they are identified for you.

Do *not* think you can make your way through a class without a book; you cannot. Your textbooks are a necessary expense, and you will incur these costs throughout your program, so plan for it.

Buying Used Books

You might be thinking you will purchase used books to save some money. Before you do that, however, do some research to make sure used materials will serve your needs adequately.

In some cases, you can acquire a used book that is exactly the same as the new version you would buy, and it is indeed a better deal. In other cases, you must buy the new version of the text. To know whether a used book is indeed a wise buy, ask a few questions:

- Is the used book *exactly the same edition* as the required book for the course? Do the ISBNs match?
- What condition is the used book in? Is it missing any pages? Does it have highlighting or margin notes from the previous owner that will disrupt your own readings?
- Were there any supplements, such as CDs, DVDs, guidebooks, or access codes for websites, that came with the original book? Are these included with the used book?

Check out all these factors before you decide to buy used books.

Orienting Yourself Online

The Biography (Bio)

You will want to check into your class and figure out what you need to do. Quite often the first task is to post a personal biography. You may want to write a standard bio and keep it. Save it to a file, so you can use it for every class.

- Emphasize professional and perhaps previous school experience.
- Keep your bio short and succinct. If you bio is too long, you risk the chance others will find it boring and thus not read it all.
- Steer away from providing too much personal information. You are introducing yourself to strangers for the first time, not posting your life story. You definitely should not post your phone number and address. You can probably trust everyone in your class, but you can never be too careful. Do not view your bio as an opportunity to "sit on the psychiatrist's couch."

Create a bio with relevant information that another student and faculty member would want to read about you. This is not a forum for divulging your innermost thoughts.

As other students post their bios, you may want to comment and look for things you have in common. Responding is a great way to connect with other students and begin creating a learning community. Remember, the bio exchange is the introduction to the class.

The Syllabus

After you post your bio and begin to look around in the class space for course materials, seek out the syllabus and assignments. A *syllabus* is an outline of assignments in the class and their due dates. Think of the syllabus as your bible. You should study the syllabus, learn the syllabus, and love the syllabus, and we are going to explain why.

First, keep in mind that the syllabus can be overwhelming if you look at all the assignments and think you have to do all of them *today*. You will do a little at a time, a bit each day, building toward the finish of the course. Do not be overwhelmed. Keep it in perspective.

Look at the syllabus and understand the policies unique to your instructor and what he or she thinks is most important. Some faculty members emphasize participation; some emphasize the format of the paper; whatever the instructor's priority is should be stated in the syllabus, although it is not always obvious. You may have to review the entire document to find it.

Consider what is worth the most points in the class, and focus on those assignments. If you have a project worth 20% of the course grade, you will want to spend the most time with that assignment. If you have an assignment worth only 5%, you may consider if you had to miss something, that would be the assignment to miss.

It is all about strategy and figuring out what can give and what cannot. Certainly we do not advocate ever missing assignments, which not only hurts your grade, it also affects your learning. However, you are a working adult with commitments and may have to let something go. If you do, it is good to know ahead of time where the leeway is.

Make sure you understand due dates, which can be tricky in an online environment because of the time zones. Some schools require that assignments be posted by the time zone where the server is, usually at the corporate headquarters of the school. Others require that assignments be submitted by the student's time zone. Yet others require the assignment be due by the faculty member's time zone.

Due dates and times vary with each course, so make sure you are clear on them. Often there is a penalty for a late submission, and these penalties can add up quickly. Do not fall victim to this. Submitting work late can hurt your grade in no time at all. If you find yourself in a situation where you are unable to submit your assignment on time, find out how late an assignment can be. Even if you submit the assignment late, you may be able to earn some points, and some points are better than none.

Completing Assignments

After you have reviewed the syllabus and completely understand the requirements, begin to answer any questions posted for the class discussion, and complete your readings and assignments. Making a good first impression with both the instructor and fellow learners is important. Do this by posting answers to the questions that are complete and thoughtful, not too wordy, yet add to the conversations.

Oftentimes students comment that answering the same discussion question as all the other students is difficult because the others have already "captured the answer." Here are a few suggestions:

- Be the first one to answer the question.
- Do not read the other students' answers until you post yours.
- Read all of the other students' messages, research the topic, and then provide a completely different viewpoint.
- Connect the question with real life by detailing your answer with relevant information from your own life experiences or issues in the news or pop culture.

Doing assignments online is no different than doing assignments for an on-ground class. These assignments generally require the same attention and detail. Consider how much latitude you have regarding the assignments. If possible, double-dip. In other words, arrange it so an assignment for class also serves a purpose for your job. Or if you happen to be taking two classes, do an assignment that applies to both classes. This takes a lot of preplanning and thought, but being efficient in this way can help save you time in the long run. Considering alternate applications of course topics also helps you retain that information.

If you are highly scheduled and like to see when you can complete obligations by mapping it out, you might print out a calendar of due dates. Then you can personalize it with actual days and times you know you will have open to work on the different assignments.

Class Gets Under Way

You posted your bio, you studied the syllabus, and you have a plan/strategy to be a success. You will need to continue to focus on other elements of managing the class. Knowing what resources to have available is helpful. Sometimes it varies by class.

Determining What to Print

Too often, students think they need to print every document for the class. Perhaps you really need the printed documents, but think it through beforehand.

The one document you should definitely print is the syllabus. And if there is a class calendar, print that too. However, as far as the other documents, it is quite possible you will not need to print them. Printing too many materials can cause you problems:

- In determining which ones are really important for continued reference
- In having documents cluttering your office
- In having a printer that is constantly out of ink

You have to print what you need to be comfortable, but before you go crazy printing everything, really ask yourself if you need it or if it is something you could look up again later in the electronic environment. How much you need to print will vary by class. For example, in a quantitative class, you may print more materials than you would in an English class because you may have to work out the equations, samples, and so on. However, one could argue that in an English class, you may want to edit your paper using a pen and paper. For each new circumstance, you will need to reconsider what makes sense to print.

A viable alternative to printing materials is to save the documents to your desktop for easy retrieval. Save the key documents, and if you end up referring to them regularly, print them out. If you do not refer to them often, then just having them readily available on your machine may be enough.

Now you have started your class. You know what is going on and you know the commitments, but perhaps others do not. Think about sharing your experience with them. Be sure to include them in your world; the more they understand, the more likely they will be there to support you.

We encourage you to journal your feelings as you begin class. Never forget that excitement you feel. Remembering this feeling will help you become reenergized as you become discouraged or tired. And you will. The key will be to keep going even after that excitement wears off.

→ MORE POWER TO YOU

Now is your chance to explore this chapter's topics further. Check out the sites listed here. Enjoy expanding your knowledge and *more power to you!*

Preparing for Classroom Learning
http://www.studygs.net/classrm.htm

Influencing Teachers
http://www.studygs.net/attmot2.htm

Be Proactive
http://www.stevepavlina.com/blog/2004/11/be-proactive/

If any of these websites are not available or you wish to seek out additional information, we encourage you to do your own online search. Consider the concepts covered in the chapter that are most important to you, and think of various terms that could be used to describe them. For this chapter, some potential keywords to search include:

> *preparing online class*
> *online student resources*

When searching online, consider different ways to express ideas. Remember to use synonyms and related words. Try phrasing things in different ways. And always review more than the first few pages of search results.

For more specific information on searching online, refer to Chapter 9.

Maintaining Your Online Success

14

Power Up by:

- Setting up a filing system to organize important course documents. Staying organized will help you stay efficient.

- Taking steps to prepare for the next class. Find out what you need to do to enroll. Order your books and materials early.

- Planning for contingencies. Be prepared for emergencies or the unexpected. Back up your files regularly, either electronically or with hard copies.

- Thinking twice before you discard books. The books from previous classes can provide resource material in subsequent courses. They can also become valuable references beyond your academic career.

- Taking time to relax and enjoy the reprieve if you have a break between classes. But do not become too comfortable or you may not want to go back to school.

- Remembering that each instructor and each course will be different. Learn from your past experiences, but be open-minded about the future.

- Rewarding yourself for a great accomplishment. Acknowledge your continued success as you finish each class.

- Maintaining a positive outlook. Cultivate your belief in yourself and your potential for success.

I n closing, we talk about continuing your education. You will see that beginning is easy. You have heard people talk about the "honeymoon period" or how the "newness wears off," and these stages may apply to you as you go through your program.

When you begin school, you will be full of excitement and drive, and that alone can keep you going for the first few classes. But the truth is, at some point in your program you may feel down and discouraged about how much more there is to do. You may wonder if it is all worth it, and you may even consider not continuing. This chapter addresses what it takes to maintain your online success and continue when you feel like hanging it up.

Staying Organized

As you progress through the program and each class, your knowledge will grow. But so will the number of textbooks and electronic documents you have to keep track of. Staying organized will help you stay efficient.

Computer Files

We suggest you set up a filing system to store important documents. You may choose to use a hard-copy filing system, but we recommend that you save work on the computer as much as you can. It will save both space and paper.

Use your desktop and create folders. Ideally you have a folder for each class, and in that folder you store all the documents you created for the class.

Take the time to develop your own logical system of filing. Be sure you use brief but descriptive names for all your documents, and even numbers when it is called for. Logical naming of folders helps you easily determine their content after the memory of the particular assignment has faded. The first time you do a large paper with multiple drafts, you will be glad you chose a relevant title for the document and saved the versions using numbers 1 to 4.

You may not see the need for multiple files at first, but as work piles up, you will wish you had it carefully marked and stored. It will make locating the files in the future so much simpler.

We suggest you keep everything: your assignments, your in-depth posts, your answers to discussion questions. You cannot be sure now what may come in handy later. You may be able to build on what you have done for future assignments and posts. For example, if you decide in your business program to focus your papers on Wal-Mart, you could use the same introduction with the company history for each paper. You may also find other bits of information you could reuse.

Textbooks for Future Reference

When you finish a class, you may be tempted to sell your books. There may be compelling reasons to do so. Perhaps you need the money or they take up too much space.

However, keep in mind that you are in an academic program and the concepts and ideas will often be related or build on one another. You may find the books from previous classes useful for resource material. By continuing to use your books as references, you reinforce your memory about the concepts you learned in those classes.

You may also discover that certain books can become valuable references well beyond your academic career: You might talk to people who work in your chosen field to find out what books they have found helpful in their work. All of your textbooks might not be worthy of becoming lifetime references. But consider which ones might, and keep them on hand.

Emergency Backup

As you progress through the program, always have a plan to back up your work. You need to consider what would happen if your computer were to crash or be infected with a destructive virus, or if a natural disaster occurred.

We all know the computers are not completely reliable. *We strongly recommend that you back up your documents periodically.* You could do this by

- Using a whole drive designed specifically for the purpose.
- Using a small portable thumb or flash drive.
- Saving documents on backup disks.
- Printing hard copies and keeping them in a safe place.
- E-mailing copies to an alternative e-mail account.

If you use a machine backup, make sure the backup system itself contains enough memory to hold everything you need to save.

Whichever option you choose, back up regularly. Weekly is usually good, and daily is better. This kind of planning is easy to dismiss or overlook but can save your life, if not your sanity.

You will work hard completing assignments as you move through your program. Do not let some unforeseen glitch cause your hard work to be lost.

The Master Juggler: You

You will have so much to manage while you are completing your academic program. Acquiring an education while working and trying to stay involved with family and friends is a juggling act. You will find yourself trying to figure out what you can give up and what you must keep in order to survive.

Planning Ahead

You will always need to be looking ahead and calculating your time constraints and how they can be managed. For example, if you have children and they are out of school for the summer, you may not want to take a challenging class at that time. You might want to wait until the fall when everyone's lives are more structured. It may be easier then for you to fit in more time for class.

The holidays can also lead to increased stress. You are busy in school as well as trying to step up to all the commitments that come along with the holidays: social obligations, family gatherings, and shopping, for example. As you select your courses and plan your schedule for the semesters ahead, be sure to consider all the possible factors that can make demands on your time.

One of your authors remembers some of the conflicts between family and school. In particular, she recalls how classes fell during a few holiday seasons. She once had a class that ended December 23, the day before Christmas Eve. She had a huge paper due. She had to finish it because the policy at the school was that all assignments had to be in when the class ended. It was stressful, but it was worth it to be done before the festivities started.

Another year, she had an assignment due, but the class was not ending; it would continue after a two-week break over Christmas. She ended up submitting the assignment late and taking a hit on the points, but she was okay with that because it was more important for her to be sane and available for her kids over the holidays.

As you can see, it is a matter of give and take, determining what is best for each situation and adapting to the circumstances. Strategize for success and determine what will work for you at any given point.

One Class Follows Another and Another

As you are nearing the end of your first class, in fact, any time you are nearing the end of a class, consider what you need to do to prepare for the next class.

What are the enrollment policies at your institution? You will need to find out whether you are automatically enrolled in your next class or whether you are responsible for enrolling yourself.

You will need to know what materials are required. As we have already advised, order your books early, so you can begin working on the next class as soon as possible.

If you have a break between classes, take time to relax and enjoy the reprieve, but do not become too comfortable or you may not want to go back to school. Studies show the longer you are away from school, the harder it will be to go back. If you are concerned about that, gather your books and start reading and preparing for the next class. Get a jump start on it!

As you finish one class and close that door, remember you are starting from square one again in your next class. You have to study the syllabus. You have to learn the faculty member's idiosyncrasies. It is up to you whether you make the same mistakes or learn from your past experiences in subsequent classes. Remember, each instructor is different, so do not expect things to play out as they have before. Adaptability and an open mind are key characteristics to cultivate as you progress through your program.

Celebrate Your Achievements

As you finish a class, reward yourself for a great accomplishment. If you can afford to take yourself out to lunch or dinner, that's great. But if all you can do is reach your own arm around to pat yourself on the back, then that's enough. Acknowledge your continued success. You deserve it. Do not forget and let it slide. Do not undermine the importance of a reward.

One student we know told us that every time she finished a class, she and her husband would go to happy hour for a cold beer and chicken wings. It was her little treat for a job completed. Plus, it allowed her time to reconnect with her husband before jumping into the next class. Do not overlook the importance of taking the time to appreciate your own effort and sharing your success with those close to you.

Goodbye and Good Luck

This book has been filled with tips. We do not think it covers everything at all. We continue to learn and to think of new ideas.

Online learning is dynamic, which makes creating tips for this environment ever changing too. You will learn new ideas and apply different strategies as you progress through the program, which is what will make you successful. Each of us has to discover our own recipe for success.

Further, we live in an ever-changing landscape: of technology, of obligations, and of individual circumstances. So we have to be flexible and remember what worked at one point in our life may not work at another point, even with school.

You will probably be in school for two years or more. Children will get older, jobs may come and go, you will have both happy and sad times, and through it all, school will go on. You have to stay flexible and figure out how to accomplish your goals. Just as a tree bends in the wind, you will become a stronger and better person for the experience of completing your degree.

Following are some closing thoughts for your education. What can you add?

- Going to school is not easy, but it should be invigorating. You should be excited.

- Keep a journal and record your thoughts when you finish a class. When you feel down, read those thoughts and remind yourself why you are doing this.

- You are worthy of this experience. You have made some sacrifices, and there are more to come, but you will emerge a better person: more experienced, more educated, more confident. Surround yourself with supportive people who will be there just to listen and encourage you.

- Work hard, but remember, you have a life too. Do not neglect yourself or the special people in your world. Strive for balance.

- Be a good listener, ask questions, and keep an open mind. Stick to your goals, and do not be afraid of failure. Sometimes it can teach you as much, if not more, than success.

- Always enjoy the education. Worry less about the final product, and enjoy the new ideas, concepts, and people that you are being introduced to through your classes.

- *Appreciate the journey.* Believe in yourself and believe in your potential for success. We do!

We hope we have confirmed your desire to attend school online and perhaps even made it stronger. Going to school is both a privilege and the opportunity of a lifetime. We wish you the best!

→ MORE POWER TO YOU

Now is your chance to explore this chapter's topics further. Check out the sites listed here. Enjoy expanding your knowledge and *more power to you*!

18 Ways to Reward Yourself
http://www.weightwatchers.com/util/art/index_art.aspx?tabnum=1&art_id=1911

Six Tips to Earning More Money After Graduation
http://www.associatedcontent.com/article/184544/five_tips_for_earning_more_money_after.html

Staying Inspired and Motivated
http://www.soarwithme.com/articles.php?article_id=59

If any of these websites are not available or you wish to seek out additional information, we encourage you to do your own online search. Consider the concepts covered in the chapter that are most important to you, and think of various keywords that could be used to describe them. For this chapter, some potential terms to search include:

organizing computer files
lifelong learner

When searching online, consider different ways to express ideas. Remember to use synonyms and related words. Try phrasing things in different ways. And always review more than the first few pages of search results.

For more specific information on searching online, refer to Chapter 9.

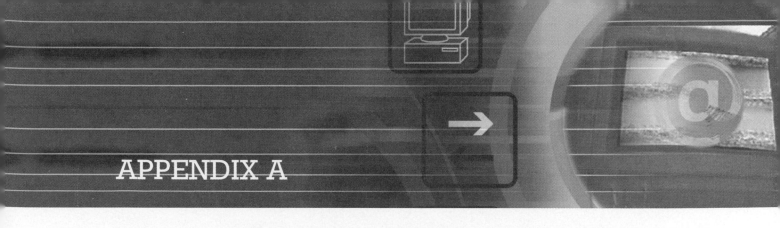

APPENDIX A

Financing Your Education

Many schools offer financial aid. Usually if a school is accredited, it can offer financial aid, which comes in the forms of grants, loans, and scholarships. Do not be shy or reserved about seeking help financially. It is there for you.

This appendix only touches on the vast subject of financial aid. We are not experts on this subject and would not want to lead you astray, but we do think it is important to introduce you to the basics.

Grants are often awarded to students who are in dire need of financial help. Grants are given by the government and you are not required to pay the money back.

Financial aid can be given based on two factors. Need-based financial aid is for those who meet certain criteria that show they are unable to pay for school on their own. Non-need-based financial aid is available to students who choose to finance their education rather than pay for it up front. All financial aid must be paid back; however, the type you qualify for will determine if you will accumulate interest while in the program as well as when you will begin repayment. Some loans do not accumulate interest; others do. Some require you pay them back immediately when graduating; others recognize a six-month grace period. Check with your financial aid officer and find out what you qualify for and what would work for you. Note only that a number of private banks lend money for school. It used to be financial aid was loaned by government entities, but that is not the case anymore.

Be careful about overextending on financial aid. You do have to pay it back, and although you will graduate and be earning more money, you do not want to devote all of your earnings into repaying loans.

Scholarships are another great way to finance your education. Do not think scholarships are only available to students just graduating or students not in your situation. Check with your financial aid office for scholarship information and also search online.

Scholarships are often awarded by companies, charities, and small interest groups. Scholarships are not paid back. It is your money to use for education. Often you have to apply for the scholarship and may be required to fulfill an obligation such as write a paper, but that is well worth it.

Financial aid usually requires you maintain a certain grade-point average to continue to qualify. Check what that is so you make sure you do not lose your funding.

APPENDIX B

Understanding the Importance of Accreditation

The purpose of programmatic accreditation in higher education is to provide a professional review of the quality of an educational program. When a school seeks accreditation for its programs, it is opting to have the quality of its program compared with established national or regional standards.

Benefits of Accreditation

To receive federal grants and loans, students must attend an accredited university. If you are not sure which school/program is best for you, look at accredited schools to be assured of a higher quality program and to help narrow down the search.

Employers frequently ask if a college or university is accredited before deciding to provide tuition assistance to current employees and when evaluating the qualifications of new employees.

If you wish to transfer credits seamlessly from one institution to another, having credits from an accredited university is key. At an accredited school, the faculty and staff are involved in evaluating the quality of the instruction and the end-product curriculum, which helps ensure a holistic review of a program.*

*The authors would like to express gratitude to our friends at the Institute for Advanced Education in Geospatial Sciences (IAEGS) for their LMS research that was used in this appendix. To learn more about IAEGS, visit http://geoworkforce.olemiss.edu/.

REFERENCES

Baikie, K., and Wilhelm, K. (2005). Emotional and physical health benefits of expressive writing. *Advances in Psychiatric Treatment*, *11*, 338–346. Retrieved August 23, 2007, from http://apt.rcpsych.org/cgi/content/abstract/11/5/338

Bureau of Labor Statistics. (1999). 1999 Education requirements and job growth. Retrieved December 9, 2004, from http://www.bls.gov/opub/ted/1999/Dec/wk1/art02.htm

Bureau of Labor Statistics. (2004). Projected employment in high-paying occupations requiring a bachelor's or graduate degree. Retrieved March 12, 2005, from http://www.bls.gov/opub/ted/2004/mar/wk3/art03.htm

Carnevale, D. (2005). Employers still prefer traditional degrees over online learning, study finds. *The Chronicle of Higher Education*, *52* (5), A43.

Dictionary.com Unabridged. (vol. 1.1). (2007). Random House, Inc. Retrieved June 3, 2007, from Dictionary.com, http://dictionary.reference.com/browse/plagiarism

Gardner, H. (1983). *Frames of mind: The theory of multiple intelligences*. New York: Basic Books.

Gross, R. (1999). *Peak learning*. New York: Tarcher/Penguin.

Hamner, W., & Harnett, D. (1974). Goal setting, performance, and satisfaction in an interdependent task. *Organizational Behavior and Human Performance*, *12*, 217–230.

Hill, L. (2001). Learning styles: An examination of learning styles and my personal discovery of my own. Retrieved June 6, 2007, from http://www.authorsden.com/visit/viewarticle.asp?id=1421

Internet Tutorials: Boolean searching on the Internet: A primer in Boolean logic. (n.d.). Retrieved August 23, 2007, from http://www.internettutorials.net/boolean.html

Kerka, S. (1996). Journal Writing and Adult Learning. ERIC Digest No. 174. Retrieved August 23, 2007, from ERIC Clearinghouse on Adult Career and Vocational Education, http://www.ericdigests.org/1997–2/journal.htm

Locke, E. (1968). Towards a theory of task motivation and incentives. *Organizational Behavior and Human Performance*, *3*, 157–189.

Myers & Briggs Foundations. (n.d.). Retrieved June 3, 2007, from http://www.myersbriggs.org

National Center for Education Statistics. (n.d.). Retrieved June 15, 2007, from http://nces.ed.gov

Rhodes, J. (1998). Vision, reading, and computer uses: An interview with distinguished optometrists. Retrieved June 25, 2007, from http://wcbword.com/interviews/williams.html

Rowland, G., Lederhouse, A., and Satterfield, D. (2004). Powerful learning experiences within coherent learner groups. *Performance Improvement Quarterly*, *17* (2), 46–65. Retrieved June 15, 2007, from ProQuest.

The Sloan Consortium. (2007). Retrieved June 15, 2007, from http://www.sloan-c.org

Using Wildcards. (n.d.). Retrieved June 15, 2007, from http://apps.caes.uga.edu/impact/searchhelp.cfm

INDEX

Index

NOTE TO STUDENT:

On the following pages are two signs you can tear out and hang on your door or office space when you are studying and/or testing. Oftentimes the people in our lives need to be reminded we need our quiet time. We have found this technique to be useful to avoid distractions while studying.

DO NOT DISTURB:

STUDENT STUDYING

DO NOT DISTURB: STUDENT TESTING